ANTI-PARLIAMENTARY COMMUNISM

Anti-Parliamentary Communism

The Movement for Workers' Councils in Britain, 1917–45

Mark Shipway

MACMILLAN
PRESS

First published 1988

Published by
THE MACMILLAN PRESS LTD
Houndmills, Basingstoke, Hampshire RG21 2XS
and London
Companies and representatives
throughout the world

Printed in Hong Kong

British Library Cataloguing in Publication Data
Shipway, Mark
Anti-parliamentary communism: the movement
for workers' councils in Britain, 1917–45.
1. Communism—Great Britain—History
—20th Century
I. Title
322.4'2'0941 HX243
ISBN 0–333–43613–X

Contents

List of Tables

Acknowledgements

I would like to take this opportunity to record my thanks for all the help I received during the various stages of researching and writing this book, from its origins as a doctoral thesis to its present form. In particular, I would like to mention by name the following people: David Howell, who supervised my work in the Department of Government at the University of Manchester during 1981–5; my friend and comrade John Crump, who commented on successive drafts with meticulous attention to detail and unwavering commitment to socialist principle, and who helped to sustain my efforts with his unflagging interest and encouragement; Bob Jones, who also commented on my written work, shared his own extensive knowledge of the subject with me, suggested sources to pursue, and lent me rare material in his possession; and those members of the Wildcat group whose ideas found their way into this book, and who made many useful suggestions about what to retain and omit when the text was being edited for wider publication.

Leeds MARK SHIPWAY

List of Abbreviations

AAUD	Allgemeine Arbeiter-Union Deutschlands (General Workers' Union of Germany)
AEU	Amalgamated Engineering Union
AFB	Anarchist Federation of Britain
APCF	Anti-Parliamentary Communist Federation
AWRU	All-Workers' Revolutionary Union
BSP	British Socialist Party
CLS	Communist League of Struggle
CNT	Confederacion Nacional del Trabajo (National Confederation of Labour)
CO	Conscientious Objector
Comintern	Communist International (Third International)
CP(BSTI)	Communist Party (British Section of the Third International)
CPGB	Communist Party of Great Britain
CWP	Communist Workers' Party
ECCI	Executive Committee of the Communist International
EWO	Essential Works Order
FAI	Federacion Anarquista Iberica (Iberian Anarchist Federation)
GIC	Groep van Internationaal Communisten (Group of International Communists)
ILP	Independent Labour Party
IUDA	Industrial Union of Direct Actionists
IWW	Industrial Workers of the World
KAI	Kommunistische Arbeiter-Internationale (Communist Workers' International) (Fourth International)
KAPD	Kommunistische Arbeiter-Partei Deutschlands (Communist Workers' Party of Germany)
NCL	No-Conscription League
NEP	New Economic Policy
NUSM	National Union of Scottish Mineworkers
NUWM	National Unemployed Workers' Movement
POUM	Partido Obrero de Unificacion Marxista (United Marxist Workers' Party)
SATC	Socialist Anti-Terror Committee

SLP	Socialist Labour Party
SPD	Sozialdemokratische Partei Deutschlands (Social Democratic Party of Germany)
SPGB	Socialist Party of Great Britain
SWMF	South Wales Miners' Federation
SWRP	Scottish Workers' Republican Party
TGWU	Transport and General Workers' Union
TUC	Trades Union Congress
USM	United Socialist Movement
UWO	Unemployed Workers' Organisation
UWP	United Workers' Party
WSF	Workers' Suffrage Federation/(from May 1918) Workers' Socialist Federation

Introduction

This book developed out of an interest in a political movement known as 'left' or 'council' communism, which achieved brief prominence – particularly in Germany – at the end of the First World War.

Before the war the future left communists generally belonged to the left wing of the social democratic parties of the Second International. After these parties had lined up in support of their respective ruling classes at the outbreak of the armed conflict in 1914, the left communists were soon to be found among the revolutionary minority which called on the working class to 'turn the imperialist war into civil war'. At the same time they also began to formulate a radical critique of the social democratic ideas which had led to the Second International's integration into capitalist society and to its support for the war.

The left communists were quick to acclaim the 1917 Russian revolution and in its wake participated in the formation of communist parties as constituents of a new, Third International. The left communists confidently expected their Russian comrades' support in the struggle against the treacherous social democratic and trade union leaderships, and against outmoded forms of working-class action such as parliamentarism. These hopes were soon dashed, however, when the Third International adopted the tactics which Lenin had outlined in his notorious attack on the left communists, *'Left-Wing' Communism, An Infantile Disorder*.

Besides disagreeing with the Bolsheviks over the most appropriate tactics for use in the class struggle in Western Europe, the left communists were also critical of the direction taken by events within Russia itself, especially after the introduction of the New Economic Policy (1921), which they regarded as a 'reversion to capitalism'. Eventually the left communists argued that Russia was a capitalist state run by the Bolsheviks and that the Third International's policies simply reflected the interests of the Russian capitalist state in the field of foreign policy. Thus the left communists were driven to form a new – anti-Bolshevik – Fourth International, in which the interests of the world revolution would take precedence over the interests of any of the new International's constituent national parties. Consequently the term 'left' communism soon became obsolete, since the 'orthodox' communists (that is, the Bolsheviks) were now recognised as belonging to the *capitalist* political spectrum. Thereafter the left communists became more widely known as 'council' communists, because of their emphasis on workers' councils (or soviets), rather than political parties, as the means which the working class would use to overthrow capitalism and administer communism.

In the chapter of *'Left-Wing' Communism, An Infantile Disorder* which dealt with the revolutionary movement in Britain, Lenin's attack was mainly directed against a group called the Workers' Socialist Federation. The WSF had started out as an organisation of militant suffragists, but its political views were transformed in the direction of revolutionary communism by the impact of the Russian revolution. The WSF existed until mid-1924 and changed its name several times during this period, so for the sake of convenience it is usually referred to in this book as the *Dreadnought* group, after the title of its weekly publication the *Workers' Dreadnought*, which was edited by Sylvia Pankhurst.

It was as a history of the *Dreadnought* group – left communism's representatives in Britain – that this book was originally conceived. As the work of researching the *Dreadnought* group's ideas and activities during 1917–24 progressed, however, it was exciting to discover that other anti-parliamentary communist organisations existed in Britain at that time and that anti-parliamentary communist ideas survived the *Dreadnought*'s demise.

As well as in the pages of the *Workers' Dreadnought* anti-parliamentary communist ideas were also put forward by a newspaper called the *Spur*, which was edited by Guy Aldred. Whereas Sylvia Pankhurst and her comrades were chiefly influenced by post-First World War left communism, Guy Aldred and his comrades drew much of their inspiration from nineteenth-century anarchists such as Bakunin. The *Spur* was not the publication of any particular organisation, but had close links with several revolutionary propaganda groups throughout Britain. As far as the history of anti-parliamentary communism is concerned the most significant of these was the Glasgow Anarchist Group, an organisation which could trace its lineage back through a succession of Clydeside-based groups which had propagated an anarchist-influenced version of anti-parliamentarism since the 1890s.

In 1920 the Glasgow Anarchist Group renamed itself the Glasgow Communist Group in order to express its affinity with the Russian revolution and its support for revolutionary unity in Britain. However, the Glasgow group also soon became disillusioned with the tactics foisted on the Western European revolutionary movement by the Bolsheviks, and in 1921 it took the initiative in the formation of an Anti-Parliamentary Communist Federation to directly oppose the Russian-backed Communist Party of Great Britain.

The APCF sustained the anti-parliamentary communist tradition in Britain until the end of the Second World War. During this time it suffered two splits in its ranks. The first of these took place in 1933–4, when Guy Aldred and some of his comrades broke away to form the United Socialist Movement. The second split took place in 1937, with the departure of some anarchists who were later involved in the formation of the Glasgow Anarchist Federation at the beginning of the Second World War. In this book the APCF is regarded as the genuine standard-bearer of anti-parliamentary communism in Britain during the 1930s and 1940s, but the ideas of the USM and the Anarchists are also examined and discussed.

As research brought more and more information to light about the history of anti-parliamentary communism in Britain, the need for an accurate, comprehensive and sympathetic study of the subject became increasingly obvious. Biographies of Sylvia Pankhurst dwell at length on her pre-1917 suffragist ideas and activities; references to her years as an anti-parliamentary communist are conspicuous only by their absence. Nor are the histories of the early years of the CPGB much more enlightening. The *Dreadnought* group participated in the communist unity negotiations which preceded the formation of the CPGB, but its ideas were at odds with the tactics which the CPGB eventually adopted. This enables historians of the CPGB to portray the *Dreadnought* group as an 'infantile' tributary flowing into the Leninist mainstream, later to emerge as an effluent which disappears into the void. None of them assess anti-parliamentary communist ideas in their own right, and even their most banal 'factual' comments about the anti-parliamentarians are frequently mistaken.

Guy Aldred and his comrades have escaped such treatment, but only because they withdrew from the unity negotiations at an early stage. Their reward for this has been that historians ignore them altogether – a fate which has also befallen the anti-parliamentary communists active in Britain after 1924. Only the few present-day revolutionary groups which acknowledge a political debt to the past work of the anti-parliamentary communists have shown any interest in setting the record straight. Yet all too often even these groups' accounts are flawed by superficial research and a tendency to bend the facts to suit their own preconceptions.

This book is, therefore, the first serious, lengthy and detailed account of the theory of anti-parliamentary communism and of the history of the groups which adhered to this theory in Britain between the two world wars. Yet it would be misleading to give the impression that it has been written simply out of a concern to establish the historical truth. There is a political assumption underlying this book's choice of subject. That is, that the anti-parliamentary communists are worthy of our attention because the views they held place them among the relatively small number of groups and individuals which have put forward a genuine alternative to worldwide capitalism.

This alternative, which the anti-parliamentarians described interchangeably as socialism or communism, was far removed from what is popularly understood by these terms, such as the policies of the Labour Party or the system which developed in Russia after 1917. For reasons which this book will explain, the anti-parliamentary communists regarded the Labour Party as a capitalist organisation and Russia as a capitalist state. The socialism/communism advocated by the anti-parliamentarians meant the complete abolition of the system which forces the dispossessed majority into dependence on wage slavery, producing wealth for exchange in a market economy, to the profit of a privileged few who rule society in their own interests. It would involve wrenching the world's productive resources out of the hands of their present controllers, and transforming and developing them to produce wealth directly for use, so that everyone's individually-determined needs would be provided in abundance.

Political organisations popularly identified with socialism/communism have often paid lip service to such ideas. On attaining power, however, they have always maintained in existence the very money–market–wages system they purported to oppose. At no time have the measures advocated by the anti-parliamentarians ever been put into practice in any of the so-called socialist or communist states in the world. Capitalism still exists everywhere, with all the consequences of its normal way of functioning: unemployment, war, relentless insecurity and material deprivation for the vast majority of the world's inhabitants, and so on. As long as this state of affairs continues groups such as the anti-parliamentary communists will always be important, because the socialist/communist ideas they propagated offer the working class its only solution to the wars and barbarism which the present world system holds in store. As the anti-parliamentarians frequently warned: 'All Else Is Illusion.'

The relative obscurity in which the anti-parliamentary communists expended most of their efforts has made the job of researching some parts of their history a difficult task. It can be confidently asserted, however, that enough material has been located to form the basis of a detailed and comprehensive account of what the anti-parliamentarians were doing and thinking at each stage of the period covered. What is just as certain is that this book is unlikely to be the final word on the subject. For example, not long after the original research for this book had been completed and submitted for examination as a doctoral thesis, a comrade in Norway informed me that in an archive in Copenhagen he had come across correspondence revealing the practical solidarity given to two council communist refugees from Nazi Germany by anti-parliamentarians in Glasgow in the mid-1930s. Unfortunately, this discovery came too late for its findings to be included in this text. Nevertheless, it is to be hoped that this book will inspire others to take an interest in its subject, and to make similar discoveries which will help to correct, improve or expand the account presented here. If this happens the hard work which has gone into writing this book will have been well worth the effort.

Part I
Basic Principles 1917–24

1 'Anti-Parliamentarism' and 'Communism'

The term 'anti-parliamentary communism' begs two questions. First, what is 'anti-parliamentarism'? Secondly, what is 'communism'? This opening chapter is intended to answer these questions. It begins with a chronological account of the history of the anti-parliamentary communist groups in Britain during 1917–24, followed by an examination of the meanings attached to 'parliamentarism' and 'anti-parliamentarism' in the debates over tactics which took place within the revolutionary movement during these years. After a discussion of the deeper philosophy of anti-parliamentarism that informed its adherents' views on a wide range of issues, the chapter ends with an explanation of the anti-parliamentarians' conception of communism.

BREAKING WITH SUFFRAGISM: THE IMPACT OF THE RUSSIAN REVOLUTION

The association between the Pankhursts and Votes For Women is so firmly established in most people's minds that it may come as a surprise to find Sylvia Pankhurst occupying such a prominent place in this account of *anti*-parliamentarism. Most descriptions of Pankhurst's life end, or leave an unexplained gap, where this account begins – with Sylvia Pankhurst still a militant suffragist, but on the brink of a major change in her ideas.

Until 1917 Pankhurst's political ambitions were summed up in the aims of the Workers' Suffrage Federation, the organisation which she had founded (as the East London Federation of Suffragettes) in 1914: 'To secure Human Suffrage, namely, a Vote, for every Woman and Man of full age, and to win Social and Economic Freedom for the People.' In July 1917 the WSF changed the name of its newspaper from the *Woman's Dreadnought to the Workers' Dreadnought* and expanded its statement of aims slightly in order to clarify that 'Social and Economic Freedom for the People' would be established 'on the basis of a Socialist Commonwealth'.

The WSF argued that the vote would enable women workers to exert influence over the fundamental decisions affecting their lives.

Universal suffrage would 'make Parliament obedient to the people's will'.[1] If it was the will of the people that a socialist society should be established, they could bring this about by electing socialists to Parliament. A prerequisite of this strategy was that the suffrage should be extended to every woman and man.

The centrality of the suffrage issue in the WSF's political outlook was reflected in its response to the February Revolution in Russia. The news that the Tsarist autocracy had been overthrown and that 'a constituent assembly is to be elected by the men and women of Russia by secret ballot and on the basis of Universal Suffrage'[2] was one of the main reasons why the WSF reacted favourably towards the February Revolution.

We can gauge how far the WSF was from anti-parliamentarism at this stage by contrasting its views with those of Guy Aldred, whose rejection of the idea that universal suffrage would produce governments which reflected and responded to ordinary people's wishes was evident in his own response to the February Revolution. In May 1917 Aldred wrote: 'We know that the vote does not mean freedom . . . In Britain, our parliament has been a sham. Everywhere parliamentary oratory is bogus passion, universal suffrage an ineffective toy gun of the democracy at play in the field of politics. Why celebrate the triumph of the toy in the land of the ex-Czar?.'[3]

While the February Revolution evoked very different responses from Aldred on the one hand and Pankhurst on the other, the October Revolution in Russia acted as a catalyst in the WSF's ideas which would eventually lead it to adopt the position already held by Aldred and his comrades. This change began in dramatic fashion. The WSF's statement of intent, 'To Secure a Vote for every Woman and Man of full age, and to win Social and Economic Freedom for the People on the basis of a Socialist Commonwealth', no longer appeared in the *Workers' Dreadnought* after the issue dated 19 January 1918, and the following week's issue carried an article by Sylvia Pankhurst praising the Bolsheviks' dissolution of the Constituent Assembly in Petrograd just eight days previously.

In March 1917 the WSF had looked forward to the establishment of the Constituent Assembly with keen anticipation; in January 1918 the Bolsheviks dispersed the very same Assembly before its first meeting – with Pankhurst's endorsement. Until 1917 the WSF had viewed events such as the February Revolution through the prism of the suffrage issue; after 1917 it would view issues such as suffrage through the prism of the October Revolution.

It was the emergence of the soviets in Russia, seen as the means by which the revolution had been carried out and as the administrative machinery of the post-revolutionary society, which caused the WSF to reject the parliamentary route to socialism. The group's commitment to 'Popular Control of the Management of the World'[4] was not abandoned; it was simply felt that soviets (committees of recallable delegates elected by and answerable to mass meetings of working-class people) would be far better able to bring about this goal than parliaments. In her article on the dissolution of the Constituent Assembly Sylvia Pankhurst argued: 'As a representative body, an organisation such as the All-Russian Workers', Soldiers', Sailors' and Peasants' Council is more closely in touch with and more directly represents its constituents than the Constituent Assembly, or any existing Parliament.'[5] Likewise, the view of the WSF Executive Committee was that soviets were 'the most democratic form of government yet established'.[6]

The WSF's recognition of the superiority of the soviet form quickly cast doubts on the parliamentary approach to which the group had previously adhered. In February 1918 Sylvia Pankhurst asked:

> Is it possible to establish Socialism with the Parliament at Westminster as its foundation? . . . We must consider very seriously whether our efforts should not be bent on the setting aside of this present Parliamentary system . . . and the substitution for it of a local, national and international system, built upon an occupational basis, of which the members shall be but the delegates of those who are carrying on the world's work.[7]

Similar doubts about the possibility of establishing socialism by parliamentary means and tentative suggestions of soviets as an alternative were also raised by the rest of the WSF. Resolutions adopted at the WSF's Annual Conference in May 1918 showed that the organisation had not yet rejected parliamentarism completely. For example, one resolution urged workers in Britain to elect 'International Socialists' to Parliament and not to vote for any candidate who supported the war. However, another resolution argued that 'Parliament organised on a territorial basis and government from the top are suited only to the capitalist system', and called for the organisation of 'a National Assembly of Local Workers' Committees . . . which shall render Parliament unnecessary by usurping its functions'.[8] The Conference's decision to change the organisation's name from the Workers' *Suffrage* Federation to the Workers' *Socialist* Federation also signified a growing rejection of parliamentarism, as did the removal of the slogan 'Socialism, Internationalism, Votes For All' from the masthead of the *Workers' Dreadnought* in July 1918, and its replacement with a simple appeal 'For International Socialism'.

By the time of the general election at the end of 1918 the WSF's views on parliamentarism were still in a state of transition. When a group of Sylvia Pankhurst's admirers in Sheffield asked her to stand as a candidate in the Hallam constituency, the *Dreadnought* reported that Pankhurst had declined the invitation: 'in accordance with the policy of the Workers' Socialist Federation, she regards Parliament as an out-of-date machine and joins the Federation in working to establish the soviets in Britain'.[9]

Other responses to the election were less clear-cut. When a General Meeting of the WSF was questioned about its attitude it replied that the WSF 'would not run candidates and would only support Socialists, but that it could not prevent members working for Labour candidates if they wished to'.[10] Furthermore, the following statement by Sylvia Pankhurst could be interpreted as supporting involvement in the election in order to spread revolutionary ideas: 'The expected General Election interests us only so far as it can be made a sounding-board for the policy of replacing capitalism by Socialism, and Parliament by the Workers' Councils. We shall be at the elections, but only to remind the workers that capitalism must go.'[11]

Thus despite the WSF's growing anti-parliamentarism, in the end it gave support to three Socialist Labour Party candidates (J.T. Murphy, Arthur MacManus and William Paul) and also to David Kirkwood and John Maclean.[12] Indeed, Pankhurst herself travelled to Glasgow in mid-November 1918 to open a Grand Sale Of Work in aid of Maclean's campaign fund.

Pankhurst's support for Maclean enables us to draw another comparison between the WSF's views at this point and the anti-parliamentary position as represented by Guy Aldred. In June 1918 Aldred had opposed Maclean's decision to stand for Parliament, citing the 'Marxian truism that the workers for their own political purpose – which is the social revolutionary one of expropriating the ruling class – cannot seize and use parliamentary machinery of the capitalist state'. This was Aldred's rendition of Marx's statement in *The Civil War in France*, that 'the working class cannot simply lay hold of the ready-made State machinery, and wield it for its own purposes'.[13]

Aldred advised Maclean to 'make your programme analagous to the Sinn Fein programme only with Socialism and not mere nationalism for its objective'.[14] At the 1918 general election the Irish nationalist party Sinn Fein had said that its elected Members of Parliament would boycott Westminster and establish their own parliament in Dublin. In the context of communist candidatures the 'Sinn Fein' tactic meant that

> Successful candidates would not go to parliament, but would remain in their constituencies till they had a quorum, then they would constitute an assembly, insisting on the right to represent the district which elected them. Thus a dual authority is established, which could possibly spread like wild-fire, as these innovations do, and eventually challenge the state.[15]

The election of a communist candidate standing on the 'Sinn Fein' programme would be an expression of the voters' opinion that 'political authority should be withdrawn from Parliament and represented in Councils or Soviets created by and responsible to the workers'.[16] These references to 'dual authority' and 'Councils or Soviets' suggest that besides the obvious influence derived from the Irish nationalists, the example of the 1917 Russian revolution also entered into the thinking behind the 'Sinn Fein' tactic advocated by Aldred.

Only by 1919 could the WSF be said to have finally arrived at a fully-fledged anti-parliamentary position. In March of that year Sylvia Pankhurst wrote: 'Circumstance are forcing the Socialists of every country to choose whether they will work to perpetuate the Parliamentary system of government, or to build up an industrial republic on Soviet lines. It is impossible to work effectively for both ends.'[17] It soon became clear which choice the WSF had made. A resolution 'to ignore all Parliamentary and Municipal elections and to expose the futility of workers wasting their time and energy in working for these ends' was submitted for inclusion on the 1919 Annual Conference agenda. In June the resolution was approved and became WSF policy.[18]

On the recommendation of a courier from the newly-formed Third International the Conference instructed the WSF Executive Committee to take steps towards linking up with the new International and with other communist groups in Britain. WSF delegates were told by the Executive Committee to 'stand fast' on the position of 'No Parliamentary Action' in their discussions with other groups.[19]

Guy Aldred's favourable comments about the WSF's attitude around this time indicate the extent of the change which had taken place in the WSF's views in the space of two years; in May 1919 Aldred observed that 'the *Workers' Dreadnought*, under the editorship of our comrade, Sylvia Pankhurst, has been making great strides intellectually speaking, and seems now to have become a definite Revolutionary Marxian Anarchist weekly with a clear outlook on the question of Soviet Republicanism as opposed to Parliamentarism'.[20]

In July 1919 Pankhurst attempted to enlist Lenin's support for the WSF's anti-parliamentary stance in the communist unity negotiations. In a letter to the Bolshevik leader she suggested that 'if you were here, I believe you would say: Concentrate your forces upon revolutionary action; have nothing to do with the Parliamentary machine. Such is my own view.'[21]

However, Pankhurst's belief was soon disillusioned when she received Lenin's reply. After a few conciliatory remarks about anti-parliamentarians being among 'the best, most honest and sincerely revolutionary representatives of the proletariat', Lenin announced that he personally was 'convinced that to renounce participation in parliamentary elections is a mistake for the revolutionary workers of England'.[22] This was not the sort of response that anti-parliamentarians in Britain had hoped or expected to receive. The example of the Russian revolution had been instrumental in causing the WSF to *abandon* notions that parliamentary action could play any role in the revolutionary struggle – how quickly Lenin had forgotten the lessons of his own revolution!

Furthermore, the little anti-parliamentarians in Britain knew about Bolshevism had led them to identify it with the anarchist variety of anti-parliamentarism which inspired Aldred and his comrades. In *State and Revolution* (first published in English in 1919), Lenin had returned to Marx's *The Civil War in France* in order to revive the idea of smashing, rather than taking over, the existing state apparatus. In its own day Marx's argument had been regarding by his anarchist critics (such as Bakunin) as a retraction of his previous view that state power had to be conquered as a prelude to social change, and as an admission that anarchist views on this issue were correct. We have already seen how Guy Aldred based his opposition to John Maclean's parliamentary candidature on the arguments in *The Civil War in*

France. Thus it is hardly surprising that Aldred should have regarded *State and Revolution*, which put forward the same line of argument, as one of the 'immense services rendered to the cause of the workers' world revolution by Lenin'.[23] Reviewing Lenin's pamphlet in December 1919 Aldred wrote that the author, 'in showing the revolutionary one-ness of all that is essential in Marx with all that counts in Bakunin, has accomplished a wonderful work'.[24]

Aldred summed up his perception of the affinity between Bolshevism and anarchist anti-parliamentarism when he wrote: 'No man can be really and truly an Anarchist without becoming a Bolshevist . . . no man can be really and truly a Bolshevist without standing boldly and firmly on the Anarchist platform.'[25] Other anti-parliamentarians shared this view. For example, one of the topics which Willie McDougall of the Glasgow Anarchist Group spoke about when he toured Scotland as a *Spur* 'missionary' in the winter of 1919–20 was 'Lenin's Anarchy'.[26]

THE ANTI-PARLIAMENTARIANS AND THE FORMATION OF THE CPGB

The communist unity negotiations, which had provoked Pankhurst to seek Lenin's views, continued throughout the rest of 1919 and most of 1920. One of the most contentious issues was whether or not the communist party should engage in parliamentary action. There was basic agreement that Parliament was not a suitable administrative form for communist society and that the revolution would not be carried out through Parliament. Both of these tasks would be fulfilled by the workers' soviets. Disagreement arose, however, over whether or not Parliament could be put to any use pending the revolution. The British Socialist Party and the Socialist Labour Party supported the use of election campaigns for propaganda purposes and Parliament as a 'tribune' from which to make revolutionary speeches. These tactics were also advocated by the Bolsheviks who termed them 'Revolutionary Parliamentarism'. The other main participants in the negotiations – the WSF and the South Wales Socialist Society – opposed Revolutionary Parliamentarism in favour of complete abstention from any involvement in parliamentary activity.

Guy Aldred had already proposed the 'Sinn Fein' tactic as one attitude communists could adopt towards elections, and in October 1919 he suggested two other options. Communists could use elections to measure the level of support for communism and to 'demonstrate the supreme political strength and unity of the Communist Party, as a prelude to revolutionary action'. Alternatively, communists could 'organise a disciplined boycott of the ballot box'. Aldred favoured the organised boycott, but could support either tactic 'without any violation of principle'.[27]

The 'bottom line' of Aldred's position was that under no circumstances should successful communist candidates take their seats in Parliament; in his opinion Revolutionary Parliamentarism, which required communists to enter Parliament and use it as a platform for revolutionary propaganda, was a contradiction in terms, because 'there can only be revolutionism OR parliamentarianism'.[28] Lenin's support for the tactic was a 'fatal compromise'.[29]

When it became clear that unity in Britain would have to be based on terms dictated by the Bolsheviks, anti-parliamentarians such as Aldred therefore faced the choice of compromising their principles or excluding themselves from the unity negotiations. In May 1920 the Glasgow Anarchist Group had renamed itself the Glasgow Communist Group to express its support for communist unity, and announced that it stood for 'the Dictatorship of the Proletariat, the Soviet Republic, anti-Parliamentary agitation, and the Third International'. At the same time, however, the Group had also stated that it would not be party to 'any Unity Convention willing to . . . support men and women sitting in the capitalist Parliament House'.[30] In October 1920 the Group acknowledged that this combination of views amounted to an untenable position when it declared that it had 'suspended' its support for the Third International 'until such time as that body repudiates its "wobbling" on the question of Parliamentary Action'.[31]

The WSF tried to pursue a different course of action. In August 1920 Aldred's comrade Rose Witcop criticised the WSF for having been 'prepared to waive the question of parliamentary action for the sake of unity'.[32] This seems to have been a fair assessment of the WSF's attitude during early 1920. Sylvia Pankhurst suggested that parliamentary action was 'not a matter of principle but of tactics, always provided, or course, that Parliamentary action by Communists is used in a revolutionary manner'.[33] Within the WSF Executive Committee there was 'a very strong feeling against Parliamentary action,' but WSF delegates to the unity talks were advised that 'we might leave the question of Parliamentary Action to be worked out by the party as the situation developed'.[34] Contrary to most accounts of the unity negotiations, therefore, it was not parliamentary action which proved to be the insurmountable obstacle in the way of unity between the WSF and the other groups, but the other contentious issue of affiliation to the Labour Party.

After the annoucement of a Communist Unity Convention to be held in London on 1 August, at which policy decisions would be settled by majority votes binding on all participants, the WSF called an 'Emergency Conference' of 'left wing' communist groups (that is, those opposed to affiliation and parliamentary action). This was originally intended to enable the 'left wing' communists to plan their strategy in advance, since the proposed Unity Convention was bound to be dominated by 'right wing' (that is, pro-parliamentary and pro-affiliation) delegates.[35] In the event, however, the participants at the 'Emergency Conference' (held in London on 19–20 June) decided to take no further part in the unity negotiations. Instead, they proceeded to form themselves into the 'Communist Party (British Section of the Third International)' on a platform of seven 'cardinal points' which included 'refusal to engage in Parliamentary action'.[36]

Besides the WSF the other founder-members of the CP(BSTI) were the Aberdeen, Croydon and Holt Communist Groups, Gorton Socialist Society, the Manchester Soviet, Stepney Communist League and the Labour Abstentionist Party. Fortunately it has been possible to discover a little about who some of these groups were and what they stood for.

An exchange of correspondence between the Aberdeen Communist Group and one of its critics was published in the Glasgow *Forward* in 1920. The critic paraphrased the Group's views as follows: 'Lenin has been guilty of some fatal compromise, and Guy Aldred is entirely wrong in seeking to use the ballot box in order to register the strength of his following. Johnnie Maclean is a reformist . . . Willie Gallacher is a job hunter.' In reply, William Greig of the Aberdeen group explained that it stood for a 'clear-cut Revolutionary, anti-Parliamentary, anti-Trade Union, anti-Reform policy'. He was opposed to trade unions because they split the working class into '1,300 different sections' and he described parliamentary elections as 'job hunting expeditions at the polling booths of the capitalist class'.[37]

The Stepney Communist League had been a founder-member of the national Communist League, formed on the initiative of the Socialist Labour Party's London District Council in March 1919 and consisting mainly of a few SLP branches plus some of the groups associated with Guy Aldred, such as the Glasgow Anarchist Group. The WSF was also affiliated. The League stood for the formation of workers' committees to 'resist all legislation and industrial action directed against the working class, and ultimately assuming all power, establish a working class dictatorship'.[38]

The Labour Abstentionist Party published its programme in May 1920. The Party's aim was 'The Collective Well-Being of the People', and its 'Tactical Methods' included 'Securing the election of Parliamentary Candidates pledged to abstain from taking their seats' and 'Propagation of the Futility of Parliamentary Action'.[39]

The secretary/treasurer of the Labour Abstentionist Party, E. T. Whitehead, became secretary of the CP(BSTI) at the June conference and was soon soliciting Guy Aldred's support. Whitehead told Aldred that

> we are definitely against parliamentary action. This does not mean that we are necessarily against taking part in elections, but the party is against running candidates for the present. It will always be dead against any candidates taking their seats, and should it decide to run them, they would have to adopt your ['Sinn Fein'] programme as suggested by you in the May *Spur*.[40]

Aldred spurned Whitehead's approach: partly because he was opposed to the way in which the CP(BSTI)'s programme had been 'foisted on the movement' by a conference of 'delegates' with no real mandates from the groups they claimed to represent, but mainly because of the inconsistency of an avowedly anti-parliamentary organisation declaring itself the 'British Section' of an organisation committed to Revolutionary Parliamentarism.[41] This inconsistency, which had led the Glasgow Communist Group to 'suspend' its support for the Third International rather than compromise its adherence to anti-parliamentarism, perplexed the CP(BSTI) for several months after its formation, and the party's attempts to resolve the problem had fractious consequences.

In *'Left-Wing' Communism, An Infantile Disorder* (written during April–May 1920), Lenin had just directed a strong attack against anti-parliamentary tendencies within the various Western European communist groups. Regarding the situation in Britain Lenin stated that 'British Communists *should* participate in parliamentary action' and that communist unity in Britain should be based on '*obligatory* participation in parliament'.[42] During the summer of 1920 extracts from Lenin's pamphlet were published in the revolutionary press in Britain. Because of the prestige Lenin enjoyed in the eyes of most British revolutionaries, his pamphlet undoubtedly exerted considerable influence in the debates about parliamentary action. This became clear when the decisive Communist Unity Convention was held on 31 July–1 August. In a message addressed to the delegates Lenin repeated that he was 'in favour of participation in Parliament'[43] and it was duly decided by 186 votes to 19 that the Communist Party of Great Britain would adopt Revolutionary Parliamentarism as one of its tactics. At the same time, the Second Congress of the Third International was being held in Moscow. Various resolutions advocating Revolutionary Parliamentarism were adopted and the tactic was also included among the International's Twenty-One Conditions of Admission.

Lenin's pamphlet, his letter to the Communist Unity Convention, and the decisions of the Second Congress, all emphasised the conflict inherent in the CP(BSTI) declaring itself *against* parliamentary action and *for* the Third International. The British delegates to the Second Congress, Sylvia Pankhurst among them, left Russia with instructions to unite in a single party within four months of their return, on the political basis of the resolutions adopted by the Congress. Initially the CP(BSTI) remained defiant. At a conference in Manchester on 18–19 September it voted to accept the Third International's Conditions of Admission 'with the reservation that the passages referring to the discipline to be applied to parliamentary representatives does not affect our Party, which does not take Parliamentary action'.[44]

Soon afterwards, Sylvia Pankhurst outlined her views on what course of action the CP(BSTI) should follow. Arguing that the tactic of Revolutionary Parliamentarism was likely to be abandoned at the next Congress of the International, she advised the CP(BSTI) to accept the International's terms of admission and unite with the CPGB to form a single, united Communist Party in Britain.[45]

This advice was based on the impressions Pankhurst had formed whilst attending the Second Congress in Moscow. There had been a sizeable presence of anti-parliamentary delegates from various groups throughout Europe and America. Pankhurst believed that if they held to their views and grew in strength they would be able to form an anti-parliamentary majority by the time the Third Congress was held. Pankhurst also had informal discussions with Lenin, during which he told her that parliamentary action and affiliation to the Labour Party were 'not questions of principle at all, but of tactics, which may be employed advantageously in some phases of the changing situation and discarded with advantage in others. Neither question, in his opinion, is important enough to cause a split in the Communist ranks.' According to Pankhurst, Lenin 'dismissed' the issue of parliamentary action as 'unimportant'; if the decision to employ Parliamentary action had been a mistake it could be 'altered at next year's Congress'.[46] Judging by the advice Pankhurst gave the CP(BSTI), she seems to have been won over by Lenin's persuasive assurances.

Subsequently, at a conference in Cardiff on 4 December, the CP(BSTI) voted to accept fully all Statutes and Theses of the International – although, once again, 'it was made abundantly clear in the argument that this vote did not mean that this party had in the slightest degree changed its views on the advisability of Revolutionary Parliamentarism for Britain'.[47]

Not all CP(BSTI) members agreed with this decision. The four Manchester branches, which between them claimed to have 200 members (a third of the party's total membership), resigned from the party in protest, regarding the decision to unite with the CPGB on the basis of a programme including a commitment to parliamentary action as a 'sell-out' to parliamentarism.[48] E. T. Whitehead replied that as far as he was aware 'no single member of this Party is prepared to be a member of a party which adopts revolutionary Parliamentarism as one of its tactics'.[49] Unity with the CPGB and affiliation to the Third International would involve joining organisations committed to the *possibility* of using Revolutionary Parliamentarism, but the CP(BSTI) would still be free to argue against the tactic ever being put into practice. To this end, Sylvia Pankhurst advised the anti-parliamentarians to 'keep together and form a strong, compact left block' within the CPGB and to 'insist that the constitution of the Party should leave them free to propagate their policy in the Party and in the Third International as a whole'. The *Workers' Dreadnought* would continue to appear, as 'an independent organ giving an independent support to the Communist Party from the Left Wing standpoint'.[50]

The CP(BSTI) finally united with the CPGB at a second Communist Unity Convention held in Leeds at the end of January 1921. This provoked an immediate response from those anti-parliamentarians who had doubted the compatibility of opposition to parliamentary action and support for the Third International. The Glasgow Communist Group began publication of a new paper (the *Red Commune*), because 'there is no other party organ in this country . . . that stands fearlessly for Communism. They all urge or compromise with, in some shape or form, parliamentarianism.' The new platform of the Glasgow Communist Group advocated 'Anti-Parliamentary Activity; (a) Boycotting the Ballot Box; (b) Communist Anti-Parliamentary or Sinn Fein Candidature'. The Glasgow Group also invited all anti-parliamentarians to 'unite with us in an anti-Parliamentary Federation or Party'.[51] As a result a conference was held in Glasgow at Easter 1921 at which the Anti-Parliamentary Communist Federation was formed as a direct challenge to the pro-parliamentary CPGB. The Glasgow Communist Group became the Central Branch of the new organisation.

OPPOSITION TO PARLIAMENTARISM AFTER THE FORMATION OF THE CPGB

The CP(BSTI)'s expectation that it would be able to put forward anti-parliamentary views freely within the CPGB turned out to be mistaken. In September 1921 Sylvia Pankhurst was expelled from the CPGB because the *Dreadnought*'s repeated criticisms of CPGB policy contravened party discipline as laid down in the Conditions of Admission.[52] Many of Pankhurst's comrades were forced out of the CPGB on similar charges.

The position that Aldred and the Glasgow Communist Group had adopted – that anti-parliamentarism and support for the Third International were mutually exclusive commitments – proved to be more perceptive. In 1921, while Aldred was serving a one-year prison sentence for sedition arising out of the publication of the *Red Commune*, Rose Witcop went to Russia to sound out the possibility of the APCF acquiring 'associate membership' of the Third International. This could be granted to 'groups or parties . . . who in due course would be prepared to join the national Communist Party of their country'. Aldred was not prepared to contemplate unity with the CPGB, but 'he was not opposed to the mission seeking information and financial backing'. Witcop attended the Third Congress of the International and 'received promise of solid financial backing for the *Spur*, payment of all legal and other expenses of the High Court trial at Glasgow [the *Red Commune* sedition case], maintenance for Guy Aldred whilst in prison, and financial backing when liberated'. However, such support would only be given 'on condition that she could secure the promise by Aldred and the Anti-Parliamentary Communist Federation of acceptance of membership of the Communist Party and the Moscow line'. Since this would have required the APCF to abandon its anti-parliamentary principles, when Guy Aldred was released from prison in mid-1922 all contacts between the APCF and the Third International were severed.[53]

Following her expulsion from the CPGB Sylvia Pankhurst involved herself in efforts to regroup anti-parliamentary communists at a national and international level. The anti-parliamentary Communist Workers' Party of Germany (KAPD), which had been excluded from the International following the Third Congress, had announced that it was a forming a Fourth International. The *Workers' Dreadnought* quickly declared its support for the KAPD's initiative[54] and during the winter of 1921–2 Pankhurst began organising a Communist Workers' Party in Britain. In February 1922 the new party published a brief set of principles which included the statement that it was resolved 'to take no part in elections to Parliament and the local governing bodies, and to carry on propaganda exposing the futility of Communist participation therein'.[55]

Anti-parliamentarism also featured in the programme of the All-Workers' Revolutionary Union, an organisation formed on the *Dreadnought* group's initiative in September 1922. The AWRU was set up as 'One Big Union' which would unite workers in the struggle to overthrow capitalism and then function as the administrative machinery of the post-revolutionary communist society. The AWRU's statement of principles declared: 'The AWRU rejects all responsibility for the administration of the capitalist State or participation in the elections to Parliament and the local governing bodies.'[56]

The programmes adopted by the Communist Workers' Party and the All-Workers' Revolutionary Union set the tone for Sylvia Pankhurst's remarks about the general election held in November 1922: 'We expect nothing from the General Election. It belongs to the Capitalist civilisation which is nearing its end. With that civilisation Parliaments and Cabinets as we know them today will disappear. We are looking forward to the advent of Communism and its industrial councils.'[57]

In the November general election Guy Aldred fulfilled his intention of putting into practice the 'Sinn Fein' tactic by standing in the Glasgow constituency of Shettleston. This caused some dissension within the ranks of the APCF: the 'anarchist faction' within the group 'asserted its opposition to the use of the ballot box even as a weapon against parliamentarism', and the APCF refused to give official support to Aldred's campaign. The APCF's decision was somewhat inconsistent, considering that its forerunner, the Glasgow Communist Group, had endorsed the 'Sinn Fein' policy as a valid anti-parliamentary tactic in the *Red Commune* in February 1921. Nevertheless, 'repudiating the election as a group, the comrades still helped, unenthusiastically, as comrades'.[58]

Aldred's election address stated: 'I stand for the complete and final overthrow of the present social system and the immediate establishment of a Socialist Commonwealth.' He rejected all canvassing, electioneering and promises of reforms. In opposition to 'the capitalist State and the Parliamentary system of Government', he urged workers to 'discover and evolve into a new political or social structure their power on the industrial field'. If elected he would refuse to swear the oath of allegiance to the monarchy or take his seat in Parliament.[59] The result was: J. Wheatley (Labour) 14 695 votes; T. Ramsay (National Liberal) 9704; G. Aldred (Communist) 470.

When the Glasgow Communist Group announced its support for the 'Sinn Fein' tactic in February 1921 the *Workers' Dreadnought* had commented: 'It is a puzzle to us how to reconcile the anti-parliamentarism of the platform of this Group with its tactics of running anti-parliamentary candidates pledged not to take the oath and pledged not to sit.'[60] Consequently, the *Dreadnought* criticised Guy Aldred's Shettleston campaign, dubbing him an 'Anti-Parliamentary Parliamentarian'.[61] In June 1923 Aldred and Pankhurst spoke in opposition to each other in a debate in London, and according to Aldred Pankhurst 'proclaimed herself a convinced anti-parliamentarian and again denounced my Shettleston candidature'. Aldred continued: 'In the *Workers' Dreadnought* for 7th July, 1923 Sylvia Pankhurst returned to her attack on me for the Shettleston campaign and again sneered from the absolute Anti-Parliamentarian standpoint of one who believed in boycotting the ballot box entirely.'[62]

When Sylvia Pankhurst visited Glasgow in November 1923 to address two Scottish Workers' Republican Party municipal election meetings, the APCF made the most of its opportunity to turn the tables. The SWRP had used a *Dreadnought* account of the Poplar Board of Guardians' instigation of a police baton charge on a demonstration of unemployed workers as the basis of a leaflet distributed when Poplar Board member George Lansbury addressed Glasgow Trades Council in October 1923.[63] This was the only link between

Pankhurst and the SWRP, and Pankhurst claimed afterwards that she had spoken *against* parliamentarism at the two meetings.[64] However, her appearance on the platform of a group contesting twelve seats in the municipal elections proved irresistible to the APCF. They distributed a leaflet for the occasion entitled 'Sylvia's Anti-Parliamentary Comedy', in which Pankhurst's criticisms of Aldred were returned in good measure: 'How can the person who urges you to "boycott the ballot box" also advise you to "Vote Red Labour" [the SWRP's campaign slogan]? . . . If it is wrong to support a candidate pledged *not* to take his seat, is it not *more* wrong to support candidates who intend to take their seats?.'[65]

Nevertheless, Pankhurst's appearance on the SWRP platform did not mean that she had changed her attitude towards elections or Parliament. During the 1923 general election she called for propaganda to expose the futility of involvement in Parliamentary elections.[66] The APCF also distributed leaflets urging workers to boycott the ballot box.[67] By the time of the 1924 general election the *Workers' Dreadnought* had ceased publication, but anti-parliamentary propaganda was sustained by the APCF, who repeated that workers 'have nothing to gain from voting. Consequently they should boycott the ballot box.'[68]

REVOLUTIONARY PARLIAMENTARISM

We now turn to a more detailed examination of the precise meanings attached to 'parliamentarism' and 'anti-parliamentarism' during the period covered by the preceding chronological account. After 1917 the anti-parliamentary communists' efforts to define their opposition to parliamentarism were mainly provoked by the Bolsheviks' advocacy of Revolutionary Parliamentarism as a tactic to be adopted by the Third International's member parties. Therefore an examination of the communist theory of anti-parliamentarism is best considered in the context of this tactic.

The Bolsheviks were not suggesting that communists should enter Parliament in order to agitate for reforms. The Third International had been founded on the premise that the era in which reformist legislation benefitting the working class was possible had come to an end, and that '*The epoch of the communist revolution of the proletariat*' had begun.[69] Nor were the Bolsheviks suggesting that the revolution could be carried out 'within the framework of the old bourgeois parliamentary democracy'. The 'most profound revolution in mankind's history' required 'the creation of new forms of democracy, new institutions', which the experience of the revolution in Russia had revealed to be the soviets or workers' councils.[70]

The anti-parliamentary communists in Britain agreed with the Bolsheviks on these points. Rose Witcop stated that 'it is impossible for the working class to gain its emancipation by Act of Parliament',[71] and the WSF argued that the 'guiding and co-ordinating machinery' of the revolutionary struggle 'could take no other form than that of the Soviets'.[72]

The Bolsheviks, however, drew a distinction between 'the question of parliamentarianism as a desirable form of the political regime' and 'the question of using parliament for the purpose of promoting the revolution'.[73] Although the revolution itself would be carried out by soviets and not by Parliament, this did not rule out the possibility of using Parliament to 'promote the revolution' in the meantime. Whether or not communists chose to use Parliament in this way was entirely a tactical matter:

> 'Anti-parliamentarianism' on principle, that is, the absolute and categorical rejection of participation in elections and in revolutionary parliamentary activity, is therefore a naive and childish doctrine which is beneath criticism, a doctrine which is . . . blind to the possibility of revolutionary parliamentarianism.[74]

The Bolsheviks acknowledged that the abstentionist position was 'occasionally founded on a healthy disgust with paltry parliamentary politicians',[75] but they criticised abstentionists for not recognising the possibility of creating 'a new, unusual, non-opportunist, non-careerist parliamentarism'.[76] According to the Bolsheviks, Parliament was a 'tribune' of public opinion which revolutionaries could and should use to influence the masses outside, while election campaigns should also be used as an opportunity for revolutionary propaganda and agitation. This was what the Bolsheviks meant by 'Revolutionary Parliamentarism'. As Lenin put it, 'participation in parliamentary elections and in the struggle on the parliamentary rostrum is *obligatory* for the party of the revolutionary proletariat *precisely* for the purpose of educating the backward strata of *its own class*'.[77] However, the anti-parliamentary communists in Britain doubted that this tactic could be put to any effective use and advanced three main arguments against it.

First, the aim of winning votes would come into conflict with the aim of putting across revolutionary propaganda: 'the way to secure the biggest vote at the polls is to avoid frightening anyone by presenting to the electors diluted reformist Socialism . . . Whatever party runs candidates at the election will trim its sails'.[78] In her letter to Lenin in July 1919 Sylvia Pankhurst explained that

> our movement in Great Britain is ruined by Parliamentarism, and by the County Councils and Town Councils. People wish to be elected to these bodies . . . All work for Socialism is subordinated to these ends; Socialist propaganda is suppressed for fear of losing votes . . . Class consciousness seems to vanish as the elections draw nigh. A party which gains electoral successes is a party lost as far as revolutionary action is concerned.[79]

Secondly, the anti-parliamentary communists disagreed that Parliament could be an effective platform for revolutionary speeches. The *Dreadnought* pointed out that 'most people do not read the verbatim reports of Parliamentary debates'. The capitalist press never gave revolutionary speeches the prominence enjoyed by the utterances of capitalist politicians, and only reported 'those least wise, least coherent sentences . . . which the Press chooses to select just because they are most provocative and least likely to convert'.[80] Guy Aldred argued that 'the value of speeches in Parliament turn upon the power of the press outside and exercise no influence beyond the point allowed by that press'. As long as newspapers' contents remained dictated by the interests of their capitalist owners, revolutionary speech-making in Parliament would be 'impotent as a propaganda activity'.[81] In his Shettleston election address Aldred maintained that 'street-corner oratory educates the worker more effectively than speeches in Parliament'.[82] This being the case there was little to be gained by entering Parliament; as the Glasgow Anarchist Group argued, 'fighters for Revolution can more effectively spend their time in propaganda at the work-gates and public meetings'.[83]

Thirdly, the anti-parliamentary communists pointed out that 'it is the revolutionary parliamentarian who becomes the political opportunist'.[84] They saw 'nothing but meance to the proletarian cause from Communists entering Parliament: first, as revolutionary Communists, only to graduate later, slowly but surely, as reformist politicians'.[85] No matter what their initial intentions might be, communist MPs would soon 'lose themselves in the easy paths of compromise'.[86]

As Pankhurst argued in September 1921, 'the use of Parliamentary action by Communists is . . . bound to lead to the lapses into rank Reformism that we see wherever members of the Communist Party secure election to public bodies'.[87]

When they sought to explain why out-and-out revolutionaries became tame reformists after entering Parliament, the anti-parliamentary communists referred to the class nature of the capitalist state, of which Parliament was a part. The entire function and business of Parliament was concerned with the administration and palliation of the capitalist system in the interest of the ruling class. Parliament was 'the debating chamber of the master class'.[88] Anyone who entered Parliament and participated in its business automatically shouldered responsibility for running capitalism. 'The result of working class representatives taking part in the administration of capitalist machinery, is that the working class representatives become responsible for maintaining capitalist law and order and for enforcing the regulations of the capitalist system itself.'[89] The only way to avoid such lapses into reformism or outright reaction was to shun any participation in capitalism's administrative apparatus – and that meant rejecting any notion that communists should enter Parliament.

The Bolsheviks' most telling response to the anti-parliamentarians' case was to argue that while opportunism, careerism and reformism were characteristics of *capitalist* politicians, there was no reason why *communists* should inevitably end up behaving in the same manner. Willie Gallacher, whose anti-parliamentary views were criticised by Lenin in *'Left-Wing' Communism, An Infantile Disorder*, recalled arguing with Lenin that 'any working class representative who went to Parliament was corrupted in no time'. Lenin then asked Gallacher:

> 'If the workers sent you to represent them in Parliament, would you become corrupt?'
> I answered: 'No, I'm sure that under no circumstances could the bourgeoisie corrupt me.'
> 'Well then, Comrade Gallacher,' he said with a smile, 'you get the workers to send you to Parliament and show them how a revolutionary can make use of it.'[90]

In retrospect, however, this was an argument from which the anti-parliamentary communists emerged victorious. The CPGB *did* use election campaigns to advocate all sorts of reformist demands. The few MPs who represented the CPGB in Parliament *did not* use

Parliament as a platform for revolutionary speeches. Soon after the 1922 general election Sylvia Pankhurst observed that the CPGB's MPs had 'told the House of Commons nothing about Communism . . . Yet it is to secure Parliament for speeches on Communism, and for denunciations of Parliament as an institution, that they claim to have sought election'.[91] Where they won places on elected bodies CPGB members *did* participate in reformist or reactionary administration of parts of the capitalist state. The anti-parliamentary communists' case was strengthened by every 'incorruptible' communist who turned reformist. There was no need to develop any *systematic* explanation for this phenomenon for, in practice, it inevitably occurred, and the anti-parliamentarians were able to point to a never-ending series of examples to support their contentions.

WORKING-CLASS SELF-EMANCIPATION

The anti-parliamentarians' case against Revolutionary Parliamentarism was based on political principles which found expression not only in opposition to the use of elections and Parliament as weapons in the class struggle, but also in every other aspect of their political ideas and activities. It is to a discussion of these underlying principles that we now turn.

The *Spur* argued that anyone who sought to abolish capitalism by first gaining control of Parliament was going the wrong way about it, because 'Parliament is not the master of capitalism, but its most humble servant'.[92] The state, including the Parliamentary apparatus, arose from the conflict between social classes and serves the interests of the ruling class. But the fundamental *source* of the capitalist class's power lies in its ownership and control of the means of production. Therefore, the Glasgow Anarchist Group argued, '*the State cannot be destroyed by sending men to Parliament, as voting cannot abolish the economic power of the capitalists*'.[93] In order to achieve revolutionary social change the working class had to organise its power not in Parliament but on the economic field. As Guy Aldred put it: 'the working class can possess no *positive* or *real power* politically until the workers come together on the industrial field for the definite purpose of themselves taking over directly the administration of wealth production and distribution on behalf of the Workers' Republic'.[94] Parliamentary action was therefore a futile diversion from the real tasks facing the working class. It was necessary for workers to 'look, not to Parliament, but to their own Soviets'.[95]

In order to convey this view to the rest of the working class, it was the duty of revolutionaries to reject parliamentary activity 'because of the clear, unmistakeable lead to the masses which this refusal gives'.[96] The *Dreadnought* group believed that 'the revolution can only be accomplished by those whose minds are awakened and who are inspired by conscious purpose'.[97] The working class's attachment to Parliament would have to be broken as much in the minds of working-class people as in their activities:

> For the overthrow of this old capitalist system, it is necessary that the people should break away in sufficient numbers from support of the capitalist machinery, and set up another system; that they should create and maintain the Soviets as the instruments of establishing Communism. To do this, the workers must be mentally prepared and must also possess the machinery which will enable them to act.[98]

Revolutionaries could not assist this process of 'mental preparation' if they denounced Parliament as a capitalist institution whilst leading workers to the polling booths to elect communist candidates into that institution. Such behaviour would only create confusion. The use of elections and the Parliamentary forum was 'not the best method of preparing the workers to discard their faith in bourgeois democracy and Parliamentary reformism',[99] since 'participation in Parliamentary elections turns the attention of the people to Parliament, which will never emancipate them'.[100]

The anti-parliamentary communists emphasised the importance of widespread class consciousness because they believed that the revolution could not be carried out by any small group of leaders with ideas in advance of the rest of the working class: 'the revolution must not be the work of an enlightened minority despotism, but the social achievement of the mass of the workers, who must decide as to the ways and means'.[101] Parliamentary action restricted workers to a subordinate and passive role as voters and left everything up to the 'leaders' in Parliament: 'Any attempt to use the Parliamentary system encourages among the workers the delusion that leaders can fight their battles for them. Not leadership but MASS ACTION IS ESSENTIAL.'[102] Opposition to parliamentarism was vital, therefore, in order to 'impress upon the people that the power to create the

Communist society is within themselves, and that it will never be created except by their will and their effort'.[103]

The term 'parliamentarism' was in fact used by anti-parliamentarians to describe *all* forms of organisation and activity which divided the working class into leaders and led, perpetuated the working class's subservience, and obstructed the development of widespread revolutionary consciousness. These reasons for opposing parliamentarism – in the widest sense of the term – were expressed in 1920 by the Dutch revolutionary Anton Pannekoek, who was one of the foremost theoreticians among the left communists in Germany:

> parliamentary activity is the paradigm of struggles in which only the leaders are actively involved and in which the masses themselves play a subordinate role. It consists in individual deputies carrying on the main battle; this is bound to arouse the illusion among the masses that others can do their fighting for them . . . the tactical problem is how we are to eradicate the traditional bourgeois mentality which paralyses the strength of the proletarian masses; everything which lends new power to the received conceptions is harmful. The most tenacious and intractable element in this mentality is dependence upon leaders, whom the masses leave to determine general questions and to manage their class affairs. *Parliamentarianism inevitably tends to inhibit the autonomous activity by the masses that is necessary for revolution.*[104]

Parliamentary action – in the strictest sense – was a *paradigm*, that is, the *clearest* example of the sort of activity which anti-parliamentarians opposed; but other forms of action were also open to criticism on precisely the same grounds. For example, Sylvia Pankhurst also described trade unionism as a 'parliamentary' form of organisation, since it 'removes the work of the union from the members to the officials, [and] inevitably creates an apathetic and unenlightened membership'.[105]

The principle of working-class self-emancipation implied that the revolution could be carried out only by an active and class conscious majority of the working class. The anti-parliamentary communists' opposition to electoral and parliamentary activity was an expression of this principle, since parliamentary action obscured the vital point that Parliament was useless as a means of working-class emancipation and diminished the capacity for action by the working class as a whole. Opposition to parliamentary forms of organisation and activity was the 'negative' aspect of the principle of working-class self-emancipation; its positive aspect was expressed in the anti-parliamentary communists' support for all forms of working-class activity which encouraged the development of the class's own consciousness and capacity to act by and for itself.

•

THE MEANING OF COMMUNISM

The belief that widespread class consciousness was one of the essential preconditions of revolutionary working-class action – a belief which played such an important part in determining the anti-parliamentarians' opposition to parliamentary action – also meant that descriptions of socialism or communism (the two terms were used interchangeably) occupied a prominent place in the anti-parliamentarians' propaganda. The anti-parliamentary communists believed that 'until the minds and desires of the people have been prepared for Communism, Communism cannot come',[106] and that 'since the masses are as yet but vaguely aware of the idea of Communism, its advocates should be ever vigilant and active in presenting it in a comprehensible form'.[107] The subject of the final section of this chapter is the idea of communism which the anti-parliamentary communists presented to the masses.

According to the anti-parliamentarians, communist society would be based on common ownership of all wealth and means of wealth-production. The abolition of private property would be decisive in overthrowing capitalism: 'Social revolution means that the socially useable means of production shall be declared common-wealth . . . It shall be the private possession of none.'[108] As soon as private property had given way to common ownership all men and women would stand in equal relationship to the means of production. The 'division of society into classes' would 'disappear'[109] and be replaced by 'a classless order of free human beings living on terms of economic and political equality'.[110] Communism would also mean the destruction of the state, which, as an institution 'erected for the specific purpose of protecting private property and perpetuating wage-slavery',[111] would disappear as a consequence of the abolition of private property and of the division of society into classes. This classless, stateless human community based on common ownership of the means of production would also involve production for use, democratic control and free access. These three features of communist society will now be explained and examined.

Under capitalism, virtually all wealth is produced in the form of commodities, that is, goods which are produced to be sold (or otherwise exchanged) for profit via the market. In other words, there is no *direct* link between the production of wealth and the satisfaction of people's material needs. Such a link is established only tenuously, if at all, through the mediation of the market and the dictates of production for profit. Regardless of their real material needs, people's level of consumption is determined by whether or not they possess the means to purchase the things they require. What the system of commodity production means in practice is that the class in society which owns and controls the means of production accumulates vast extremes of wealth, while the class which is excluded from ownership and control of the means of production – the vast majority of the world's inhabitants – exists in a state of constant material insecurity and deprivation. The solution to this problem would be: 'The overthrow of Capitalism and its system of production for profit and the substitution of a system of Communism and production for use.'[112] Communism would abolish the market economy and undertake production to satisfy people's needs directly.

This takes us to the second feature of communist society mentioned earlier – democratic control, or 'the administration of wealth by those who produce wealth for the benefit of the wealth producers'.[113] Just as the struggle to overthrow capitalism would involve the conscious and active participation of the mass of the working class, so too in the post-revolutionary society of communism would the mass of the people be able to participate actively in deciding how the means of wealth-production should be used. In institutional terms this would be realised through the soviets or workers' councils, which would be 'the administrative machinery for supplying the needs of the people in communist society'.[114] The soviets would be 'councils of delegates, appointed and instructed by the workers in every kind of industry, by the workers on the land, and the workers in the home'.[115] Council delegates would be 'sent to voice the needs and desires of others like themselves'.[116]

In this way 'the average need and desire for any commodity [meaning here, any object] will be ascertained, and the natural resources and labour power of the community will be organised to meet that need'.[117] Decisions about what to produce, in what quantities, by what methods and so on, would no longer be the exclusive preserve of a minority as they are in capitalist society. Instead, the soviet decision-making machinery would 'confer at all times a direct individual franchise on each member of the community'.[118] All decisions concerning production would be made according to the freely-chosen needs and desires expresssed by all members of society.

We come now to the third feature of communist society mentioned earlier: free access. The abolition of commodity production and the establishment of common ownership would mean an end to all forms of exchange: 'Money will no longer exist . . . There will be no selling, because there will be no buyers, since everyone will be able to obtain everything at will, without payment.'[119] Selling and buying imply the existence of private property: someone first has to have exclusive ownership of an object before they can be in a position to dispose of it by selling it, while someone else first has to be excluded from using that object if the only way they can gain access to it is through buying it. If common ownership existed there would be no reason for people to have to buy objects which they already owned anyway. In short, access to wealth would be free.

As a classless society of free access and production for use, communism would also mean an end to exchange relations between buyers and sellers of the particular commodity *labour power* (that is, between the capitalist and working classes, or bourgeoisie and proletariat). No-one's material existence would depend on having to sell their ability to work in return for a wage or salary. Sylvia Pankhurst wrote that 'wages under Communism will be abolished'[120] and that 'when Communism is in being there will be no proletariat, as we understand the term today'.[121] The direct bond between production and consumption which exists under capitalism would be severed: there would be no 'direct reward for services rendered'.[122] People's needs would be supplied 'unchecked' and 'independent of service'.[123] On the basis of the principle that 'each person takes according to need, and each one gives according to ability',[124] everyone would share in the necessary productive work of the community and everyone would freely satisfy their personal needs from the wealth created by the common effort.

The establishment of free access to the use and enjoyment of common wealth would facilitate the disappearance of the state's coercive apparatus. The concept of 'theft', for example, would lose all meaning. Thus, 'Under Communism, Courts of Justice will speedily become unnecessary, since most of what is called crime has its origins in economic need, and in the evils and conventions of capitalist society'.[125] For the same reasons, 'stealing, forgery, burglary, and all economic crimes will disappear, with all the objectionable apparatus for preventing, detecting and punishing them'.[126]

Common objections encountered by advocates of communism are that a society based on free access to wealth be open to abuse through greed and gluttony, and that there would be no incentive to work. Such assertions are often based on a conception of human nature which sees people as inherently covetous and lazy. The standard communist response is to deny that any such thing as human nature exists. What these opponents of communism are referring to is human *behaviour*, which is not a set of immutable traits but varies according to material circumstances. Such a distinction (between human nature and human behaviour) is useful in making sense of some of the anti-parliamentarians' arguments. However, a conception of human nature does appear to lie beneath other arguments that they used – albeit a conception radically different from that which sees people as naturally idle beings. Rose Witcop argued that 'the physical need for work; and the freedom to choose one's work and one's methods' were in fact basic human needs and urges.[127] Indeed, this could be taken as another example of capitalism's inability to satisfy basic human needs. Within the capitalist system workers are not free to choose what work they do and how they do it. Such decisions are not made by the workers, but by their bosses. Only 'when the workers manage the industries', Sylvia Pankhurst argued, would they be able to make decisions about the conditions of production 'according to their desires and social needs'.[128]

At this point it might be helpful to draw a distinction between 'work', meaning freely-undertaken creative activity, and 'employment', meaning the economic compulsion to carry out tasks in order to earn a living. The anti-parliamentarians felt that an aversion to the latter was perfectly understandable, since employment in this sense could be seen as 'unnatural': 'a healthy being does not need the whip of compulsion, because work is a physical necessity, and the desire to be lazy is a disease of the capitalist system'.[129] In a communist society employment, or forced labour, would give way to work in the sense of fulfilment of the basic human need for freely-undertaken creative activity. As Guy Aldred pointed out, the urge to satisfy this need was evident in workers' behaviour even under capitalism; communism would provide the conditions for its most complete fulfilment: 'Men and women insist on discovering hobbies with which to amuse themselves after having sweated for a master. Does it not follow that, in a free society, not only would each work for all, but each would toil with earnest devotion at that which best suited and expressed his or her temperament?.'[130] Sylvia Pankhurst shared Aldred's expectations: in her vision of communism 'labour is a joy, and the workers toil to increase their skill and swiftness, and bend all their efforts to perfect the task'.[131] Thus the severance of all direct links between 'services rendered' and 'rewards' would not result in any lack of inclination to work, because in a communist society work would be enjoyable and satisfying in itself, instead of simply a means to an end.

The anti-parliamentary communists approached the problem of abuse of free access in a number of ways. First, on a common sense level, Rose Witcop pointed out that 'a man can consume two lunches in one day only at his peril, and wear two suits of clothing, or make a storehouse of his dwelling, only to his own discomfiture'. In the unlikely event of anyone wanting to discomfit themselves in such a way, 'we will be content to humour such pitiful perverseness. It is the least we can do'.[132]

Secondly, the anti-parliamentary communists argued that greed was a behavioural response to the scarcity which characterised capitalist society. Different material conditions would produce other forms of behaviour. The establishment of communism would 'provide a soil in which the social instincts of mankind will rapidly develop. The anti-social propensities not being stimulated by unbearable economic pressure will tend consequently to die out.'[133] Sylvia Pankhurst also argued that as a behavioural response to scarcity greed would disappear when the circumstances which stimulated it were abolished. While suggesting that a communist society would not permit anyone to 'hoard up goods for themselves that they do not require and cannot use', she went on to argue: 'the only way to prevent such practices is not by making them punishable; it is by creating a society in which . . . no-one cares to be encumbered with a private hoard of goods when all that they need is readily supplied as they need it from the common storehouse'.[134]

These comments suggest a third way of ovecoming the problem of abuse of free access. 'Over-indulgence' presupposed a continuation of scarcity: if one person consumed more than their 'fair share' there would be insufficient left over for everyone else. However, if there was sufficient wealth to satisfy everyone's needs, no matter how much any individual wanted to consume, then the problem of abuse of free access would disappear, along with any need to refute such an objection with arguments concerning altruism, human nature and so on. This was the main way in which the anti-parliamentary communists addressed the problem of abuse of free access. According to Sylvia Pankhurst, in a communist society there would be 'Abundance for all'[135] and people's needs would be satisfied 'without stint or measure'.[136]

The question of how a communist society would be able to provide abundance was tackled in a number of ways.

First, the meaning of abundance was related to the level of needs which people in a communist society might be expected to express. Rose Witcop observed 'how few things we really need': food, clothing and shelter by way of material essentials, and work, comradeship and freedom from restrictions by way of non-material essentials.[137] This might sound more like austerity than abundance – but if a communist society satisfied only these basic needs and nothing more it would still be a vast improvement on capitalism for most of the world's population, since capitalism has never shown itself capable of providing even these most basic of needs for more than a small minority of the world's inhabitants.

Even if abundance is defined merely as the adequate provision of basics such as food, clothing and shelter, this still begs the question of how communism would be able to provide everyone with such things when capitalism patently cannot. To answer this question we must move on to a second argument put forward by the anti-parliamentary communists. Through its constant development of the means of production and distribution capitalism itself had laid the technological foundations upon which a society of abundance could be built. So long as the level of production remained fettered by the dictates of production for profit via the market, the potential for abundance which capitalism had created would never be realised. The communist revolution would smash these fetters and institute direct production for use. New inventions and technology in the field of production would be applied to the satisfaction of human needs. They would 'constantly facilitate' greater and greater increases in society's productive capacity and 'remove any need for rationing or limiting of consumption'.[138] In short, there would be 'plenty for all'.[139]

Thirdly, the anti-parliamentary communists argued that levels of production would also be boosted by integrating into socially-useful productive activity the vast numbers of people whose occupations were specific to a money–market–wages system:

> Just consider the immense untapped reservoirs for the production of almost unlimited supplies of every imaginable form of useful wealth. Think of the scores of millions of unemployed, not forgetting the useless drones at the top of the social ladder. Estimate also the millions of officials, attendants, flunkeys, whose potentially valuable time is wasted under this system. Consider the wealth that could be created by the huge army of needless advertising agents, commercial travellers, club-men, shop-walkers, etc., not to mention the colossal army of police, lawyers, judges, clerks, who are ONLY 'NECESSARY' UNDER CAPITALISM! Add now the scandalous waste of labour involved in the military machine – soldiers, airmen, navymen, officers, generals, admirals, etc. Add, also, the terrific consumption of energy in the manufacture of armaments of all kinds that is weighing down the productive machine. Properly used, these boundless supplies of potential wealth-creating energy, could ensure ample for all – not excluding 'luxuries' – together with a ridiculously short working day. Likewise, there would be pleasant conditions of labour, and recreation and holidays on a scale now only enjoyed by the rich![140]

Finally, the anti-parliamentary communists argued that communism had to be established on a global scale, so that to assist its aim of bringing about abundance for all communism would have the productive capacity and resources of the entire world at its disposal.

Only when abundance was not assumed did the anti-parliamentary communists fall back on a view of people as naturally altruistic beings. Sylvia Pankhurst acknowledged the possibility of 'some untoward circumstance' producing 'a temporary shortage'. To cope with scarcity in such circumstances everyone would 'willingly share what there is, the children and the weaker alone receiving privileges, which are not asked, but thrust upon them'.[141]

When the anti-parliamentarians described themselves as communists, therefore, they meant that they stood for the establishment of a classless, stateless society based on common ownership and democratic control of the world's resources, in which money, exchange and production for profit would be replaced by production for the direct satisfaction of people's needs and free access to the use and enjoyment of all wealth.

The description of communism was a vital element in the anti-parliamentarians' propaganda, since it held out the prospect of a solution to the problems confronting working-class people every day of their lives. However, the description of communist society was more than just a pole-star guiding the direction of the class struggle. After the Russian revolution the anti-parliamentary communists were confronted with a regime under which, it was widely believed, the distant goal of communism was actually being brought into reality. In Chapter 2 one of the issues which will be discussed is the extent to which the anti-parliamentarians were able to evaluate this claim by using the conception of communism outlined above as their yardstick.

2 The Russian Revolution

For better or worse the events of the Russian revolution and its aftermath influenced virtually all the areas of anti-parliamentary communist thought discussed in Chapters 1–4 of this account. Particular aspects of the revolution's impact–such as the way in which perceptions of the soviets' role during and after the revolution changed the WSF's view of Parliament as an instrument of social change – are mainly dealt with in Chapters 1, 3 and 4. This chapter concentrates on the anti-parliamentary communists' interpretation of the revolution itself, their theoretical and practical responses to it, and their assessment of the changes which took place in Russia after 1917.

FROM THE FEBRUARY TO THE OCTOBER REVOLUTION

During 1917 two demands dominated the WSF's propaganda: extension of the suffrage to every adult woman and man, and an end to the war. Because of these emphases in its own politics the WSF welcomed the February Revolution in Russia. The tyrannical Russian monarchy had been overthrown, clearing the way for government by a constituent assembly elected on the basis of universal suffrage. Moreover, since the overthrow of the Tsar had been motivated by war-weariness and a desire for peace on the part of the Russian workers and peasants, it seemed logical to conclude that these same workers and peasants would proceed to elect a government pledged to end Russia's involvement in the war. If this happened the other belligerent countries would surely be quick to follow Russia's example.

The WSF's views were not shared by Guy Aldred and his comrades. Aldred conceded that the new Russian government might be 'more enlightened' than its predecessor and that a republic might be 'saner' than a monarchy, but if the experience of parliamentary democracy in Britain was anything to go by the establishment of a similar system in Russia gave little cause for celebration. 'We know that tomorrow, the apostle of socialism will be jailed again in Russia, for sedition and what not. And so "we do not celebrate the Russian revolution". We prefer to work for Socialism, for the only possible social revolution, that of the world's working-class against the world's ruling-class.'[1] Aldred and his comrades also differed from the WSF in their views about how to end the war. While the WSF regarded peace as something for the people to demand and for governments to negotiate, anti-parliamentarians such as Rose Witcop advocated direct action by the working class. 'The suggestion of telling the Government what we want points to the incapacity . . . to grip the spirit of the Russian people. In Russia they did not reason with or explain to the Czar . . . they just *gave the Government to understand* by downing their bayonets!'. In addition to the view implied by this remark – that mutiny among the armed forces would be one way of bringing the war to an end – Witcop also called for 'industrial action' and 'no bargaining with Governments'.[2]

Despite their contrasting responses to the February Revolution, writers in the *Spur* and the *Dreadnought* agreed that the struggle in Russia was unlikely to come to a halt at whatever had been achieved in February.

In October 1917 Glasgow Anarchist Group member Freda Cohen reported widespread dissatisfaction in the ranks of the Russian army and 'some rumour of the peasants seizing the land'. To all close observers of events it was obvious that the struggle going on in Russia was 'not, as it seemed at the beginning, simply a political or anti-Czarist one'. According to Cohen 'the struggle going on there in broad daylight, just reflects the self-same struggle that has been, and is going on underground, all over the world'. By this Cohen meant the *class* struggle between the capitalists and the working class, and she predicted that the Russian workers would not be content with 'settling down in the old work-a-day world with no other gain than a new set of masters and newly forged chains'.[3] Sylvia Pankhurst had hinted at a similar prognosis a few months earlier when she had asked rhetorically: 'Is it not plain that still the Russian Revolution is continuing: still the struggle is going on: still the hold of the capitalists is upon the country and only in part is it overthrown?'[4]

Following the February Revolution the *Dreadnought* had drawn attention to the situation of dual power which existed between the Provisional Government appointed by the Duma and the 'Council of Labour Deputies' responsible to workers and soldiers.[5] At the end of June 1917 it reported that the 'Council of Workers' And Soldiers' Deputies' was now capable of overthrowing the Provisional Government should it wish to do so. Discussing the various Russian political parties' attitudes towards this situation the *Dreadnought* explained that while the Mensheviks were disinclined to support any seizure of power by the workers' and soldiers' councils,

> The Maximalists and Leninites, on the other hand, desire to cut adrift from the capitalist parties altogether, and to establish a Socialist system of organisation and industry in Russia, before Russian capitalism, which is as yet in its infancy, gains power and becomes more difficult than at present to overthrow. We deeply sympathise with this view.[6]

Thereafter the *Dreadnought* continued to note the growing strength of the Bolsheviks and to express its agreement with their aims. In August, for example, mass desertions from the army and rapidly-falling living standards in Petrograd were said to be winning support for 'the position adopted at the outset by Lenin . . . namely, that Free Russia must refuse to continue fighting in a capitalist War'. The *Dreadnought* added that Lenin's view was 'a position which we ourselves have advocated from the first'.[7]

At the end of September the *Dreadnought* reported with 'great satisfaction' that 'the Socialists who are variously called Bolsheviks, Maximalists and Leninites have secured a majority on the Council of Workers' and Soldiers' Delegates'. For the benefit of its readers the report outlined the main points of the Bolshevik programme:

> The Maximalists are the International Socialists who recognise that this is a capitalist War and demand an immediate peace, and who desire to establish in Russia not a semi-Democratic Government and the capitalist system such as we have in England, but a Socialist State. They desire Socialism, not in some far away future, but in the immediate present. The Maximalists desire that the CWSD [Council of Workers' and Soldiers' Delegates] shall become the Government of Russia until the Elections for the Constituent Assembly have taken place.[8]

Finally, when it heard that the Bolsheviks had seized power in the October Revolution the *Dreadnought* announced its wholehearted support for this turn of events: 'the latest revolt of the Russian Revolution, the revolt with which the name of Lenin is associated, has been brought about in order that the workers of Russia may no longer be disinherited and oppressed. This revolt is the happening which definitely makes the Russian Revolution of the twentieth century the first of its kind'. The seizure of power was described as a 'Socialist Revolution' with 'aims and ideals' which were 'incompatible with those of capitalism'.[9]

The *Spur*'s immediate reaction echoed this assessment of the October Revolution's nature and historic significance. An article signed by 'Narodnik' drew comparisons with the French Revolution of 1789; like its historic predecessor, the October Revolution was 'a social revolution in the fullest meaning of the word; a radical changing of all the economic, political and social arrangements; a grand attempt to reconstruct the whole structure of society, upon an entirely new foundation'.[10]

WAR AND INTERVENTION

While the *Spur* group regarded the October Revolution as a herald of the social revolution of the world's working class against the world's ruling class to which Guy Aldred had referred after the February Revolution, the WSF welcomed it more as a blow struck for world peace, and responded by demanding the conclusion of a peace to end the world war and by campaigning against Allied military intervention in Russia.

In contrast to the Bolsheviks' revolutionary defeatist wartime slogan of 'turn the imperialist war into civil war', the peace appeals issued by the new Bolshevik government called for a 'just, democratic peace' based on no annexations, no indemnities, and the right of nations to self-determination. This policy, which 'contained an element of calculated appeal to American opinion and to such radical opinion in other countries as might be sympathetic to it',[11] immediately struck a sympathetic chord with the WSF. Sylvia Pankhurst had already suggested in August 1917 that the WSF should make a new banner bearing the slogan 'Negotiate For Peace On The Russian Terms: No Annexations: No Indemnities',[12] and after the October Revolution Pankhurst's articles in the *Workers' Dreadnought* frequently linked the call for peace on these terms with the fact that these were also the Bolsheviks' demands. In December 1917, for example, Pankhurst stated: 'We take our stand on the Russian declaration: "No annexations, no indemnities, the right of the peoples to decide their own destiny".'[13]

When peace negotiations between Russia and Germany opened at

Brest-Litovsk towards the end of 1917, the WSF argued that other belligerent governments should follow Russia's example – 'The Russian Socialist Government is showing us the way to obtain a just Peace' – and urged the British labour movement to give 'strong backing for the Russian negotiators at Brest-Litovsk'.[14] While the talks were in progress Sylvia Pankhurst pointed out that 'whilst some capitalist sections would endeavour to cajole the Russian Socialists [such as the German government, which had agreed to negotiate], others would coerce them'.[15] Opposition to such coercers' – governments which sought to overthrow the Bolshevik regime by military intervention and aid to the Bolsheviks' internal enemies – became the predominant element in the WSF's response to the Russian revolution after Russia's withdrawal from the war in March 1918. Harry Pollitt recalled that his 'main sphere of activity at this time was with the Workers' Socialist Federation, doing propaganda for Russia. Sylvia Pankhurst was, of course, the leading spirit in the Federation . . . I covered the greater part of London with her group. We held meetings on Saturday nights and Sunday mornings, afternoons and evenings'. Even 20 years later, by which time he had become a high-ranking member of the CPGB, Pollitt's experience of working with the WSF in the anti-interventionist 'Hands Off Russia' campaign forced him to admit that the WSF had been 'made up of the most self-sacrificing and hard-working comrades it has been my fortune to come in contact with'.[16] This gives a revealing insight into the importance which the WSF attached to opposing intervention, and the amount of time and effort which it put into the campaign. Opposition to intervention was also a persistent theme of Sylvia Pankhurst's articles about international affairs in the *Workers' Dreadnought* until the threat of intervention finally came to an end in the autumn of 1920.

The WSF's campaign against intervention was aimed at three targets. One of these was the British government. In March 1918 Sylvia Pankhurst wrote of the 'urgent need that the Governments of all Europe should feel the pressure of the workers in their respective countries to prevent the crushing of Socialism in Russia'.[17] At its 1918 Annual Conference the WSF called on the British government to bestow legal recognition on its Russian counterpart and to initiate peace negotiations on the Bolshevik terms of no annexations, no indemnities and the right of nations to decide their own destinies.[18]

Secondly, the WSF's campaign was intended to influence the organised labour movement in Britain. A *Dreadnought* editorial addressed to delegates attending the January 1918 Labour Party conference urged the labour movement to 'bring every means at its disposal to support the Russian Socialist Government, the first working class Government that the world has ever seen'.[19] This meant protesting against foreign intervention in Russia.

Thirdly, the WSF's campaign was aimed at rank and file workers. At the end of 1919 the WSF demanded recognition of the Russian government, withdrawal of aid to its internal enemies and an end to intervention, and called for the organisation of a rank and file conference to make these demands and to censure the leaders of the Labour Party, TUC and Triple Alliance for their failure to organise militant opposition to intervention.[20] In July 1918 the WSF participated in the formation of a People's Russian Information Bureau which was intended to increase British workers' awareness of developments in Russia and so arouse them from their role as 'passive spectators' and 'inarticulate tools in the great struggle between the old regime of capitalism and the uprising workers of the world'.[21] The WSF believed that workers in the Allied countries held 'the key to the situation', since 'the International Capitalist war against the Workers' Soviet Republics cannot be carried on a day without the assistance of Allied workers'. Accordingly, in July 1918 the WSF called for a 'Workers' Blockade Of The Counter-Revolution', by means of an international general strike which would force the 'International Capitalists' to make peace with the 'Soviet Republics'.[22]

In the main, therefore, the WSF's efforts were directed towards encouraging workers in Britain to act as a pressure group to try to influence the British government's policies in favour of the interests of the Russian government. Only occasionally did the *Dreadnought* hint at a different approach to the survival of the Bolshevik regime. In April 1919 Sylvia Pankhurst argued that the 'most effectual way' to end 'the war against the Soviets of Russia' would be to 'set up the Soviets in Britain'.[23] Similarly, on May Day 1920 she wrote that there would be no peace with the Russian regime, nor with any other 'Communist republic' which might be established, 'whilst capitalism rules the powerful nations of the world'.[24] These comments suggested that the fate of the Russian revolution depended on the overthrow of capitalism elsewhere in the world – that the best way to defend the Bolshevik regime would be to attack the capitalist regimes. As will become apparent later, however, the infrequency with which the WSF put forward such a line of argument is particularly significant in view of the *Dreadnought* group's subsequent reappraisal of the events of this period.

'SOCIALISM IN THE MAKING'

The amount of time and energy which the WSF put into the 'Hands Off Russia' campaign invites an examination of what the WSF thought it would be protecting when it called for defence of Soviet Russia.

Several of the comments quoted already from the *Workers Dreadnought* referred to the 'socialist' or 'working class' government in Russia, and to Russia as a 'soviet' or 'workers' ' republic. The WSF believed that the October Revolution had given the Russian working class control of state power. This belief was based on the view that the soviets or workers' councils were in charge of post-revolutionary Russian society. Since the soviets were exclusively working-class organisations, and Russia was being ruled by the soviets, this meant that the working class was now exercising its own power over society as a whole.

The *Dreadnought*'s accounts of the changes taking place in Russia after the revolution were frequently published under the headline 'Socialism In The Making', implying that the Russian working class was presiding over a society in which socialism was being built. The ideas which the anti-parliamentarians put forward during 1919–21 concerning this notion of a 'transitional period' provide one of the most striking examples of how the Russian revolution and its aftermath made an impact on the views of the anti-parliamentary communists in Britain.

In August 1921 Sylvia Pankhurst wrote: 'Frankly, we do not believe that society will reorganise itself without the use of force on both sides, because the present system is maintained by force.'[25] In its attempts to seize and maintain power the working class would encounter violent resistance from the ruling class. The revolutionary period would be akin to 'civil war'.[26] The *Dreadnought* group repeatedly argued that for the duration of this period of revolutionary civil war the working class would have to exercise a dictatorship over the rest of society through its soviets.[27] This was a view shared by Guy Aldred and his comrades. In 1920 Aldred wrote of the need for 'a transitional period during which the workers must protect the revolution and organise to crush the counter-revolution. Every action of the working-class during that period must be organised, must be power-action, and consequently dictatorial.'[28] When the 'dictatorship of the proletariat' became a contentious issue amongst anarchists who interpreted anarchy literally as the abolition of *all* authority, Aldred insisted that 'there can be no efficient pursuit of working class emancipation without the establishment of the proletarian dictatorship'.[29] He was, moreover, quite prepared to defend the implication of this view – that anarchists who did not support the dictatorship were in effect counter-revolutionaries: 'those Anarchists who oppose the dictatorship of the proletariat as a transitional measure are getting dangerously near assisting the cause of the reactionaries, though their motives may be the highest. As a believer in the class struggle, I do not share their infatuation for abstract liberty at the expense of real social liberty.'[30]

Supporters of the proletarian dictatorship saw it as a temporary expedient: 'The dictatorship in so far as it is genuine and defensible, is the suppression by Workers' Soviets of capitalism and the attempt to re-establish it. This should be a temporary state of war.'[31] The dictatorship would be necessary until the counter-revolution had been quelled and the expropriated ruling class had 'settled down to accept the new order'.[32] With the disappearance of social classes, the dictatorship – initially the political expression of working-class power over the rest of society – would gradually wither away: 'As the counter-revolution weakens, the Soviet Republic will lose its political character and assume purely useful administrative functions.'[33]

Pending the achievement of a completely classless society, however, the working class would have to adopt a series of transitional measures. As long as the state of civil war continued the workers would have to disarm the ex-ruling class and create their own 'Red Army'.[34] Anyone attempting to reintroduce economic exploitation or refusing to undertake socially useful work would be deprived of political rights: 'No person may vote, or be elected to the Soviets who refuses to work for the community, who employs others for private gain, engages in private trading, or lives on accumulated wealth. In the Soviet community such persons will soon cease to exist.'[35] This system would be enforced in part through the administration of 'revolutionary justice' by judges elected by and answerable to the soviets.[36]

During the transitional period work would be compulsory for everyone. Sylvia Pankhurst suggested that 'in the early stages before the hatred of work born of present conditions has disappeared, the community might decide that an adult person should show either a certificate of employment from his workshop or a certificate from his doctor when applying for supplies from the common storehouse'.[37] In other words the compulsion to work would come from material necessity, since only those people who had first made a contribution to production would be allowed to satisfy their needs from the communal storehouses.

Sylvia Pankhurst was explicit that during the transitional period a wages system would still exist: 'after long experience of Capitalism . . . it would be difficult to abolish the wage system altogether, without first passing through the stage of equal wages'.[38] No indication was given of how long this 'stage' or 'era' might have to last, nor was there any suggestion as to how the step from the equal wages system to a wageless society might be effected. Equal wages would be accompanied by free provision of staple necessities and 'equal rationing of scarce commodities' until the application of technology began to produce wealth in abundant quantities.[39]

Workers' labour power was not the only commodity which would be subject to buying and selling during the transitional period. The CP(BSTI)'s programme assumed that all exchange transactions should be under the exclusive control of the state: 'For the period in which money and trading shall continue, local and national Soviet banks will be set up and shall be the only banks.'[40]

Practically all the features of the anti-parliamentarians' description of the transitional period were also features of early post-revolutionary Russia. During 1918–20 a civil war raged as the White forces and foreign powers tried to overthrow the newly-established Bolshevik regime. The Red Army was created to defend the state against this onslaught. During the same period the economic system known as War Communism came into being. Work became, in effect, compulsory for all: 'On every wall . . . "He who does not work, neither shall he eat", was blazoned abroad.'[41] Staple necessities were provided free and scarce commodities strictly rationed: 'At its lowest, in the first quarter of 1921, only 6.8 per cent of "wages" were paid in money, the rest being issued free in the form of goods and services.'[42] Efforts were made to reduce wage differentials with the aim of achieving equality of wages. The State Bank and all private banks were seized, nationalised and amalgamated into the People's Bank of the Russian Republic. State finance came under the control of the Supreme Council of National Economy. Attempts were made to bring all trade under state control: there was 'a resolute attempt to suppress free trade in essentials. Private trade in a wide range of consumers' goods was forbidden.'[43]

Thus the anti-parliamentary communists in Britain used the specific experience of post-revolutionary Russia as a model for all future communist revolutions. This reveals a great deal about the anti-parliamentarians' view of the Russian revolution and the society which emerged afterwards. They would not have generalised from the Russian example in such a manner had they not believed that the October Revolution had been a working-class, communist revolution, and that Russian society after 1917 was in the midst of a transition towards a communist society.

THE 'REVERSION TO CAPITALISM'

While such an assessment sums up the anti-parliamentarians' view of Russia during the first three years after the revolution, a very different point of view emerged thereafter. Until 1921 the anti-parliamentarians believed that although the Russian workers had not yet achieved their final goal they were still progressing in the right direction. What characterised the *Dreadnought*'s analysis from the end of 1921 onwards, however, was the identification of a reversal in the direction of events – in fact, a 'reversion to capitalism'.[44]

An early intimation of this view appeared in the *Dreadnought* in September 1921, when Sylvia Pankhurst referred to 'the drift to the Right in Soviet Russia, which has permitted the re-introduction of many features of Capitalism'. Pankhurst also noted 'strong differences of opinion amongst Russian Communists and throughout the Communist International as to how far such retrogression can be tolerated'. In the same issue of the *Dreadnought* A. Ironie drew attention to the the recent re-establishment of payment for basic necessities, restoration of rents, and reinstatement of property to expropriated owners. Ironie argued that the Bolsheviks could not 'justify their claims to being the means of transition towards common-ownership whilst the decrees quoted above witness a retrogression in the opposite direction'.[45]

These two articles marked the beginning of the *Dreadnought* group's thoroughgoing reassessment of the society which had emerged in Russia.

Whereas in August 1918 the *Dreadnought* had reported that the revolution had established a system of collective workers' control of industry,[46] in January 1922 Sylvia Pankhurst argued that 'in Russia, as a matter of fact . . . there is an antagonism between the workers and those who are administering industry'. A 'theoretically correct Soviet community' where 'the workers, through their Soviets, which are indistinguishable from them, should administer' had 'not been achieved'.[47]

During the earliest days of the revolution the *Dreadnought* had also applauded the expropriation of large landowners and the redistribution of land amongst the peasantry. In May 1922, however, Pankhurst cited 'the fact that the land of Russia is privately worked by the peasants' as evidence that socialism *did not* exist in Russia.[48]

The *Dreadnought*'s belief that the Russian working class exercised a dictatorship over society through its soviets was also called into question. In July 1923 Sylvia Pankhurst wrote that 'the term "dictatorship of the proletariat" has been used to justify the dictatorship of a party clique of officials over their own party members and over the people at large'.[49]

One of Pankhurst's last articles in the *Dreadnought* on the subject of Russia and the Bolsheviks made a wholly unfavourable assessment of the party she had once admired for its apparent determination to establish socialism 'in the immediate present', and of the country previously taken as a model for the post-revolutionary society. The Bolsheviks, Pankhurst wrote,

> pose now as the prophets of centralised efficiency, trustification, State control, and the discipline of the proletariat in the interests of increased production . . . the Russian workers remain wage slaves, and very poor ones, working, not from free will, but under compulson of economic need, and kept in their subordinate position by . . . State coercion.[50]

As we have seen, the *Dreadnought* group's ideas about the post-revolutionary transition to communism were modelled on the period when the policy of War Communism was in operation in Russia. In February 1921, however, War Communism was abandoned in favour of the New Economic Policy (NEP). This was regarded by the *Dreadnought* group as the decisive turning-point in the fortunes of the revolution. Between March and August 1921 private trade was legalised and an agricultural tax in kind introduced (allowing peasants to sell their surplus produce for profit); small-scale nationalisation was revoked; leasing of enterprises to private individuals began; and payment of wages in cash, charges for services, and the operation of trade and industry on an explicitly commercial basis, were all instituted. Thus in September 1921, when Pankhurst first referred to Russia's 'reversion to capitalism', she supported her argument by pointing to the 're-introduction of many features of Capitalism, such as school fees, rent, and charges for light, fuel, trains, trams and so on'. The 'retrogressive' changes noted by A. Ironie were also introduced under the NEP.[51] The *Dreadnought* group's belief in the direct links between the abandonment of War Communism, the introduction of the NEP, and the 'revival of capitalism' was made explicit in December 1921, when Sylvia Pankhurst referred to 'Russia's "new economic policy" of reversion to capitalism'.[52]

The following two years witnessed a series of events which the *Dreadnought* group interpreted as confirming its view that the introduction of the NEP had set Russia on course for a return to capitalism. The first such event occurred in December 1921, when the Executive Committee of the Communist International adopted the United Front tactic. The *Dreadnought* group regarded this as complementary to the NEP: the latter made concessions to capitalism within Russia, the former advocated co-operation with capitalist parties outside Russia. In Pankhurst's opinion, the adoption of the tactic proved that 'the Russian Soviet Government and those under its influence have abandoned the struggle for the International Proletarian Revolution and are devoting their attention to the capitalist development of Soviet Russia'.[53]

Shortly after denouncing the United Front the *Dreadnought* reported that the Russian government had invited people with technical qualifications to emigrate to Russia to exploit coal and iron concessions in the Kuznets Basin area. Sylvia Pankhurst saw that the 'Kuzbas' scheme would regenerate capitalist social relations between owners of capital and wage labourers, and asked: '*What is to become of the Russian workers' dream of controlling their own industry through their industrial soviets?* . . . for the natives of Kuzbas, it seems that another Revolution will be needed to free them from the proposed yoke.'[54]

Russia's participation at the Genoa conference in April 1922 – convened after a meeting of Allied industrialists had agreed that Europe's economic recovery depended on 'large-scale investment in Soviet Russia' and 'the exploitation of Russian resources'[55]

– was regarded as further proof of the Bolsheviks' willingness to place Russian workers 'under the yoke of the foreign capitalist', and that 'the principles of Communism in Russia' were 'being surrendered'.[56]

Another apparent indication of the Bolshevik regime's surrender to capitalism was pointed out in 1923, when the German Communist Party was attempting to organise insurrections in various regions of Germany. Trotsky was reported as having ruled out Russian intervention in Germany even if events reached the point of civil war and revolution, since the Russian government was more interested in maintaining the confidence of the foreign capitalists who had invested in Russia: 'Leon Trotzki and his colleagues are prepared to put their trade with international capitalists and the agreements they have made with capitalist firms, before Communism, before the proletarian revolution and the pledge they have made to the German comrades to come to their aid in the hour of need.'[57]

The events outlined above were regarded by the *Dreadnought* group as *symptoms* of Russia's 'reversion to capitalism'. When it came to suggesting *causes* the group put forward an explanation which can be separated into five inter-related parts.

First, the group adhered to the view that all societies had to pass through certain stages of historical development. The Bolsheviks' attempt to establish socialism in a basically feudal society had been 'in defiance of the theory that Russia must pass through capitalism before it can reach Communism'. The Bolsheviks had 'made themselves the slaves of that theory'[58] because they had found it impossible to leap straight from feudalism to communism and consequently had been forced to take on the task of initiating the era of capitalism themselves. The theory of stages of development was bound up with the anti-parliamentary communists' view of communism as a society of free access to wealth. If capitalism had not fulfilled its historic role of developing the forces of production to the point where production of wealth in abundance became possible, one of communism's essential preconditions would be lacking and any attempt to establish a communist society would founder. Thus 'the state of Russia's economic development and the material conditions with which she is faced' had 'rendered inevitable the failure of the Soviet Government to maintain a fighting lead in the world revolutionary struggle'.[59]

Secondly, the *Dreadnought* group regarded the Russian peasantry as an anti-communist force: 'In Russia the ideal of the land worker was to produce for himself on his own holding and to sell his own products, not to work in co-operation with others.' Socialism would find 'its most congenial soil in a society based on mutual aid and mutual dependence', not in a country where an individualistic peasantry overwhelmingly outnumbered any other class.[60] In 1917 Sylvia Pankhurst had welcomed the redistribution of land among the peasants; later, she criticised the Bolsheviks for having done exactly what she herself had once recommended: 'Instead of urging the peasants, and leading the peasants, to seize the land and cut it up for *individual ownership*, the right course was to have endeavoured to induce them to seize the land for *common ownership*, its products being applied to common use.' The Bolsheviks' support for individual rather than common ownership – an attempt to 'save time by refraining from bringing the land workers to a state of communism' – had led 'directly and inevitably to reaction'.[61]

A third part of the explanation for the 'reversion to capitalism' concerned working-class control of production. The *Dreadnought* argued that 'until the workers are organised industrially on Soviet lines, and are able to hold their own and control industry, a successful Soviet Communist revolution cannot be carried through, nor can Communism exist without that necessary condition'.[62] This necessary condition had not been fulfilled in Russia; 'though the Soviets were supposed to have taken power, the Soviet structure had yet to be created and made to function'.[63] To support this view the *Dreadnought* quoted the Bolshevik Kamenev's report to the seventh All-Russian Congress of Soviets in 1920: 'Even where Soviets existed, their general assemblies were often rare, and when held, frequently only listened to a few speeches and dispersed without transacting any real business'.[64] Such evidence led the *Dreadnought* to abandon its view that Russian industry was controlled by the workers through their own industrial soviets: 'Administration has been largely by Government departments, working often without the active, ready co-operation, sometimes even with the hostility of groups of workers who ought to have been taking a responsible share in administration. To this cause must largely be attributed Soviet Russia's defeat on the economic front.'[65]

This reference to administration by government departments, as opposed to by the workers themselves, leads to the fourth part of the

Dreadnought's explanation. In one of the first *Dreadnought* articles questioning the authenticity of Russia's claims to communism, A. Ironie had written: 'The realisation of Communism, i.e., not Communist Partyism, but the common-ownership and use of the means of production, and the common enjoyment of the products, still remains a problem to be solved by the creative genius of the people freely organising themselves; or not at all.'[66] Ironie's counter-position of the party and the self-organised working class implied that the interests of the Bolsheviks and those of the Russian workers had conflicted. Only the conscious participation of the whole working class would assure the success of the communist revolution; Ironie's remarks suggested that this essential precondition had been lacking in Russia. Any attempt to establish communism by a small group acting on behalf of the working class would result only in the dictatorial rule of a minority – not communism, but Communist-Partyism.

The final part of the explanation put forward by the anti-parliamentary communists focused on the failure of working-class revolution elsewhere in Europe, and the Russian regime's consequent isolation. Sylvia Pankhurst argued that other countries' 'failure to become Communist' held back 'the progress of Russian Communism'.[67] There was a limit to the advances the revolution could make, surrounded by a hostile capitalist world. Ultimately, the Bolsheviks' fate would depend on whether or not the revolution could be extended beyond Russia's boundaries. The introduction of the NEP – seen as inaugurating the 'reversion to capitalism' – was attributed to 'the pressure of encircling capitalism and the [revolutionary] backwardness of the Western democracies'.[68] Russia's isolation could be overcome either through the world revolution or through succumbing to the pressure of encircling capitalism and compromising with the capitalist powers. In the *Dreadnought* group's opinion the Bolsheviks had concluded that the first of these options was no longer viable; consequently, the second option had been forced upon them. In November 1922 Sylvia Pankhurst wrote in an Open Letter to Lenin: 'It seems that you have lost faith in the possibility of securing the emancipation of the workers and the establishment of world Communism in our time. You have preferred to retain office under Capitalism than to stand by Communism and fall with it if need be.'[69] The symptoms of the 'reversion to capitalism' – outlined earlier – were all taken as evidence of the Bolsheviks' determination to retain state power, even at the cost of Russia's reintegration into the world capitalist economy and the abandonment of communism.

While the *Dreadnought* group argued that the failure of revolutions elsewhere in Europe had forced the Bolsheviks to break their isolation by negotiating with capitalist governments, other anti-parliamentary communists pointed out that the converse was also true: these same negotiations acted as a brake on the emergence of revolution outside Russia. At the Third Congress of the Communist International in 1921 the Communist Workers' Party of Germany (KAPD) delegate Sachs observed that

> agreements and treaties which contributed to Russia's economic progress also strengthened capitalism in the countries with which the treaties were concluded . . . Sachs referred to an interview given by Krasin to the *Rote Fahne* in which the British miners' strike was said to have interfered with the execution of the Anglo-Soviet Trade agreement.[70]

A similar observation had been made by Guy Aldred in 1920. When he learned of Lenin's support for Revolutionary Parliamentarism Aldred was strongly critical of this tactic, yet he realised why Lenin had been forced into making his 'Fatal Compromise': 'Circumstances are compelling [Lenin] to give up his dream of an immediate world revolution and to concentrate on conserving and protecting the Russian revolution.'[71] Such compromises would be 'inevitable until the world revolution makes an end of the present false position in which Lenin and his colleagues find themselves'.[72] Yet the reformist policies of the Communist International could also reinforce Russia's isolation. Lenin was counting on the support of parliamentary reformists in Western Europe to bring temporary protection to the Russian regime, but the regime in Russia could only be saved permanently by the world revolution. It was not the parliamentary reformists who would inaugurate this revolution, but the anti-parliamentary communists, on whom Lenin had now turned his back: 'Desiring not to weaken the Russian revolution by declaring war on the political opportunists and parliamentarians, Lenin has succeeded in endangering that revolution by proclaiming war on the anti-parliamentarians and so on the world revolution itself.'[73]

The reformist policies advocated by Lenin caused Aldred and his comrades to 'suspend' their support for the Communist International. Lenin had chosen to take whatever measures were necessary to defend the Bolshevik regime; the *Spur* group had chosen to continue to work for the world revolution. 'Lenin's task compels him to compromise with all the elect of bourgeois society whereas ours demands no compromise. And so we take different paths and are only on the most distant speaking terms.'[74]

THE CAPITALIST STATE AND THE COMMUNIST INTERNATIONAL

When Aldred argued that the different priorities chosen by Lenin and the *Spur* group had forced them to part company, it was tantamount to arguing that the Bolshevik regime's interests no longer coincided with, or were perhaps even opposed to, those of the world revolution. There was the potential in Aldred's argument to conclude that since the Bolshevik-dominated Communist International was the instrument of the Russian regime's foreign policy, if the policies of the Communist International were counter-revolutionary it could only be because the Russian regime itself was also counter-revolutionary.

This was the argument put forward by some anti-parliamentary communist groups, such as the Communist Workers' Party of Germany (KAPD). Following its exclusion from the Communist International after the Third Congress in 1921, the KAPD initiated the formation of a new, Fourth International – the Communist Workers' International, or KAI. The Manifesto of the KAI argued that 1917 had been a 'dual revolution': '*In the large towns it was a change from capitalism to Socialism; in the country districts the change from feudalism to capitalism. In the large towns, the proletarian revolution came to pass; in the country the bourgeois revolution.*' Initially, the incompatible objectives of the communist working class and the capitalist peasantry had been submerged in an alliance against their common enemy, the feudal aristocracy, but once this ruling class had been overthrown and the counter-revolution suppressed the 'absolute, insurmountable contradictions – *class contradictions*' – between the working class and the peasants burst forth. The Bolsheviks capitulated to peasant demands in 1921 when they brought in the New Economic Policy, which introduced '*capitalist production for profit for the whole of agricultural Russia*'. Production for profit in industry soon followed. As with every other nation state, Russia's foreign policy was shaped by its dominant domestic interests. Since the NEP had turned Russia into a 'peasant–capitalist' state, 'the desires and interests of the peasants in their capacity as capitalist owners of private property' were now 'directing the course of the Soviet Government in foreign policy'. And since 'The Third Congress of the Third International has definitely and indissolubly linked the fate of the Third International to present Soviet Russia', the policies of the International were now being dictated by the interests of a capitalist state.[75]

The starting-point of the KAPD's critique – its opposition to policies adopted by the Communist International – was shared by Guy Aldred. But unlike the German left communists, Aldred did not explain the objectively counter-revolutionary nature of the Communist International's policies by reference to the counter-revolutionary character of the Russian regime. There were two main reasons for this. First, Aldred and his comrades maintained a distinction between the policies pursued internationally by the Bolsheviks, through their control of the Communist International, and the policies they pursued domestically through their control of the Russian government. The former may have been counter-revolutionary, but in Aldred's opinion this did not necessarily imply that the same could be said of the latter. Compared to the KAPD and the *Dreadnought* group, in fact, Aldred and his comrades were remarkably uncritical of the Russian regime. In November 1923, for example, in an article headlined 'Hail Soviet Russia!!', Aldred wrote: 'To the Communist International we send our greetings and declare that there can be *no* united front with parliamentary labourism and reformism . . . The Communist International must be Anti-Parliamentarian in action and stand for the unity of the revolutionary left.' In other words, Aldred's differences with the Third International were essentially *tactical* disagreements over Revolutionary Parliamentarism and the United Front. Although the International had adopted certain mistaken policies, it remained at heart a sound revolutionary organisation. In the same article, Aldred's criticisms of the International were strictly separated from his remarks about the Russian regime itself, for which he had nothing but praise: 'This month Soviet Russia celebrates her sixth birthday. We send our revolutionary greetings to our comrades, the Russian Workers and Peasants, who have triumphed over all forces of counter-revolution and pestilence, and made Russia the beacon light of socialist struggle and the Soviet principle the rallying point of the world's toilers.'[76]

PERSECUTION OF REVOLUTIONARIES IN RUSSIA

The other reason for Aldred's lack of criticism of the Bolshevik regime lay in his dislike of certain people who *were* critical of the Bolsheviks. Until 1925 Aldred's view of Russia was apparently governed by the maxim, 'my enemy's enemy is my friend'.

In September 1923 Aldred responded to criticisms of Russia made by W. C. Owen, in the London anarchist journal *Freedom*, by stating: 'We are not uncritical admirers of the Bolshevik regime and we are willing to side with left-wing criticism. But we do demand that the critics shall be free from reproach and suspicion.' In Aldred's opinion, Owen did not satisfy this criterion since he had 'ratted to capitalist patriotism' by supporting the First World War.[77] The terms for any discussion about Russia were thus established: if a critic's revolutionary credentials were not impeccable Aldred would automatically regard any criticisms he or she made as groundless.

In mid-1924 the APCF's journal, the *Commune*, published letters from various anarchist organisations complaining about the persecution of revolutionaries in Russia. To begin with Aldred was reasonably open-minded. He acknowledged that 'if men and women, who have served faithfully the working class, are suffering in Russian dungeons, then we, who protest against workers being imprisoned in capitalist prisons, must raise our voices in solemn protest'. Yet he was not convinced that the anarchists' allegations were true, and so concluded by requesting

> from whatever source such information is forthcoming, details concerning the imprisonment and exile 'of persecuted revolutionists in Russia'. Are there social revolutionaries in exile and imprisoned in Russia? What are their names, revolutionary records, and present offences? Let us have the facts. We can judge for ourselves whether their crimes were those of revolution or counter-revolution.[78]

Despite the deluge of information which this appeal brought forth, Aldred remained sceptical. In August 1924 he repeated: 'We want the truth. The cry of "safeguarding the revolution" can be used as an excuse for tyranny. The cry of "Anarchism and Liberty" may conceal a counter-revolutionary conspiracy. We want to cut through phrases and get down to facts.'[79]

Some of the *Commune*'s correspondents were baffled by Aldred's scepticism. When Aldred asked whether genuine revolutionaries really were being persecuted in Russia, Alexander Berkman replied: 'One might justly assume that these questions are asked by a gentleman just arrived from the moon. It is incomprehensible to me, at least, that an editor of a revolutionary publication should ask such questions – *seven years later*, so to speak; that is, after seven years of Communist dictatorship in Russia.'[80] Aldred defended his attitude by referring to the dubious credentials of some of the people involved in publicising allegations of persecution, and he invited the Bolsheviks to refute the allegations or else explain and justify their actions.

Until the end of 1924 Aldred had been careful not to portray Emma Goldman as a 'dubious' critic, since he believed that her record as a revolutionary was irreproachable, but the controversy soon became so heated that this concession was tossed aside. Aldred wrote that Goldman's criticisms of the Bolsheviks were indistinguishable from White propaganda, and that opponents of anarchism and communism were happily quoting her remarks in support of their own reactionary causes.[81] In the February 1925 issue of the *Commune* Aldred referred pointedly to the keenness with which capitalist publishers – hardly renowned for their enthusiasm to see anarchists' writings in print – had rushed to publish Goldman's denunciation of the Bolshevik regime, *My Disillusionment in Russia*. In April Aldred demanded that the 'revolutionary scab' and 'ex-anarchist' Goldman should be 'boycotted and condemned by every worker for her infamous associations. She is a traitor to labour's struggle who should be "fired" with enthusiasm – from each and every proletarian assembly.'[82]

While Aldred was certainly not unique in adopting this attitude towards Goldman's criticisms of the Bolsheviks, he was foolish to let the personal animosity he felt towards certain individuals, which in its origins had little to do with the issues at stake, interfere so severely with the clarity of his political perception and judgement. By contrast, the record of the *Workers' Dreadnought* group was far more impressive. Throughout 1921–4 the *Dreadnought* group expressed solidarity with communist opposition groups in Russia and published several opposition manifestoes received from Russia.

On 3 September 1921 an article by Alexandra Kollontai, outlining the views of the Workers' Opposition, appeared in the *Dreadnought*, and between April and August 1922 there followed a serialisation of Kollontai's text, 'Russian Workers v. Soviet Government'. The

Dreadnought group soon declared, however, that the 'so-called' Workers' Opposition was 'unprincipled and backboneless'[83] and transferred its support to the Group of Revolutionary Left-Wing Communists of Russia, which had been formed after splitting from the Bolshevik party around March 1922. The *Dreadnought* described this group as 'the genuine Communists in Russia, who are making a stand against the United Front and state capitalism and who are upholding the standpoint of the Communist Workers' Party of Germany'.[84] In one of its manifestoes the Russian group attacked opportunism and reformism in the Bolsheviks' domestic and international policies, criticised the Communist International for becoming 'bound up with the capitalism which is being newly introduced into Russia', and condemned the United Front tactic as a policy intended to promote the 'proposed reconstruction of capitalist world economy'.[85]

In December 1923 the *Dreadnought* published the manifesto of the Workers' Group. Formed in March 1923 as 'a direct offshoot of the Workers' Opposition', the Workers' Group's best-known member was Gabriel Miasnikov, 'an old worker-Bolshevik, and a party member since 1906', who was expelled from the party in February 1922.[86] Miasnikov was associated with clandestine opposition to the Bolsheviks in Russia until the late 1920s, when he escaped to Paris.

After spending nearly eighteen months vigorously refuting allegations that genuine revolutionaries were being persecuted by the Bolsheviks, the article Guy Aldred wrote for the eighth anniversary of the Russian revolution in November 1925 was itself filled with references to 'our persecuted comrades in Russia' and 'our comrades rotting in the Soviet prisons'.[87] Ironically, among the persecuted comrades Aldred had in mind were communists such as Miasnikov, whose case the *Dreadnought* had been championing for a long time.The APCF's sudden conversion to the *Dreadnought* group's point of view is discussed in Chapter 5.

THE 'REVERSION' ARGUMENT: AN ASSESSMENT

When it comes to assessing the anti-parliamentary communists' attitude towards Russia after 1917, it would be hard to avoid dwelling on some of the confusions and inconsistencies in their ideas.

The argument that there was a 'reversion to capitalism' in Russia after 1921 implied that during 1917–21 Russia was socialist/

communist in nature. When it tried to explain why this 'reversion' had taken place, however, the *Dreadnought* group failed to bring to light any new factors that had come into play after 1921 which had not also influenced events before then.

The *Dreadnought* group argued that the Bolsheviks had been forced to introduce capitalism in Russia because their attempt to pass straight from feudalism to communism had run aground on an unavoidable 'law of history' – the necessity of the capitalist era. If such a 'law' did exist, however, the constraints it placed on the options open to revolutionaries would surely have been no less strict in 1917 than they were four years later. Another of the group's explanations was that it had proved impossible to establish communism in a society dominated by a petit-bourgeois peasantry. Yet the petit-bourgeois aspirations of the Russian peasants were surely just as strong in 1917 as they were in the following years. The *Dreadnought* group also argued that Russian industry, and society in general, was controlled by the government, rather than the workers' councils, and that there was an antagonistic relationship between the state and the working class. However, Sylvia Pankhurst herself acknowledged that 'though the Soviets were supposed to have taken power' in 1917, in actual fact 'the Soviet structure had yet to be created and made to function'.[88]

The 'reversion to capitalism' argument appears even more implausible when the nature of the 'communism' which the *Dreadnought* group claimed existed in Russia during 1917–21 is examined. According to the description outlined in Chapter 1, the anti-parliamentarians saw communism as a stateless, classless, moneyless, wageless society. However, in the so-called 'transitional period' (which the anti-parliamentarians modelled on post-revolutionary Russia) the state, classes, money and wages – in fact, *all* the features of capitalism that a genuinely communist revolution would abolish – still existed. The usual Leninist riposte to this is that the transitional period is neither capitalist nor communist in nature, but is occupied by a third type of social formation called 'socialism'. However, such a distinction between socialism and communism was completely foreign to the anti-parliamentary communists, for whom the two terms were synonymous. Judging by the anti-parliamentary communists' own definitions, therefore, it was not communism which existed in Russia during the so-called 'transitional period' after 1917, but capitalism.

Some of the other inconsistencies and confusions in the *Dreadnought* group's views can be explained by the changes which took place in the group's own political ideas between 1917 and 1924, and hence in its criteria for evaluating what was happening in Russia. The standpoint from which the *Dreadnought* group viewed events in Russia changed considerably during 1917–24. During 1917–18, for example, the group assessed the significance of the Brest-Litovsk peace negotiations between Russia and Germany according to their contribution towards world peace. When world revolution became the group's major preoccupation, its assessment of negotiations between Russia and other states was different. In October 1921, for example, Sylvia Pankhurst predicted that 'all attempts by Soviet Russia to conciliate and negotiate with the forces of Capitalism will turn out to have been gravely mistaken',[89] and three years later she argued that 'as soon as the Soviet Government began to negotiate with capitalist governments it placed itself upon the inclined plane which leads to the surrender of principle and the abandonment of the revolutionary conquest'.[90]

The present-day observer can view the Russian revolution and its aftermath from a priviledged vantage point, resting on more than 60 years of hindsight. The *Dreadnought* group had to form its views on the spot, without any such advantages. In retrospect it is relatively easy to argue that the *Dreadnought* group's view of Russian society during 1917–21, and the policies the group supported during those years, were mistaken; that at no time after 1917 was anything remotely resembling communism established in Russia; and that since there had been no departure from capitalism in Russia the notion that a 'reversion' to capitalism had taken place there was wrong. However, to expect the *Dreadnought* group to have admitted all this at the beginning of the 1920s, and to have extended its criticisms of Russia right back to 1917, is perhaps to expect the group to have shown an almost superhuman degree of mental toughness and theoretical rigour. These steps, which seem easy to trace today, were ones which the anti-parliamentary communists in Britain never took. After the end of 1925, when the APCF began to revise its own attitude towards Russia, the view it adopted was the one which the *Dreadnought* group had propagated, contradictions included.

Even so, the balance sheet of the *Dreadnought* group's attempts to grapple with the Russian question was far from being entirely negative. In the critique of Russia inherited by the APCF from the *Dreadnought* group, the burden of inconsistencies weighed comparatively lightly when set alongside that critique's many positive aspects. If in the years after 1925 the APCF had been confronted with the emergence of a regime resembling War Communist Russia, it is conceivable that the negative aspects of the *Dreadnought* group's legacy might have led the APCF to support such a regime. Yet no such circumstance ever arose. As we will see in later chapters, circumstances were such that the APCF was always able to assert the positive points of the critique pioneered by the *Dreadnought* group: that Russia was not communist, but state capitalist, and that when the communist revolution did arrive the ruling class in Russia would have to be swept aside with all the rest of the world's capitalists. As a guide to the positions which the anti-parliamentary communists were to adopt towards the crucial issues of the day during the next 20 years, the validity and value of these conclusions drawn by the *Dreadnought* group turned out to be unaffected by having been reached through faulty explanations.

3 The Labour Party

Despite the limitations imposed by their relatively small numbers, the anti-parliamentary communist groups made every effort to involve themselves actively in the struggles of their fellow workers. This forced them to take up positions with regard to organisations and ideas which were dominant within the working class and through which workers' struggles were channelled. In terms of their numerical support and entrenchment within the working class, the most important of these organisations were the Labour Party and trade unions. The two remaining chapters of Part I are devoted to an examination of the anti-parliamentarans' attitudes towards these organisations.

GUY ALDRED AND THE LABOUR PARTY

Guy Aldred's account of his 'conversion' to revolutionary politics in 1906 hints at the basic elements of the anti-parliamentary communist attitude towards the Labour Party: 'My Anti-Parliamentarian and Socialist Revolt against Labourism dates from the elevation of John Burns to Cabinet rank, and the definite emergence of the Labour Party as a factor in British politics.'[1] A significant point is the connection drawn between the rise of the Labour Party and Aldred's opposition to parliamentarism. The anti-parliamentary communists believed that parliamentary action inevitably led to reformism, careerism and responsibility for the administration of capitalism. Aldred argued, for example, that 'Parliamentarism is careerism and the betrayal of Socialism',[2] and that 'all parliamentarism is reformism and opportunism'.[3] In 1906 30 of the Labour Party's 51 general election candidates were elected to Parliament. Thereafter, according to the anti-parliamentary point of view, the Labour Party could not avoid being anything but a careerist, reformist and opportunist organisation.

Every criticism which the anti-parliamentary communists made of parliamentary action in general was also applicable to the Labour Party in particular. When Labour candidates stood for election, like all other candidates they had to seek votes from 'an electorate anxious for some immediate reform'; consequently, 'the need for social emancipation' was set aside 'in order to pander to some passing bias for urgent useless amelioration'.[4] Labour's pursuit of electoral success could thus be said to be at the root of its reformism.

Aldred also argued that parliamentarians were primarily professional politicians whose own careers took precedence over the need for social change:

> the Labour movement is regarded as carrion by the parliamentary birds of prey, who start in the gutter, risk nothing, and rise to place in class society . . . the emotions of the careerist belong to the moment and express only one concern: how to exploit human wrong in order to secure power.
>
> The careerist exploits grievances. He never feels them. He never comes to grips with them. He never attempts to remove them. He uses grievances as stepping stones to office and then mocks those who have suffered.[5]

Thus a second significant point in Aldred's explanation of his arrival at the anti-parliamentary position is his reference to John Burns' career. Burns – one of fourteen children in a working-class family – was originally a member of the Social Democratic Federation and one of the 1889 dockers' strike leaders. In 1892 he was elected to Parliament on the Labour ticket, but tended to favour an alliance with progressive Liberals and did not look favourably on attempts to form an independent labour party. At the conference in 1900 which established the Labour Representation Committee, he declared himself 'tired of working class boots, working class houses, working class trains and working class margarine'.[6] By 1906 he had become President of the Local Government Board in the Liberal government. From the anti-parliamentary point of view Burns' career was seen as typical of the parliamentarians whose elevation from 'the gutter' to 'place in class society' was invariably accompanied by a steady rightwards evolution in political outlook.

The anti-parliamentarians also argued that by participating in Parliament the Labour Party upheld the class state and the capitalist system. Believing that the working class's revolutionary interests could not be expressed through Parliament, Aldred stated: 'The Labour Party is not a class party. It does not express the interests of the working class. It is the last hope of the capitalist system, the final bulwark of class-society . . . The entire outlook of the Labour Party is a capitalist outlook.'[7] In 1924 Aldred made explicit his belief that

Labour's reformism, careerism and capitalist outlook were the inevitable outcome of its parliamentarism. Referring to Ramsay MacDonald, he wrote that 'High Finance has, among its political adepts, no more devoted servant than the Labour Premier of Great Britain', and explained that 'MacDonald's record . . . is the natural and consistent expression of parliamentarism. The remedy is not the passing of MacDonald, but the destruction of parliamentarism.'[8]

This outline of Guy Aldred's attitude towards the Labour Party has been drawn from sources covering a period stretching from 1906 to the mid-1950s. As this suggests, Aldred was consistently opposed to the Labour Party throughout the period discussed in this book. The same could not be said of the *Dreadnought* group. As was the case with the issue of parliamentary action, the early history of the WSF was one of gradual advance towards a position already held by Aldred and his comrades.

THE WSF AND THE LABOUR PARTY

Far from being 'categorically opposed to any form of contact with the Labour Party' as one historian has claimed,[9] before 1920 the WSF was closely involved with the Labour Party in a variety of ways. In March 1917, for example, the WSF Executive Committee heard that Sylvia Pankhurst had attended the recent Labour Party conference as a Hackney Trades and Labour Council delegate.[10] The *Dreadnought* usually published detailed reports of Labour Party conference proceedings, and WSF members attended these conferences in order to distribute their newspaper. In April 1918 a WSF general meeting was informed that Sylvia Pankhurst had been elected to Poplar Trades Council and local Labour Party. In Pankhurst's opinion 'it was well for the WSF to be on the local Labour Party to start with', although 'the time might come when we could not continue in the Party'.[11] Accepting this view, the WSF Finance Committee agreed in September 1918 that the WSF should remain affiliated to Hackney Labour Party. At the same time Sylvia Pankhurst and Melvina Walker were appointed as delegates to the first Labour Party Women's Section conference, a report of which appeared afterwards in the *Dreadnought*.[12]

Although it was working within the Labour Party during these years, the WSF was certainly not an uncritical supporter of everything Labour did or stood for. One of the WSF's principal disagreements concerned the Labour Party's support for the war. The target for much of this criticism was Labour MP Arthur Henderson, who had joined the Coalition government in May 1915 as President of the Board of Education, before becoming a member of the new War Cabinet in December 1916. In Sylvia Pankhurst's view Henderson had 'sacrificed the interests of Socialism and the workers for the opportunity to co-operate with the capitalist parties in carrying on the War'.[13] Although Henderson resigned from the government in August 1917, in his letter of resignation addressed to Prime Minister Lloyd George he stated: 'I continue to share your desire that the war should be carried to a successful conclusion.'[14] Henderson's membership of the War Cabinet made him a widely detested figure since it implicated him in the imprisonment of socialists and the suppression of socialist propaganda, the execution of James Connolly, the introduction of industrial conscription under the Defence of the Realm Act, and the deportation of Clydeside labour leaders. Henderson was not alone in coming in for criticism, however, as the WSF levelled its attacks against the entire Labour leadership. In April 1918, for example, the *Dreadnought* stated: 'We shrink from the prospect of a Labour government manned by the Labour leaders who have co-operated in the prosecution of the War and its iniquities and who have been but the echo of the capitalist politicians with whom they have associated.'[15] Likewise, during the 1918 general election campaign the WSF criticised the Labour Party for the way it had 'crawled at the heels of the capitalist Government throughout the War'.[16]

The WSF's other main criticism concerned the programme and membership of the Labour Party. In December 1917 Sylvia Pankhurst complained that the agenda for the forthcoming Labour conference was 'loaded with palliatives, without a hint of Socialism, which alone can emancipate the workers!'[17] In March 1918 she argued that Labour's programme for 'A New Social Order' was 'mainly a poor patchwork of feeble palliatives and envisages no new order, but the perpetuation of the present one . . . Nowhere in the programme is the demand for Socialism expressed'.[18]

If the Labour Party's political programme did little to inspire Pankhurst's enthusiasm the new party constitution, published for discussion in October 1917, aroused her fears about the party's membership. Among the new constitution's proposal was the enrolment of individual members who had not passed through what Pankhurst called the 'narrow gate' of trade union membership, or membership of organisations such as the BSP or ILP. Pankhurst argued that 'the enrolment of individual members from the non-industrial classes . . . might prove a drag on the proletarian elements in the Party during the critical years which are ahead'. It would also attract self-seeking elements – 'people of no settled or deep convictions may find membership of the Labour Party a convenient method of attaining to the management of people and affairs' – while the rank and file working-class members would tend to be pushed even further into the background in the organisation and conduct of the party.[19]

The WSF put forward several proposals designed to put right the problems it had identified. When Sylvia Pankhurst attended the Labour Party conference in June 1918 she spoke in favour of Labour withdrawing from the Coalition government and ending the wartime 'political truce'. A resolution advocating the latter was passed, but Pankhurst's attempt to move an amendment to the motion adding that Labour Party members should resign from the government was ruled out on procedural grounds.[20]

The WSF's solution to the problem of Labour's war-collaborationist leadership was to elect new leaders who opposed the war. The alternative to a party under the leadership of those who had co-operated in the prosecution of the war was to 'secure International Socialist leadership in the Labour movement'.[21]

The WSF also advocated changes in the Labour Party's programme; in October 1917 Sylvia Pankhurst wrote: 'The Labour Party should set itself to draw up a strong working-class socialist programme, and should act upon it vigorously and continuously.'[22] The WSF expected this to bring four main benefits. First, an uncompromising socialist programme would deter self-seeking elements. Secondly, 'all the various smaller Socialist organisations and unattached members will gradually be pooled within [the Labour Party's] ranks'.[23] Thirdly, insistence on agreement with a socialist programme as a condition of membership would have the educational effect of raising the political consciousness of the 'large masses of people who are vaguely revolutionary in their tendencies and always ready to criticise those in power, but who have never mastered any economic or political theory'.[24] Fourthly, the adoption of a socialist programme would keep the party leaders under control. If the party was rebuilt 'on a clearly defined basis, uncorrupted by considerations of temporary political expediency', there would be no scope for the leadership to engage in reformist or opportunist manoeuvres.[25]

These proposals were all formulated in the context of working *from within* to transform the Labour Party into a genuine socialist organisation. During 1919, however, the WSF abandoned this approach and began to advocate a regroupment of revolutionaries *outside* and *against* the Labour Party.

A major cause of the WSF's change of view was the group's perception of the role played by the German Social Democratic Party (SPD), when it came to power in November 1918 in the midst of the revolutionary upheaval at the end of the war. One of the SPD's leaders, Gustave Noske, organised an alliance with the right wing para-military Freikorps to suppress and butcher the insurrectionary workers. In Guy Aldred's words, the SPD 'slaughtered to preserve the tottering power of Capitalism'.[26] For the WSF, the lesson of the SPD's leading part in crushing the German revolution was that 'when the social patriotic reformists come into power, they fight to stave off the workers' revolution with as strong a determination as that displayed by the capitalists'.[27]

A second important influence on the WSF's change of attitude towards the Labour Party was the formation of the Third International on the Bolsheviks' initiative in March 1919. Until the end of 1918 the WSF had hoped to see the social democratic Second International reconstituted, but when a definite attempt to revive the Second International was initiated at the beginning of 1919, Sylvia Pankhurst argued that it could no longer be considered 'a genuine International, because those who are today leading the Socialist movement – the Russian Bolsheviki and the Sparticists of Germany – will be absent from its councils'.[28] Subsequently the resolutions adopted by the conference in Berne in February 1919, which re-established the Second International, were criticised strongly in the *Workers' Dreadnought*, and the WSF Annual Conference in June 1919 instructed the WSF Executive Committee to link up with the new Third International.

This had important implications for the WSF's attitude towards the Labour Party. The invitation to the First Congress of the Communist International issued by the Bolsheviks in January 1919 had stated:

> Towards the social-chauvinists, who everywhere at critical moments come out in arms against the proletarian revolution, no other attitude but unrelenting struggle is possible. As to the 'centre' – the tactics of splitting off the revolutionary elements and unsparing criticism and exposure of the leaders. Organisational

> separation from the centrists is at a certain stage of development absolutely necessary.[29]

These views were reaffirmed by a resolution 'On The Berne Conference Of The Parties Of The Second International', adopted by the First Congress of the Third International in March 1919.[30] Since groups seeking to affiliate to the new International would have to adopt the same stance, the WSF's support for the Third International was obviously an important factor contributing to the group's split with the Labour Party.

The changes wrought by these factors could be seen unfolding in the WSF's internal life during 1919. In May the WSF's Bow branch was informed that three of its members (Melvina Walker, Norah Smyth and L. Watts) had been elected to Poplar Trades Council and Central Labour Party.[31] Soon afterwards the question of affiliation to Poplar Labour Party was raised at a WSF Executive Committee meeting, which accepted the view that local branches should have 'free autonomy to affiliate to Local Labour Parties'.[32] At the WSF Annual Conference in June, however, a resolution was passed instructing all branches affiliated to the Labour Party to disaffiliate.[33] The Executive Committee was instructed to begin talks with other organisations to form a communist party in Britain, and it mandated WSF delegates to 'stand fast' on the principle of 'No Affiliation to the Labour Party'.[34] A subsequent WSF membership ballot revealed that an overwhelming majority approved the Executive Committee's instructions.[35] Yet despite these decisions nearly two months elapsed before the Executive Committee learnt of Poplar WSF's expulsion from Poplar Trades Council, Melvina Walker's removal from the Executive Committee of Poplar Labour Party, and the revocation of Walker's mandate as a delegate to the Central Labour Party and London Trades Council.[36] On 20 July 1919 Poplar WSF members had

> unintentionally provoked a crisis by making an unscheduled appearance at the Labour Party's meeting against Russian intervention, commandeering a trades council lorry as a platform, and haranguing the crowds on the virtues of Sovietism. The following week Norah Smyth received a curt letter from Poplar Labour Party informing her that the WSF had been expelled.[37]

The fact that Poplar WSF had been expelled from the Labour Party, rather than resign voluntarily in line with the resolutions of the

1919 Annual Conference, indicates that some WSF members may still have been in favour of involvement with the Labour Party. The WSF's federal structure, which gave considerable autonomy to local branches and individual members, easily enabled such dissenting views to be expressed. Melvina Walker, for example, was an Executive Committee member of Poplar Labour Party *and* the WSF, despite the latter's declared opposition to the former.

By the end of 1919, however, any lingering support for WSF involvement with the Labour Party had disappeared. The Annual Conference, the Executive Committee and a ballot of the full membership had all come out against affiliation, and in February 1920 this first unequivocal statement of opposition to the Labour Party was published in the *Dreadnought*, encouraging other groups to follow the WSF's example:

> We urge our Communist comrades to come out of the Labour Party and build up a strong opposition to it in order to secure the emancipation of Labour and the establishment of Communism in our time. Comrades, do not give your precious energies to building up the Labour Party which has already betrayed you, and which will shortly join the capitalists in forming a Government of the Noske type.[38]

The final event which had led the *Dreadnought* group to make this open and unambiguous break with the Labour Party had been the first conference of the Third International's Western European Sub-Bureau, which began in Amsterdam on 3 February 1920. A resolution on trade unions adopted by the conference stated that Labourism (the pursuit of trade union interests by parliamentary means) was 'the final bulwark of defence of Capitalism against the oncoming proletarian revolution; accordingly, a merciless struggle against Labourism is imperative'. This point of view was elaborated by a resolution on 'The Communist Party and Separation of Communists from the Social Patriotic Parties', which described 'social-patriots' (that is, 'socialists' who supported the war) as 'a most dangerous enemy of the proletarian revolution', and insisted that 'rigorous separation of the Communists from the Social Patriots is absolutely necessary'.[39] During the debate about this resolution the conference chairman made it clear that the resolution precluded any member party of the Third International affiliating to the British Labour Party. When a vote was taken the only delegates against the resolution were Hodgson and Willis of the British Socialist Party; all the other delegates, including Sylvia Pankhurst and the British shop stewards' movement representative J. T. Murphy, voted in favour.

This set the final seal on the WSF's opposition to the Labour Party by appearing to lend the authority of the Third International to the WSF's position. The *Dreadnought*'s first open statement of opposition to the Labour Party appeared immediately after the Amsterdam conference, and during a discussion about the issue of affiliation to the Labour Party at a communist unity meeting on 13 March 1920, 'Pankhurst quoted the Amsterdam resolution in support of her position'.[40]

THE AFFILIATION DEBATE

It may seem odd that supporters of the Third International were debating whether or not to affiliate to the Labour Party, when the International had stated that the correct attitude towards the social democratic parties consisted of unrelenting struggle, unsparing criticism and organisational separation. The Third International did not require its supporters in Britain to transform the Labour Party into a genuine socialist organisation – as the WSF had aimed to do before 1920 – but to form a *separate* communist party within which all revolutionaries would be regrouped. This party would work to attract the working class, including those who belonged to the Labour Party, into its ranks. However, one of the tactics which was proposed to bring this about was that the communist party should affiliate to the Labour Party. As was the case with Revolutionary Parliamentarism, the tactic of affiliation to the Labour Party was heatedly debated in the unity negotiations in Britain throughout 1920.

The WSF Executive Committee's instructions to its delegates in June 1919, to stand fast on the principle of no affiliation, remained the WSF's position throughout. In March 1920, for example, the Executive Committee repeated its view that 'with regard to the Unity Negotiations . . . we should not in any event compromise on the question of Affiliation to the Labour Party'.[41] Support for the WSF's position arrived in May 1920, in the form of a comunique´from the Third International's Western European Sub-Bureau, clarifying the decisions of the Amsterdam conference. Underlining the conference's opposition to affiliation, the communique´stated that the principle of non-affiliation was of such importance that it should take precedence over the need for unity: 'Much as we should like to see a united Communist Party in England, it may be better to postpone this ideal than to compromise on important issues.'[42]

This contribution to the affiliation debate proved to be one of the Sub-Bureau's final actions. The Sub-Bureau was dominated by left communists, which was not to the liking of the Executive Committee of the Communist International in Moscow. Consequently the ECCI closed down the Sub-Bureau in May 1920 and transferred its responsibilities to the German Communist Party, which by this time had purged itself of the left communists in its ranks.

Around the same time, Lenin published his polemic against *'Left-Wing' Communism, An Infantile Disorder*, in which he argued that the British working class's attachment to social democratic organisations and ideas could only be broken if the Labour Party actually took office and proved its uselessness: 'If Henderson and Snowden gain the victory over Lloyd George and Churchill, the majority will in a brief space of time become disappointed in their leaders and will begin to support Communism.'[43] Lenin advised communists in Britain to form an electoral alliance with the Labour Party and help it to take power, so that the working class could learn through its own experience that the Labour Party was an anti-working class organisation. This was the meaning behind Lenin's notorious remark about communists supporting the Labour Party 'in the same way as the rope supports a hanged man'.[44]

As we saw in Chapter 1, the WSF's opposition to affiliation was the greatest obstacle in the way of unity with other groups in Britain. At the end of March 1920 the WSF Executive Committee proposed that 'if the BSP refuses to withdraw from the Labour Party, we get on with [the] formation of [a] Communist Party'.[45] This decision was put into practice in June 1920 when the WSF initiated the formation of the CP(BSTI), which adopted non-affiliation as one of its 'cardinal principles'.[46] At the same time, although Guy Aldred and his comrades were not involved in the unity negotiations, nor in the formation of the CP(BSTI), the Glasgow Communist Group likewise declared its refusal to 'identify itself with any Unity Convention willing to recognise the Labour Party'.[47]

At this stage the *Dreadnought* group put forward three main arguments against affiliation. First, since the Labour Party's rise to power was 'inevitable', it would be a waste of time and effort for communists to affiliate in order to assist Labour into office. Instead, communists should devote all their energies to building an organisation which would be 'ready to attack' Labour when it took power.[48]

Secondly, the *Dreadnought* group took issue with Lenin's argument that communists should affiliate to the Labour Party in order to 'keep in touch with the masses', since revolutionary propaganda could still influence Labour Party members without communists actually having to be inside the Labour Party.[49] Thirdly, the *Dreadnought* argued that affiliation was incompatible with other tactics advocated by the Third International. For example, Lenin urged communists to work closely with the Labour Party, but he also hoped to win the support of the British shop stewards' movement and the Industrial Workers of the World. These two objectives conflicted, since the IWW and the shop stewards' movement were both more or less hostile to the existing trade unions, which formed the Labour Party's backbone. Affiliation would also hinder the application of Revolutionary Parliamentarism, since communists inside the Labour Party would find it harder to be selected as Parliamentary candidates than if they maintained an independent existence.[50]

In *'Left-Wing' Communism, An Infantile Disorder* Lenin had reserved judgement on the specific issue of affiliation, since he had 'too little material at my disposal on this question, which is a particularly complex one'.[51] In June 1920, however, Quelch and MacLaine, two delegates from the pro-affiliation BSP, arrived in Russia for the Second Congress of the Third International, and they 'persuaded the Comintern leaders that the British Communist Party – when it could finally be completed – should be affiliated with the Labour Party'.[52] Consequently the 'Theses On The Basic Tasks Of The Communist International' adopted by the Congress on 19 July 1920 came out

> in favour of the affiliation of communist or sympathising groups and organisations in England to the Labour Party . . . communists must do everything they can, and even make certain organisational compromises, to have the possibility of exercising influence on the broad working masses, of exposing their opportunist leaders from a high tribune visible to the masses, of accelerating the transference of political power from the direct representatives of the bourgeoisie to the 'labour lieutenants of the capitalist class', in order to cure the masses quickly of their last illusions on this score.[53]

Lenin made two speeches at the Congress in support of affiliation. On 23 July he stated: 'Since it cannot be denied that the British Labour Party is composed of workers, it is clear that working in that party means co-operation of the vanguard of the working class with the less advanced workers.'[54] On 6 August he admitted that 'the Labour Party is not a political workers' party, but a thoroughly bourgeois party', yet cited the BSP's experience of affiliation to support his argument that 'a party affiliated to the Labour Party is not only able to criticise sharply, but is able openly and definitely to name the old leaders and to call them social-traitors'. Finally he added: 'If the British Communist Party starts out by acting in a revolutionary manner in the Labour Party and if Messrs Henderson are obliged to expel this Party, it will be a great victory for the communist and labour movement in England', because the Labour Party would have exposed its counter-revolutionary nature before its working-class supporters.[55]

Sylvia Pankhurst attended the Second Congress and spoke against affiliation in one of the debates about the tactics to be adopted by the communist party in Britain.[56] She also discussed the issue in private with Lenin, arguing that 'the disadvantages of affiliation outweighed the advantages'. However, Lenin 'dismissed the subject as unimportant, saying that the Labour Party would probably refuse to accept the Communist Party's affiliation, and that, in any case, the decision could be altered next year'. The issue of affiliation was not a question of principle 'but of tactics, which may be employed advantageously in some phases of the changing situation and discarded with advantage in others'.[57]

While the Congress of the International was taking place in Russia, the concluding communist unity convention, at which the CPGB finally came into being, was held in London. On the eve of the meeting the CP(BSTI) published an 'Open Letter to the Delegates of the Unity Convention', urging them to reject any association with the Labour Party. It argued that the Labour Party's leaders were intent on diverting the working class's struggles into harmless Parliamentary and reformist channels; that the trade unionists and parliamentarians who controlled the Labour Party had a bourgeois mentality which led them to support class collaboration and oppose class struggle; and that whereas communists stood for the dictatorship of the workers' councils, the Labour Party based itself on bourgeois parliamentary democracy.[58] Advice of a conflicting nature came in a message to the Unity Convention from Lenin, criticising the CP(BSTI) and advocating 'adhesion to the Labour Party on condition of free and independent communist activity'.[59] In the event Lenin's arguments held sway, although the Convention's vote in favour of affiliation – 100 to 85, with 20 abstentions – could hardly have been closer.

Shortly after the Unity Convention the CPGB wrote to the Labour Party asking to affiliate, but its application was rejected on the grounds that 'the objects of the Communist Party did not appear to accord with the constitution, principles and programme of the Labour Party'.[60] A lengthy series of reapplications and refusals ensued.[61] The initial rebuff was one factor which helped to ease the CP(BSTI)'s entry into the CPGB at the Leeds Unity Convention in January 1921. The *Dreadnought*'s account of the Leeds Convention noted with evident satisfaction that the affiliation tactic had thus far remained a dead letter.[62]

After entering the CPGB the *Dreadnought* group persisted in criticising the affiliation tactic. In July 1921, after the Poplar Board of Guardians (whose Labour majority included Communist Party members) had cut the rate of outdoor Poor Law relief, the *Dreadnought* asked:

> Are we to exempt from criticism the Labour Party on a particular body, because in that Labour Party are members of the Communist Party?
>
> Or are we to criticise that Labour Party and ignore the fact that the Communists are amongst the Labourists, sharing responsibility for the actions we condemn, and even initiating them, as in the matter of cutting down relief in Poplar?
>
> Should we ignore the existence of such Communists, be sure the workers would find them out.[63]

Criticism of the tactic was voiced again in August 1921, after the CPGB and the Labour Party had both chosen to stand candidates in the Caerphilly by-election. Once more the *Dreadnought* attempted to expose the problems involved in applying the affiliation tactic. If the CPGB had been affiliated to the Labour Party and none of its members had been chosen as the candidate, would it have supported the Labour candidate, even a right wing one, or would it have stood its own candidate and risked expulsion? Was the CPGB candidate at Caerphilly a ploy intended to force the Labour Party to accept the CPGB's affiliation as a lesser evil than seeing the working class vote split, or would the CPGB stand candidates no matter what? In contrast to the confusions surrounding affiliation the *Dreadnought*'s own position was clear:

> do not affiliate to the Labour Party or enter into compromising alliances within it . . . Stand aside warning the workers that the

> Labour Party cannot emancipate them, because it is merely reformist and will not sweep away the capitalist system when it gets into power . . . the best propaganda that Communists can do at this juncture is to let the Labour Party continue with its effort to become 'his Majesty's Government', and to tell the workers that all such shams must pass; that the way to emancipation is through Communism and the Soviets.[64]

Such forthright condemnation of CPGB policy was one of the reasons why Pankhurst was expelled from the party in September 1921. However, the CPGB persisted with its attempts to affiliate to the Labour Party, and it is important to examine these efforts briefly in order to form a proper assessment of the affiliation debate.

MISTAKEN ASSUMPTIONS

On the sole occasion that representatives from the Labour Party and the CPGB met face-to-face to discuss affiliation, the contributions of the various participants revealed some of the ideas behind the affiliation tactic as well as some of the problems involved in trying to apply it. At certain moments during the meeting the CPGB frankly admitted that its objective was 'to be inside the Labour Party in order to meet its enemies face to face, and to expose in front of the rank and file of the Labour movement the political trickery of [list of names] and other Labour lieutenants of the capitalist class'. Thus Arthur Henderson, one of the Labour participants, truly grasped the purpose of affiliation when he complained that the CPGB had 'no intention of being loyal . . . Mr Hodgson hopes that the present crisis will show the masses the pernicious rule of the leaders of the Labour Party. It is for that reason that they will enter the Labour Party; in order to denounce the leaders.'

At other moments, however, the CPGB representatives claimed very different intentions. When asked whether the CPGB was hoping, as Fred Hodgson had been reported as saying, 'to sever the connection between the masses and the Labour Party', Arthur MacManus replied that this 'does not represent Mr Hodgson's opinion or the Party's opinion'. According to MacManus the CPGB believed that

> any political organisation that hopes to influence the mass of the working class in this country in any particular direction in dissociation or in a detached form from the existing Labour Party, would simply be futile, and that consequently the effective way to do it was to operate their opinions inside the Labour Party and gradually pursue their opinions in such a way that if it did succeed in influencing opinion, the reformation would be based upon the Labour Party itself.

As MacManus put it later: 'We hope to make the Labour Party the Communist Party of Great Britain.'[65] These latter remarks support the view that many CPGB members sought to turn the Labour Party into a revolutionary organisation and failed to understand that the affiliation tactic was not intended to radicalise the Labour Party but to expose, discredit and destroy it.[66]

The suggestion that suporters of affiliation failed to grasp its proper aims and intentions is perhaps not surprising, considering the convoluted and manipulative thinking which lay behind the tactic. For example, Lenin advised communists to help the Labour Party into office, so that the working class could learn from its own experience that the Labour Party did not represent its interests and then join the Communist Party. What Lenin failed to explain was why workers should suddenly have wanted to join the Communist Party so soon after making the painful discovery that what that Party had advocated (a Labour government) was of no worth to them whatsoever!

The longer the Labour Party persisted in its refusal to accept the CPGB's advances, however, the more the whole debate over affiliation tended to become academic, since hardly any of the claims made on either side could actually be tested in practice. One of the few claims on which a definite judgement could be passed was the Third International's contention that if the Labour Party took office it would cure the masses of their last illusions in the labour lieutenants of the capitalist class. This idea needs to be examined closely, since it was shared by the anti-parliamentary communists.

Guy Aldred's description of Labour as 'the last hope of the capitalist system, the final bulwark of class-society'[67] suggested that only the Labour Party stood between the collapse of capitalism and the victory of communism. This was a view also held by the *Dreadnought* group. In August 1921, for example, Sylvia Pankhurst urged communists to let the Labour Party 'get into power and prove its uselessness and powerlessness'.[68] Pankhurst returned to this scenario in June 1923, when she predicted the consequences of a Labour government taking office: 'The workers, expecting an improvement in their conditions, will turn to the Left. The Labour Party, unable to alter the position of the workers without overthrowing capitalism, will see its popularity departing and the growth of Left influences.'[69] Similarly, in December 1923 Pankhurst predicted that if a Labour government failed to satisfy its supporters' aspirations 'the ideals of the workers will speedily advance beyond the Labour Party'.[70]

After the announcement of the December 1923 general election results Sylvia Pankhurst commented that 'the increase in the Labour vote is pleasing to us, because we regard it as a sign that popular opinion is on the move, and ere long will have left the Labour Party far behind'.[71] Although the Labour Party was not socialist, its opponents had portrayed it as such during the election campaign; working-class Labour voters had therefore believed that they were voting for socialism. When the Labour Party did not achieve socialism its supporters would turn elsewhere to fulfill their aspirations: 'in the intention of the electors [Labour Party government] is an evolutionary stage beyond government by the confessedly pro-capitalist parties . . The strength of the real Left movement . . . will develop as all the Parliamentary parties fail in their turn'.[72]

These expectations were put to the test in January 1924 when the Labour leader Ramsay MacDonald was invited to form a government. According to Harry Pollitt's analysis, at the end of 1924 this first Labour government was ousted from power 'because of the disillusionment of the masses with the policy of the Labour leaders'. The large majority with which the new government took office was 'in itself evidence of the workers' disgust with their leaders' pusillanimity'.[73] This sounds like the scenario envisaged by Lenin and Pankhurst – except that it was not to the Communist Party that workers had turned in disgust and disillusionment with Labour; the government which replaced Labour in office was formed by the Conservative party! Furthermore, the Labour Party received over a million *more* votes in the 1924 general election than it had done before taking office, while the CPGB's total vote, and its average per candidate, both fell.[74]

Yet the greatest illusion of the whole affiliation debate had little to do with what the CPGB could or could not achieve once it had affiliated, nor with the consequences of the Labour Party taking office. It was that the Labour Party would ever 'submit to being penetrated and manipulated by the Communists' in the first place.[75] The Labour leaders' reluctance to submit themselves to criticism, denunciation and exposure was evident at their meeting with representatives of the CPGB, and probably accounts for the contradictory interpretations of the affiliation tactic put forward by the CPGB members. Lenin did not take this factor into account: 'Communist infiltration could be real and effective only if the non-Communist "partner" consented to play the role that Lenin had written for him, that of victim and dupe. But if the partner, here the Labour Party, refused to play along, the tactic naturally failed.'[76] Lenin had sought to suppport the Labour Party as the rope supports a hanged man; the Labour Party simply refused to put its head in the noose.

ANTI-PARLIAMENTARY OPPOSITION TO THE LABOUR PARTY AFTER 1921

After Sylvia Pankhurst's expulsion from the CPGB, every organisation associated with the *Dreadnought* included opposition to affiliation among its principles. The position of the Communist Workers' Party was 'to refuse affiliation or co-operation with the Labour Party and all Reformist organisations'.[77] The All-Workers' Revolutionary Union stated that it was 'opposed to the Reformist and Counter-Revolutionary Labour Party, and rejects all affiliations and co-operation with it and other Reformist Parties'.[78] The manifesto of the Unemployed Workers' Organisation announced: 'We are opposed to affiliation to a counter-revolutionary party [such] as the Labour Party.'[79]

In November–December 1922 the Fourth Congress of the Third International approved the tactic of the United Front between the Communist and Social Democratic Parties in order to defend the working class against the capitalist offensive which had been gathering force since the end of 1920. The *Dreadnought* group completely opposed the United Front. So too did Guy Aldred. In a debate with Alexander Ritchie in the Glasgow *Worker* during 1922, Aldred explained his reasons for rejecting the tactic. The Labour Party's leaders were a collection of 'traitors' who had repeatedly betrayed the working class. Communists could not 'achieve their revolutionary purpose' by uniting with 'Mensheviks and petty reformers'. Instead of allying with the Labour Party, communists should be redoubling their efforts to 'unite with themselves'.[80] In 1923 Sidney Hanson (a

London member of the APCF) added another argument against the tactic: 'the Communist Party, seeking affiliation to the Labour Party, proposes a united front with it, and strengthens the illusion that the Labour Party is the party of the working class, the movement towards emancipation. But the Labour Party is really the anti-working class movement, the last earthwork of reaction.'[81]

LABOUR IN OFFICE

The acid test of the anti-parliamentarians' view of the Labour Party as an anti-working class organisation came when the Labour Party actually took power in Britain. The remainder of this chapter therefore concentrates on the anti-parliamentary communists' attitude towards the Labour Party in office, using the examples of local government in the East London district of Poplar (1921–3) and the first national Labour government (1924).

During 1921 an 'employers' offensive' got under way in Britain. involving a widespread attack on working-class living standards and working conditions. In its role as an employer of wage labour the state joined in this offensive. In the summer of 1921, for example, the Labour-controlled Poplar Board of Guardians reduced the rate of outdoor Poor Law relief and cut municipal employees' wages. At the time of these actions the *Dreadnought* stated: 'The Labour Party is avowedly a Reformist Party; its effort is to work towards social betterment within the capitalist system.'[82] The problem was that any party which sought to take over the administration of capitalism in order to run the system in the workers' interests would quickly discover that the initial step ruled out the proposed objective, and would find itself having to run capitalism in the only possible way: that is, *against* the interests of the working class.

In January 1922 the Poplar Board was petitioned by National Unemployed Workers' Movement members demanding 'work or full maintenance'. Under this pressure the Board approved a scale of relief in excess of the NUWM's request. At its next meeting, however, the Board found that its financial resources would not cover the promised rate of relief. The imperatives of administering capitalism had reasserted themselves. The Board cancelled its previous decision, causing hundreds of angry unemployed workers to occupy the building where the Board was meeting. Melvina Walker, a *Dreadnought* group member and 'well-known local activist', told the

Board: 'You appear to be hopeless and are merely the bulwark between us and the capitalist class to keep us in subjection.'[83]

A similar case occurred in 1923 when dock workers involved in an unofficial strike applied to the Poplar Board for relief. Their application was granted, but this precipitated another financial crisis. Faced with having to choose between taking the side of the workers or continuing to administer a part of the capitalist system, the Board opted for the latter and reduced its rates of relief. On 26 September a demonstration by the Unemployed Workers' Organisation, demanding that the Board should reverse its decision, ended in another occupation of the Board's premises. The police were summoned and with the Board's consent forced their way into the building, batoning everyone in their path (the *Dreadnought* reported 'Upwards Of Forty People Badly Hurt, Hundreds Of Slightly Wounded'). 'One thing stands out clearly', the *Dreadnought* commented:

> the result of working class representatives taking part in the administration of capitalist machinery, is that the working class representatives become responsible for maintaining capitalist law and order and for enforcing the regulations of the capitalist system itself . . . working class representatives who become councillors and guardians assist in the maintenance of the capitalist system, and, sooner or later, must inevitably find themselves in conflict with the workers . . . The batoning of the Unemployed in Poplar is the first instance of the Labour Party being brought into forcible conflict with the labouring population in defence of the capitalist system . . . As the capitalist system nears its end, the reformists who desire to prevent the catastrophic breakdown of the system will inevitably find themselves in a position of acute antagonism to the people who are striving to destroy the system which oppresses them.[84]

When the Labour Party became the national government in January 1924, the APCF changed the masthead motto of its journal from 'A Herald Of The Coming Storm' to 'An Organ Of His Majesty's Communist Opposition', implying opposition to His Majesty's government, that is, the Labour Party. The same issue also contained a lengthy article detailing the new Labour Ministers' record of anti-working class statements and actions.[85]

A month later the APCF published an article titled 'The Two Programmes'. This outlined a twelve-point 'Parliamentarian' programme and opposed each of its points with 'Anti-Parliamentarian' positions. The 'Parliamentarian' programme amounted to 'the continuation of capitalism'; among its points were:

2. Workers' Interests subservient to capitalist expediency . . .
4. Parliament – controlled by High Finance.
5. Nationalisation of some industries, yielding profits to state investors and loan sharks.
6. Political administration of Capitalism by workers . . .
11. Power left to the bourgeoisie.

Alongside each of these points the 'Anti-Parliamentarian' programme for 'the overthrow of capitalism' as set out:

2. Development of class conscious understanding. Undermining capitalist interests . . .
4. The Soviet or Industrial Council, directly controlled by the wealth-producers.
5. Socialisation of all industry.
6. No political administration of Capitalism . . .
11. All Power to the Workers.[86]

In context the 'Parliamentarian' programme was obviously meant to describe the Labour Party's policies. From the outset, therefore, the APCF was unambiguous in its opposition to the new Labour government.

The comments the *Dreadnought* group had made about the role of the Labour Party in the administration of the local capitalist state in Poplar would lead one to expect the group to have shared the APCF's attitude. In fact, this was not so. When the Labour government took office in the middle of a railway engineers' strike the *Dreadnought* stated: 'A Capitalist Government has to prove to its makers and clients – the capitalists – that it is able to ensure the best possible conditions for the business of capitalism. A Labour Government has no such duty.' The *Dreadnought* proceeded to demand the use of the Emergency Powers Act against the railway owners, and nationalisation of the railways.[87] The railway strike was followed by a dock workers' strike in February. Again the *Dreadnought* argued: 'impartiality should not be expected of a Labour Government, nor, indeed, tolerated from it . . . The duty of a Labour Goverment is to act as a friend of the workers in all cases.'[88]

Comments such as these sowed dangerous illusions. By drawing a distinction between what capitalist governments had done and what a Labour government ought to do, the *Dreadnought* implied that Labour was not a capitalist party and that workers should expect Labour's support in their struggles. However, the actions of the Labour government soon dispelled some of these illusions. During the dock strike, for example, the Labour Prime Minister Ramsay MacDonald revealed that the government planned to use strike-breakers against the dockers: 'The Government will not fail to take what steps are necessary to secure transport of necessary food supplies, and has already set up the nucleus of an organisation.'[89] Similarly, when London transport workers struck in March 1924 the government appointed a Chief Civil Commissioner to administer the Emergency Powers Act and made preparations to run bus and tram services with military and naval labour. Consequently, in March – April 1924 the *Dreadnought* group began to adopt a more critical attitude towards the Labour government:

> The Labour Government has again shown that it cannot work Socialist miracles with capitalist elements and by capitalist methods.
> The more the Labour Government applies itself to an honest attempt to ameliorate social conditions [sic] the more it is seen that the only hope of real all-round improvement is to attack the system at the root.[90]

The Labour government was defeated in the Commons on 8 October 1924 and dissolved itself the following day. After the ensuing general election Ramsay MacDonald resigned from office on 4 November. The *Workers' Dreadnought* had ceased publication in June 1924, so we lack its definitive assessment of the first Labour government's record. The APCF, on the other hand, continued to publish the *Commune* and sniped at the Labour government throughout its term in office, but did not publish a full-length appraisal of the Labour government until two years later, with the article 'Lest We Forget: The Record Of Labour Parliamentarism' in the October 1926 *Commune*. This article was also published as a pamphlet titled *'Labour' In Office: A Record*, first in 1926 and then in revised form in 1928 and 1942. These works, which belong outside the 1917–24 period, are discussed in Chapter 5. For the time being it will suffice to note that the APCF's considered opinion of the 1924 Labour government was essentially that it had 'functioned no differently from any other Capitalist Government';[91] none of Labour's actions in office had given the anti-parliamentarians cause to revise their pre-1924 views. When we examine the anti-parliamentarians' continued propagation of their ideas in the late 1920s and early 1930s, we will see that opposition to the Labour Party as an anti-working class organisation remained one of the anti-parliamentarians' basic tenets. Before that, however, this account of the anti-parliamentarians' basic principles can be completed by a discussion of the labour movement's industrial wing – the trade unions.

4 Trade Unions and Industrial Organisation

The basis of the anti-parliamentary communist critique of trade unionism was that trade unions organised workers *within* the capitalist system, as 'The Pimps Of Labour' bargaining with the capitalists over the sale of the commodity labour power.[1] The anti-parliamentarians, however, wanted to see workers organised *against* the capitalist system, for the abolition of wage labour. The anti-parliamentarians sought the replacement of trade unions with revolutionary organisations, whose primary function would be to overthrow the capitalist system and thereafter administer communist society. In keeping with the anti-parliamentary communists' views on how the revolution would be carried out, these organisations would be constituted in such a way as to enable the vast majority of workers to organise and lead *themselves*. These views help to explain the particular criticisms which the anti-parliamentarians levelled at trade unionism, and the alternative forms of organisation that they proposed.

PROBLEMS AND REMEDIES

One of the features of trade unionism criticised by the *Dreadnought* group was the opposition between the unions' leaders and officials and the rank and file membership. This was partly explained in material terms: Sylvia Pankhurst described full-time officials as 'respectable, moderate men in comfortable positions',[2] whose salaries, status and security of position elevated them to the 'middle class' and gave them a political outlook different from that of shopfloor workers. Since the trade union officials' privileges depended on the continued existence of capitalism, they had a vested interest in maintaining the *status quo* and opposing revolution: 'material interest ranges the Trade Union officials on the side of capitalism'.[3] Thus CP(BSTI) secretary Edgar Whitehead wrote: 'It cannot be too strongly impressed by Communists upon all workers that T.U.

officials, both by their secure position and their enhanced salaries, serve the maintenance of capitalism much more than they serve the cause of the emancipation of the workers.'[4]

The *Dreadnought* group also drew attention to the officials' common contempt for their members. Sylvia Pankhurst wrote that 'the apathy of the membership produces the officials' lack of faith in the capacity of the membership, and, even apart from other causes, is a source of the cynical contempt for the rank and file which so many officials display'.[5] Yet there was nothing inevitable about the rank and file's 'apathy': it was a condition which the union officials deliberately fostered, since one of the ways in which they could maintain their own positions of power and privilege was by excluding the rank and file from participating in union affairs. The officials were assisted in this by the *form* of trade union organisation:

> The members . . . resign all their authority, all their rights and liberties, as far as the Union is concerned, to the Union officials. This is an essential feature of Trade Unionism . . . The Parliamentary form of the trade unions, which removes the work of the Union from the members to the officials, inevitably creates an apathetic and unenlightened membership which, for good or evil, is a mere prey to the manipulation of the officials.[6]

Guy Aldred also observed the antagonism between the unions' officials and rank and file and the differences between these two groups' power. He explained this by reference to the trade unions' role as permanent negotiating bodies within capitalism. Unions could not hope to bargain successfully with the bosses unless they had the disciplined backing of their entire membership. Since criticisms of the union by the rank and file, or rank and file actions which the union had not sanctioned, would undermine the leaders' position *vis-a-vis* the capitalists, the leaders were forced to urge caution on the members and suppress any criticisms coming from the rank and file. In short, successful bargaining required the members to relinquish all power and initiative to their leaders; the more they did this, however, the greater would be the scope for the leaders to betray the members. Thus it was the trade unions' role as bargainers and negotiators which led to the growth of oligarchic leadership and to the likelihood of the rank and file being 'sold out'.[7]

The anti-parliamentary communists also criticised the way that unions organised workers on the basis of their sectional differences (according to craft, trade and so on) rather than on the basis of what they had in common: 'instead of preserving the vaunted unity of the working class [the trade unions] prevent it by dividing the workers into watertight compartments'.[8] Since capitalism could only be overthrown by a united working class, organisations such as trade unions, which divided the working class, were obviously counter-revolutionary. Guy Aldred argued, further, that even in reformist terms 'trade unionism has accomplished nothing so far as the well-being of the *entire* working class is concerned', since the effectiveness of unionisation depended on *excluding* other workers (such as the unskilled) from its ranks, for example through apprenticeships and the closed shop.[9] This sectional and divisive mentality also led unionised workers to spend as much time fighting each other over issues such as demarcation disputes as they spent struggling against their common enemy, the capitalists.

A final significant criticism of trade unions made by the *Dreadnought* group was that 'their branches are constructed according to the district in which the worker resides, not according to where he works'.[10] The point of this particular criticism was that since the unions did not organise workers where they were potentially most powerful – that is, at the point of production – they did not measure up to the requirements of the sort of revolutionary organisations sought by anti-parliamentarians.

During 1917–20 the *Dreadnought* group proposed certain measures to overcome the problems outlined above. First, reactionary or reformist trade union officials should be replaced by revolutionaries: 'The first thing you must do, if you really want to overthrow the capitalist system and to establish Communism, is to get rid of your reformist and palliative-loving leaders.'[11]

Secondly, action should be taken to 'alter the structure of the Unions so as to allow the Rank and File to have complete control'.[12] Sylvia Pankhurst sought the introduction of 'The Soviet system within the trade union movement'.[13] Instead of each section of workers being represented by full-time paid officials, all workers in each workplace would meet in general assemblies to elect and mandate delegates who could be recalled and replaced at any time. As the *Dreadnought* explained in 1923:

> the rank and file of a trade union cannot control its officials, cannot even watch them efficiently. The trade union machinery does not allow of it. The workers can only control an organisation

> which is a workshop organisation, with, when necessary, delegates appointed for specific work, instructed, subject to recall, remaining still as fellow-workers in the shop . . . The work and power of the organisation must not pass into the hands of even such delegates: it must be an organisation operated by the workers in the shop.[14]

Thirdly, a resolution drafted by Sylvia Pankhurst for a Rank and File Convention in March 1920 proposed that 'an industrial union shall be established which shall admit all workers in the industry, regardless of sex, craft or grade'.[15] Instead of being divided among several competing trade and craft unions, all workers in each industry would belong to a single union. This was intended to promote working-class unity.

The *Dreadnought*'s view during 1917–20 was that these changes could be effected through building a rank and file movement within the trade unions. The group's attitude at this stage was essentially one of critical support for the existing unions, rather than outright opposition and hostility. This was an approach which had been summed up most succinctly by the Clyde Workers' Committee, when it had declared at the time of its formation in 1915 that it would 'support the officials just so long as they rightly represent the workers, but . . . act independently immediately they misrepresent them'.[16]

THE INFLUENCE OF THE ENGINEERING SHOP STEWARDS' AND MINERS' RANK AND FILE MOVEMENTS

The *Dreadnought* group was influenced strongly in its attitude towards the trade unions by the shop stewards' movement which emerged in Britain during the First World War. Not long after the beginning of the war most trade unions had agreed to renounce strike action for the duration, and to accept any changes in established working practices and conditions needed to increase production. Consequently a shop stewards' movement, based mainly in engineering, arose to take over the defence of workers' basic interests. Many of the leading shop stewards belonged to organisations such as the SLP and BSP, and they regarded the shop stewards' movement as a form of organisation which would not only be able to defend workers' interests within capitalism, but which could also be used to overthrow capitalism and reorganise production on a socialist basis.

The most cogent expression of the shop stewards' movement's ideas was J. T. Murphy's pamphlet *The Workers' Committee* (1917). This discussed most of the critical points which would also be raised in the *Dreadnought*'s articles about trade unions: 'the conflict between the rank and file of the trade unions and their officials'; the unions' 'constitutional procedure' which demanded that 'the function of the rank and file shall be simply that of obedience'; the absence of any 'direct relationship between the branch group and the workshop group'; and the way in which the unions' sectionalism divided workers 'by organising them on the basis of their differences instead of their common interests'. In *The Workers' Committee* Murphy also outlined an alternative structure intended to bring about 'real democratic practice' in workers' industrial organisations, so that every member could 'participate actively in the conduct of the business of the society [union]'. Apathy towards union affairs – 'the members do not feel a personal interest in the branch meetings' – would be overcome by establishing a 'direct connection between the workshop and the branch'. All power would reside at workshop level: committees elected to represent the workers would exist merely to 'render service to the rank and file' and would 'not have any governing power'. These changes would be carried out as far as possible *within* the existing unions: Murphy emphasised that 'we are not antagonistic to the trade union movement. We are not out to smash but to grow, to utilise every available means whereby we can achieve a more efficient organisation of the workers.'[17]

Besides the engineering shop stewards' movement, the *Dreadnought* group's attitude towards trade unions was also influenced by the miners' rank and file movements, particularly in South Wales where the *Dreadnought* group had established close links with radical workers.[18] Militants within the South Wales Miners' Federation had addressed many of the problems of trade unionism outlined above. The most widely-known expression of some of their ideas on these issues was *The Miners' Next Step*, a pamphlet published in 1912 by a small group of socialist miners calling themselves the Unofficial Reform Committee. *The Miners' Next Step* criticised the SWMF's 'conciliation policy', which 'gives the real power of the men into the hands of a few leaders'. The more power was concentrated in the hands of the officials, the less power the membership had in deciding union affairs. (This was the argument that Guy Aldred had put forward a year earlier in the first edition of his pamphlet, *Trade*

Unionism and the Class War). Rank and file control of the union was far too indirect, while the 'social and economic prestige' of the leaders raised them to a position where 'they have therefore in some things an antagonism of interests with the rank and file'. Another criticism of the union was that 'the sectional character of organisation in the mining industry renders concerted action almost impossible'.

This critique was accompanied by constructive proposals for reforming the union. The pamphlet proposed a single organisation for all mine and quarry workers in Britain, which would enable them to achieve 'a rapid and simultaneous stoppage of wheels throughout the mining industry'. Proposals for democratisation of the union were also outlined, so as to enable the rank and file to 'take supreme control of their own organisation'. All policy initiative and ratification was to rest with the lodges, and the union executive was to become an unofficial, 'purely administrative body; composed of men directly elected by the men for that purpose'. If these reforms were carried out there would be a growing recognition that 'the lodge meetings are the place where things are really done'; rank and file apathy would disappear, and the lodges would become 'centres of keen and pulsating life'. The long-term objective of these proposals was 'to build up an organisation that will ultimately take over the mining industry, and carry it on in the interests of the workers'. This aim also applied to all other industries: the authors wanted to see 'every industry thoroughly organised, in the first place, to fight, to gain control of, and then to administer, that industry'.[19]

The strong influence of such ideas on the *Dreadnought* group's attitude towards the trade unions, and in particular the insistence of militant mining and engineering workers on the need to work *within* the trade unions, shows that some accounts of the *Dreadnought* group's attitude have been factually mistaken. For example, it is not correct to suggest that 'Pankhurst's group . . . was *unable* to prevent the Communist Party, formed in late 1920, from pledging to work within the existing trade union structure',[20] since the fact is that the *Dreadnought* group *supported* such a strategy. The CP(BSTI)'s programme stated that the party should aim to 'stimulate the growth of rank and file organisation' and 'undermine the influence of reactionary Trade Union leaders over the rank and file' by forming a CP(BSTI) branch within every local trade union branch and workplace.[21]

A circular to CP(BSTI) branches stated that the party's 'most urgent need' was 'the speedy addition to the ranks of the party of genuine class fighters from the ranks of the proletariat, especially of the organised industrial proletariat, so that the party may exercise increasing control and influence inside the organised Unions of Workers'.[22] A CP(BSTI) Industrial Sub-Committee submitted a report suggesting how this might be achieved. It stated: 'Branches should make the closest distinction between work through the NON PARTY MASS ORGANISATIONS OF OUR CLASS, and through the PARTY ORGANISATIONS.' CP(BSTI) members were to oppose 'Party Organisations' such as the Labour Party, but try to exert every possible influence within 'Non Party Mass Organisations' such as trade unions, shop stewards' and rank and file movements, and unemployed workers' organisations. In order to gain influence within such organisations party members were instructed to 'accept delegation from branches of their industrial organisations to all such bodies as Trade Union Congresses, Trade Union Executives, or to any Trades and Labour Council or similar body WHERE SUCH ACCEPTANCE OF DELEGATION DOES NOT NECESSITATE DENIAL OF THEIR COMMUNIST PRINCIPLES'. Wherever possible, party members were to 'take full and active part in building up Shop Stewards' and Workers' Committee Movements, and in all Rank and File Movements which weaken the power of officials, and lead to Rank and File Control, Mass Action, and the development of the Class Struggle'. Agitation within trade union branches was also intended to spread communist ideas, attract militant union members into the CP(BSTI), and expose the trade unions' inadequacies as revolutionary organisations.[23]

All of which demonstrates the complete inaccuracy of the claim that the *Dreadnought* group 'despised . . . participation in the work of the trade unions'.[24]

GUY ALDRED AND THE SHOP STEWARDS' MOVEMENT

One of the several significant differences between the *Dreadnought* group and Guy Aldred concerned their respective attitudes towards the shop stewards' movement. Aldred was imprisoned repeatedly after the introduction of conscription in 1916, because he refused to fight in an imperialist war from which only the capitalist class would profit. His opposition to the war also led him to oppose those workers who were not only churning out the munitions which millions of workers in uniform were using to slaughter each other, but were also seeking to profit from their strategically important position by bargaining for wage rises, reductions in working hours and so on. In Aldred's view the engineering shop stewards' movement's aims

> contained *no* suggestion of *not* erecting capitalist institutions, of *not* engaging in armament work, of asserting any sort of class-consciousness against the war. Indeed, the workers' committee flourished on war . . . The idea was merely that of improving the worker's status in the commodity struggle and not to develop his revolutionary opposition to capitalism.[25]

Aldred criticised those 'revolutionaries' who separated their industrial agitation from their opposition to the war, leaving their 'revolutionary' politics behind when they entered the munitions factory. Aldred described Willie Gallacher, for example, as someone who had 'made munitions during the war, and atoned for this conduct by delivering Socialist lectures in the dinner hour'.[26]

Aldred's attitude towards the shop stewards' movement has led one critic to dismiss him as 'a character marginal to the organised labour movement on Clydeside' because 'he condemned the munitions workers as "assassins of their own kindred" '.[27] But Aldred's attitude was shared by another figure less frequently dismissed as 'marginal' – John Maclean too was

> opposed to the way the Clyde Workers' Committee and the socialists on it were behaving . . . Most of the shop stewards were socialists and anti-war, but they had submerged their politics in workshop struggles and were not even mentioning the war inside the factories . . . This meant that no anti-war fight developed inside the factories; the men were making guns, shells and all kinds of munitions, but the all-important question was never raised.[28]

David Kirkwood, the shop stewards' leader at Beardmore's Parkhead Forge in Glasgow, was an outstanding example of the type of stewards criticised by Aldred and Maclean. Although he claimed to oppose the war, Kirkwood's own account of the war years scarcely mentions him engaging in any sort of anti-war activity. He was a willing collaborator in any scheme to increase munitions output, so long as it did not adversely affect wages and conditions, and relished the quips that it was really he (Kirkwood), and not the owner Sir William Beardmore, who was actually in charge of running Parkhead

Forge.[29] The attitude of stewards such as Kirkwood led John Maclean, in his famous May 1918 speech from the dock of the High Court, Edinburgh, to condemn not only worldwide capitalism – 'the most infamous, bloody and evil system that mankind has ever witnessed' – but also those workers who sought to exploit their powerful bargaining position in the munitions industry:

> David Kirkwood . . . said that the Parkhead Forge workers were then prepared to give a greater output and accept dilution if they, the workers, had some control over the conditions under which the greater output would accrue . . . Since he has got into position he seems to have boasted that he has got a record output. The question was put to me: Was this consistent with the position and with the attitude of the working class? I said it was not . . . that his business was to get back right down to the normal, to 'ca'canny' so far as the general output was concerned.[30]

When the war ended, however, there was no longer any political reason for Aldred not to support the shop stewards' movement. In August 1919 he expressed his approval of the forms of organisation created during the war by the movement, writing of the need to abandon 'the unwieldy, bureaucratic, highly centralised Industrial Union idea of peace-time [class] war organisation' in favour of 'a living unit of organisation in every workshop, and a federation of living units, mobilising, according to necessity, the real red army. This will be accomplished by developing our Workshop Committees.'[31] Around the same time, the Communist League, in whose formation Aldred participated, was arguing that communists should 'enter the workers' committees and councils and by their agitation and education develop and extend the growing class consciousness'. In time the workers' committees would overthrow the capitalist system and then function as the administrative machinery of communist society.[32] This was basically the same position which the CP(BSTI) put forward in more detail in 1920.

THE POST-WAR CLASS STRUGGLE

So far this chapter has concentrated on the anti-parliamentary communists' ideas up to 1920. During 1920–1 these ideas began to change, mainly in response to fluctuations in the pattern of the post-war class struggle. In Britain the shop stewards', workers' committee and rank and file movements were largely the product of certain groups of workers' militancy during the war and the short post-war boom. If the level of class struggle declined these forms of organisation were likely to disappear, along with the revolutionary expectations vested in them. This is precisely what did happen in Britain after 1920.

The high level of wartime demand for their products kept unemployment among engineering, shipbuilding and metal union workers below 1 per cent during 1915–18.[33] During the short-lived post-armistice boom (1919–20), the unemployment rate among these workers was still only 3.2 per cent. In 1921, however, unemployment shot up to 22.1 per cent, and then to 27 per cent the following year. At the same time the wage gains which engineering workers had made during the war began to be eroded. This was the background to a decline in engineering workers' militancy, reflected in the downwards trend in the statistics for strikes in the metal, engineering and shipbuilding industries (see Table 4.1).

Table 4.1 Disputes involving stoppages in the metal, engineering and shipbuilding industries, 1919–24

	Working days 'lost'	*Workers involved*
1919	12 248 000	403 000
1920	3 402 000	179 000
1921	4 420 000	63 000
1922	17 484 000	369 000
1923	5 995 000	61 000
1924	1 400 000	71 000

Source: Board of Trade Statistical Department, 1926.

The exceptional figures for 1922 were the result of a three-month engineering workers' lock-out; Harry McShane describes what happened:

> the engineers were defeated . . . and they returned to much worse working conditions. The union's defeat meant a reduction in wages, not only for them but ultimately for all trades and labourers as well. After the war I got £4 8s. a week as an engineer, but after the lock-out engineers' wages went down to £2 13s.[34]

This was the general pattern throughout the rest of British industry. Unemployment increased from 1.5 per cent in the autumn of 1920 to 18 per cent by December 1921. Cuts in wages were only partially offset by a fall in the cost of living. The number of working days 'lost' in disputes involving stoppages in all industries decreased, as did the number of workers involved (see Table 4.2).

Table 4.2 Disputes involving stoppages (all industries), 1919–24

	Working days 'lost'	*Workers involved*
1919	34 969 000	2 591 000
1920	26 568 000	1 932 000
1921	85 872 000	1 801 000
1922	19 850 000	552 000
1923	10 672 000	405 000
1924	8 424 000	613 000

Source: Board of Trade Statistical Department, 1926.

The sections of the working class which had been at the forefront of the class struggle were the ones hit hardest by the onset of the post-war depression. The national rate of unemployment in August 1922 stood at 12.8 per cent – compared with 27 per cent on Clydeside and 32 per cent in Sheffield. Engineering and shipbuilding workers accounted for 65 per cent of all unemployed workers on Clydeside, while iron, steel and engineering workers made up 70 per cent of the total in Sheffield. In Wales as a whole 44 per cent of unemployed workers were miners – a percentage which was obviously much higher in the coalmining areas themselves.[35] In his Presidential address to the South Wales Miners' Federation in July 1923, Vernon Hartshorn remarked that 'he had never known a period when the workmen had been more demoralised than they were during 1922 . . . Wages had been low, unemployment had been extensive and the owners had taken advantage of the general position to attack standard wages and customs which had been in existence for many years'.[36]

During this period the generalised class struggle of the years before 1920 gave way to defensive battles in which sections of the working class were isolated and defeated one by one. The year 1921 illustrates the change. In April the railway and transport workers' union leaders withdrew their promise of support to the miners, leaving their Triple Alliance partners to fight a three-month struggle which ended in defeat. Of the 85 million working days 'lost' in 1921, nearly 80 million were accounted for by locked-out miners. In 1921 almost two and a half times *more* days were 'lost' in strikes as there had been in 1919, but more than a third *fewer* workers were involved (see Table 4.2).

These circumstances saw a rapid decline in the rank and file activity of the shop stewards' movement. As unemployment rose known militants were frequently the first to lose their jobs through victimisation by employers: 'Soon it was a wry joke that the shop steward leaders of 1918 had become the unemployed leaders of the 1920s.'[37] The decline of rank and file activity saw power within the trade unions shift back in favour of the full-time officials, a trend consolidated by a number of major union amalgamations (which on grounds of sheer size created conditions for greater bureaucratisation) and by the spread of national collective bargaining. As Sylvia Pankhurst observed in 1922:

> Undoubtedly a strong move is being made by the Union officials to secure greater power in the Unions and to thrust the rank and file still further into the background . . . the Unions become more and more bureaucratic, more and more dominated by the capitalist influence upon the Trade Union leaders, still further removed from rank and file control.[38]

The victimisation of shopfloor activists during the 'employers' offensive' was complemented by state repression of 'subversives': 'In 1921 over 100 "communists" were arrested and jailed for variations on the theme of sedition.'[39] A leaflet issued by the APCF in 1921, in connection with the prosecution of the Glasgow Communist Group for publishing the 'seditious' *Red Commune*, referred to the 'concerted effort on the part of the ruling class . . . to suppress ruthlessly every serious advocate of social transformation in order to preserve the present iniquitous and unjust system'.[40]

'ONE BIG UNION'

The downturn in the level of class struggle and the decline of the shop stewards' movement revived an old debate among socialists in Britain. Before the First World War there had been two basic approaches to the problem of trade union sectionalism, bureaucracy and reformism. 'Amalgamationists' advocated working within the existing trade unions to convert them into industrial unions through amalgamating all the competing unions in each industry. 'Dual unionists' sought the same end (or in some cases a single union for all workers), but advocated building new unions from scratch in the belief that the existing ones were beyond reform.[41] These two camps had been able to work side-by-side in the shop stewards' movement during the war, but when the movement began to die away the division between amalgamationists and dual unionists reappeared.

Most of the leaders of the engineering shop stewards' and miners' rank and file movements entered the CPGB, where they pursued the strategy of working to reform the unions from within. After Sylvia Pankhurst's expulsion from the CPGB in 1921, the *Dreadnought* group was therefore cut off from its former influences. This partly explains why from the end of 1921 the *Dreadnought* group moved in the opposite direction and adopted a 'dual unionist' stance. In August 1921 Sylvia Pankhust wrote that the working class had to 'fight as one big union of workers to abolish Capitalism'.[42] Thereafter 'One Big Union' became the *Dreadnought* group's slogan for industrial organisation. The tactics pursued by the group during 1917–20 – the creation of rank and file movements *within* the existing unions, the replacement of reformist leaders by revolutionaries, the democratisation of trade union structures and practices, and the conversion of trade and craft unions into industrial unions – were abandoned.

This change of attitude can also be explained by the group's view that the decline of rank and file activity had ruled out any immediate prospect of success in reforming the existing unions. In January 1922 Sylvia Pankhurst argued that trade union rules and structures could not be changed 'without long and hard effort . . . it must take many years to change them appreciably'.[43] In April 1923 she argued that those who pursued the tactic of trying to change the unions' leadership were mistakenly 'following in the footsteps of the early Socialists who put Red Flaggers into office, and saw them gradually transformed into the Social Patriots you denounce today'. The central problem was not one of leadership, but of the very nature of trade unionism itself: 'You are dissatisfied with the Union officials – with all Union officials. Is it not time you ceased to blame particular individuals, and decided to abolish the institution itself?.'[44] Pankhurst also argued that the conversion of craft unions into industrial unions would still not overcome *all* the divisions within the working class: 'The working class . . . must break down its craft barriers *and* its industrial barriers.'[45]

In February 1922 the *Dreadnought* group's newly-adopted opposition to the existing unions and its rejection of working within them was expressed in the programme of the Communist Workers' Party, which sought 'to emancipate the workers from Trade Unions which are merely palliative institutions'. The party's aim was:

> To prepare for the proletarian revolution, by setting up Soviets or workers' councils in all branches of production, distribution and administration, in order that the workers may seize and maintain control.
> With this object, to organise One Revolutionary Union:
>
> (a) built up on the workshop basis, covering all workers, regardless of sex, craft, or grade, who pledge themselves to work for the overthrow of Capitalism and the establishment of the workers' Soviets;
>
> (b) organised into a department for each industry or service;
>
> (c) the unemployed being organised as a department of the One Revolutionary Union, so that they may have local and national representation in the workers' Soviets.[46]

These aims were taken a step further seven months later, when the draft constitution for an All-Workers' Revolutionary Union of Workshop Committees was published in the *Dreadnought*. The AWRU's object was 'to emancipate the working class . . . by the overthrow of capitalism and the private property and wage system', with the AWRU itself serving as 'the machinery which will enable the workers to take control of production, transport and distribution, and administer all services for the benefit of the entire community'. It would support 'every form of industrial and active proletarian struggle which furthers its ultimate aim' and engage in 'propaganda, agitation and action . . . to promote the spread of class-consciousness and Communist ideals amongst the workers'. Describing the existing unions as 'bulwarks of the capitalist system' which 'by their sectionalism and craft distinctions . . . prevent the uniting of the workers as a class', the constitution stated: 'The AWRU rejects the policy of "Boring from within" the old Trade Unions; its object is to supersede them; it fights openly against them'. The proposed conditions of membership included prohibitions on taking office in any union except the AWRU, and on participating in any trade union-promoted workshop committee. The structure of the union would take the form of tiers of workshop, factory, district, area and national councils, formed by delegates who would be 'subject to recall at any time by those who appointed them'.[47]

The proposed formation of the AWRU by the *Dreadnought* group was influenced by the example of the German left communists. During the German revolution tens of thousands of radical workers deserted the trade unions and formed revolutionary 'factory organisations'. In February 1920 these united to form the General Workers' Union of Germany (AAUD), allied to the KAPD. The Programme And Rules of the AAUD were published in the *Dreadnought* in November 1921, and the striking similarity between the AAUD and AWRU programmes points strongly to the conclusion that the *Dreadnought* group intended the AWRU to be a British equivalent of the AAUD.[48]

In a text on 'The Organisation of the Proletariat's Class Struggle' (1921), Herman Gorter of the KAPD argued that 'the factory organisation is *the* organisation for the revolution in Western Europe'.[49] However, Gorter did not believe that the working class achieve revolutionary consciousness and succeed in its struggle against capitalism simply by organising on a factory by factory basis. Among the workers in the factory organisations there would inevitably be some who had a broader and clearer view of the class struggle than their fellow-workers. This minority should not remain dispersed among the various factory organisations, but should form itself into a separate party comprising 'the most conscious and prepared proletarian fighters'.[50] This necessity was acknowledged in the AAUD's Programme And Rules: 'The AAU . . . stands for the uniting of the most advanced revolutionary proletarians in a separate political organisation of purely proletarian-Communist character. It thereby recognises the political organisations united in the Communist Workers' International as necessary to the class struggle.'[51] The political platform of the factory organisations was a simplified version of the party's programme. The factory organisations were open to all revolutionary workers, including, but not only, members of the KAPD. As Gorter explained:

> The factory organisation endows its members with the most general understanding of the revolution, e.g. the nature and significance of the workers' councils (soviets) and of the dictator-

ship of the proletariat.

The party comprises the proletarians whose understanding is much broader and deeper.[52]

The crucial difference between these arrangements and those proposed by the *Dreadnought* group was the absence from the latter of any stress on the need for the party. When the *Dreadnought* group formed the Communist Workers' Party in imitation of the KAPD, its platform consisted of six points: to spread communist ideas; electoral abstention and anti-parliamentary propaganda; refusal of affiliation to the Labour Party or any other reformist organisation; to emancipate workers from the existing trade unions; to organise 'One Revolutionary Union' as the forerunner of the workers' councils; and affiliation to the Fourth (Communist Workers') International. Seven months later the AWRU was formed. Far from being a watered-down version of the CWP (as the AAUD was of the KAPD), the AWRU adopted the CWP programme in its entirety. If anything, in fact, the AWRU's programme was *more* comprehensive than the CWP's platform. Instead of being open to 'all workers who pledge themselves to work for the overthrow of Capitalism and the establishment of the workers' Soviets' (as the CWP programme originally proposed), membership of the AWRU was conditional on acceptance of *all* the above-mentioned points. In contrast to the German left communists' conception of the relationship between Party and Union, in the *Dreadnought* group's scheme the AWRU simply superseded the CWP; the Party was now redundant, its role and programme taken over completely by the Union. Whereas Gorter argued that by itself 'the factory organisation is not sufficient'[53] and insisted on the need for separate political organisation, the *Dreadnought* group believed that the factory organisation (AWRU) *would* suffice on its own.

THE AWRU: FORERUNNER OR NON-STARTER?

The idea that the organisations formed to struggle within and against capitalism would prefigure the administrative institutions of communist society was an important aspect of the *Dreadnought* group's proposals for the establishment of 'One Big Union'. During 1917–20 the group had criticised the existing trade unions from the standpoint of wanting to see the emergence of organisations which workers would use to struggle against capitalism, overthrow the system, and thereafter administer communist society. The idea behind the formation of the AWRU – to 'create the councils in the workshops in order that they may dispossess the Capitalist and afterwards carry on under Communism'[54] – was no different. After 1920 the *Dreadnought* group had the same long-term aim as before, but sought to realise it by different means.

The terms used in the *Workers' Dreadnought* to describe the administrative machinery of communist society – such as 'a world federation of workers' industrial republics' or 'a worldwide federation of communist republics administered by occupational soviets' – reveal the group's view of the fundamental features of communist administration. It would be based on workplaces, with the basic unit being the workshop, only socially-productive workers would be able to participate in administration, and representatives would be mandated delegates. In other words, the administration of communist society would share the characteristics of the workers' organisations formed to overthrow capitalism. In February 1922 Pankhurst wrote that 'the Soviets, or workers' occupational councils, will form the administrative machinery for supplying the needs of the people in Communist society; they will also make the revolution by seizing control of all the industries and services of the community'.[55] The 'One Big Union' was an embryonic Soviet; the Soviet was a fully-developed 'One Big Union'. This is what the *Dreadnought* group meant in 1923 when it stated: 'Communism and the All-Workers' Revolutionary Union are synonymous.'[56]

Yet the historical experiences upon which the group could have drawn – such as the revolutions in Russia in 1905 and 1917 and in Germany in 1918 – contained no precedents to support the idea that soviets or workers' councils would emerge through the development of 'One Big Union'. The soviets of the Russian revolutions and the workers' councils of the German revolution did not develop from previously-existing organisations. Instead, they were created more or less spontaneously by the working class in the course of its mass struggles. Before 1921 it had been from mass strike movements that the *Dreadnought* group had expected soviets to emerge. The necessity for any pre-existing revolutionary workers' union, such as the AWRU, was not mentioned by the group during this period.

After 1921, however, circumstances had changed, and were quite unlike the situations which had prevailed in Russia and Germany.

There was little prospect of soviets emerging as a product of mass struggle – for the simple reason that there was no mass struggle going on. The declining number of strikes that did take place focused mainly on defensive, 'economistic' issues and took place among the working class section by section, rather than generally and simultaneously. A demoralised working class faced high unemployment, rank and file activity had declined drastically, and trade union amalgamations were strengthening union bureaucracies. This was hardly the most favourable climate for the construction of brand-new industrial organisations of any sort, let alone revolutionary ones. The *Dreadnought* group's idea that the AWRU might develop into a soviet-type organisation, uniting and extending strikes, developing them politically, and challenging the power of the capitalist state, bore little relation to the actual level of class struggle and the preoccupations of most workers.

If workers' councils were unlikely to emerge spontaneously, however, might not an alternative have been to force their emergence artificially, by preparing the way for their development through an organisation such as the AWRU? Even this strategy would appear to have been over-ambitious in the context of the period after 1920. It is difficult to see what activities the AWRU could actually have become involved in during these years. Its draft constitution rejected the role of bargaining and negotiating within capitalism (over wages, hours, working conditions and so on), but there was little prospect of the class struggle having any other content at this time. Apart from converting individual workers to socialism, one by one, through general propaganda, the most the AWRU could have done would have been to wait until the next upsurge in class struggle and class consciousness. Yet such an upsurge would have provided exactly the sort of circumstances in which, as the Russian and German examples had shown, soviets might have arisen, but in which the existence of the AWRU would have made little difference to whether they did or not.

Besides the unpromising circumstances prevailing in Britain after 1920, longer-term historical conditions were also stacked against the AWRU's chances of success. Dual unionism – the position adopted by the *Dreadnought* group after 1921 – had never been found to be a fruitful area in which to work, because the idea of building completely new unions from scratch appeared to be unsuitable for Britain. Dual unionism had made its greatest progress in the United States, through the Industrial Workers of the World (IWW). The working class in the USA was relatively mobile in geographical and occupational terms. The archetypal IWW members were the 'bums' who travelled around the country on the tramp or by the railroad taking work wherever they could find it. Such workers had no attachment to any particular factory or occupation; they could regard themselves as part of one big class and thus recognise the need for one big union. Moreover, a rejection of 'political' activity in favour of organisation on the job made sense to the many immigrant workers in the IWW who were denied the vote.

However, craft workers aside, the level of unionisation was relatively low in the United States; IWW recruits came predominantly from the large numbers of previously unorganised workers. Where it existed, in fact, the IWW was usually the *only* union, rather than the dual unionist model of a revolutionary organisation formed in direct opposition to an established reformist craft union. None of these factors which encouraged the growth of the IWW in the first decade of the twentieth century applied in Britain during the same period. Compared to its American comrades the British working class was relatively immobile in geographical and occupational terms, and trade union organisation was sufficiently widespread to be able to recruit previously unorganised workers into existing unions. Attempts to set up new unions necessarily had to be in rivalry to the existing unions, and so could be readily portrayed as divisive of working class unity.

In fact, the actual fate of the AWRU testifies just as eloquently to the shortcomings of its founders' ideas as all the criticisms raised so far. In reality, the AWRU does not seem to have existed at all outside the pages of the *Workers' Dreadnought*. In July 1923, ten months after the publication of the AWRU's draft constitution, an article in the *Dreadnought* addressed 'To The Miners Of Great Britain' announced that the AWRU was preparing an intensive campaign to promote the idea of building 'One Big Union' to seize control of industry and administer society. The author admitted, however, that 'There are no funds . . . We are few. The revolutionary truth has few spokesmen'.[57] Two months later the *Dreadnought* published a second article by the same author, which stated: 'From replies to the recent article . . . it is obvious that revolutionary sentiment, and the will to propagate and accomplish its end, is not dead.' This second article was titled 'Where Is The AWRU?', and in answer to this question the author wrote that 'seemingly its half-developed, swaddled form is nurtured in the minds of hundreds, aye thousands of comrades'.[58] Despite the evident optimism of these remarks, however, the AWRU seems to have disappeared without trace.

THE UNEMPLOYED WORKERS' ORGANISATION

Given the objective conditions of the period after 1920, and in particular the high rate of unemployment in Britain, it is hardly surprising that the AWRU made far less progress than another *Dreadnought*-sponsored body: the Unemployed Workers' Organisation.

The UWO's Manifesto, Rules and Constitution were published in the *Dreadnought* in July 1923. The UWO was set up by unemployed workers who opposed the CPGB-dominated National Unemployed Workers' Movement's 'reformist' demand for 'work or full maintenance' and its aim of affiliating to the Labour Party and TUC.[59] The *Dreadnought* group was not instrumental in establishing the UWO, but an editorial in the paper stated that 'having read its declaration of principles, and believing these were tending towards our own direction, and an improvement on those of the older organisation of the unemployed, we agreed to allow the new organisation to ventilate its views in this paper so far as considerations of space and policy may permit'.[60] The UWO's Manifesto was modelled word-for-word on the 1908 Preamble of the Chicago IWW (the 'anti-political' wing of the IWW, as opposed to the 'political' Detroit wing). In the words of the IWW Preamble, and in similar vein to the constitution of the AWRU, the UWO's Manifesto declared that 'by organising industrially we are forming the structure of the new society within the shell of the old'.[61]

Compared to the AWRU the UWO's rise was positively meteoric. According to reports published in the *Dreadnought* it recruited most of its membership among disaffected NUWM members in areas of London such as Edmonton, Poplar, Bow, Bromley, Millwall, South West Ham, Lambeth and Camberwell: 'Branch after branch is dropping away from the old Movement and joining the new. As fast as the members are dropping out of the NUWM they are coming into the UWO.'[62] In January 1924 the *Dreadnought* reported that a UWO branch was being formed in Leeds, while the total membership in London had reached 'well over 3000'. The UWO was 'still going strong and the membership is increasing by leaps and bounds'.[63]

Yet the significance of the UWO's growth should not be overestimated. According to the organisation's Manifesto the working class had to 'take possession of the earth and machinery of production, and abolish the wage system. The army of production must be organised not only for the everyday struggle with Capitalism, but also to carry on production when Capitalism shall have been overthrown.'[64] However, the UWO did not organise the 'army of production'. It organised an army *out* of production. Precisely because the UWO was an organisation of the unemployed, there was no way that it could have fulfilled the aims stated in its own Manifesto. As unemployed workers the UWO's members were in no position to wield the sort of power which would have enabled them to take over the means of production. The faster the UWO grew, the more this basic flaw in its strategy was exposed. And the faster the *unemployed* workers' organisation grew, the more it pointed to the lack of viability of any *workplace* organisations such as the AWRU.

REVOLUTIONARY ORGANISATION: TWO VIEWS

A simple lesson can be drawn from the episode of the stillborn AWRU. Mass organisations with revolutionary aspirations are a product of periods of upsurge in the class struggle, when large numbers of people are drawn into conflict with the existing order and established ideas. They cannot survive in the absence of such conditions.

In contrast to the *Dreadnought* group Guy Aldred seems to have had a greater awareness of this link between the level of class struggle and the possibilities for organisation. By 1920 Aldred had recognised that with the ebb of the post-war revolutionary wave the revolutionary potential of the shop stewards' and workers' committee movement was in decline. Disagreeing with the view that the existing workers' committees were the 'only legitimate British equivalent to the Russian soviets', Aldred argued that 'the actual Industrial Committee arises out of the commodity struggle, and tends to function as the organ of that struggle'.[65] If nothing except commodity struggles (that is, disputes over the price and conditions of sale of labour power) were on the agenda, then the workers' comittees faced one or other of two fates. Either they would 'function as the organ' of those struggles, lapsing into a form of radical trade unionism, or, if they tried to preserve their revolutionary aims, they would end up as 'small associations for propaganda . . . unable to enter into the direct proletarian struggle for emancipation'.[66]

Vernon Richards' remarks about the question of industrial organisation are pertinent here:

> To be consistent, the anarcho-syndicalist must, we believe, hold the view that the reason why the workers are not revolutionary is that the trade unions are reformist and reactionary; and that their structure prevents control from below and openly encourages the emergence of a bureaucracy which takes over all initiative into its own hands, etc. This seems to us a mistaken view. It assumes that the worker, by definition, must be revolutionary instead of recognising that he is as much the product (and the victim) of the *society* he lives in . . . In other words, the trade unions are what they are because the workers are what they are, and not *vice versa*. And for this reason, those anarchists who are less interested in the revolutionary workers' organisation, consider the problem of the *organisation* as secondary to that of the *individual* . . . we have no fears that when sufficient workers have become revolutionaries they will, if they think it necessary, build up their own organisations. This is quite different from creating the revolutionary organisations first and then looking for the revolutionaries (in the reformist trade unions in which most workers are to be found) afterwards.[67]

These comments accurately define the differences between the *Dreadnought* group and Aldred and his comrades. A common image in the *Dreadnought*'s accounts of industrial struggles was of a combative, militant rank and file restrained and betrayed by cautious, conservative union bureaucrats: 'the men were prepared to fight but were held back, and consequently let down, by the men they trusted – their officials'.[68] The attempt to set up the AWRU was premissed on the attitude criticised by Richards: that new organisations had to be created in which workers' revolutionary spirit would be allowed untrammelled expression, rather than meeting with suppression as it did in the trade unions.

Guy Aldred, on the other hand, stood closer to the position supported by Richards. Part of the reason for this was probably that Aldred had already passed through, and later repudiated, a phase when he supported dual unionism. In 1907 Aldred had helped to set up the Industrial Union of Direct Actionists, whose aim was 'to organise the workers on a revolutionary economic basis' with 'Direct Action and the Social General Strike' as its weapons.[69] In Aldred's view 'the workers had to build up their social organisation and evolve their political expression of organisation within the womb of the old society'.[70]The IUDA would fill this need. At that time, therefore, Aldred supported the sort of prefigurative organisation which the *Dreadnought* group proposed fifteen years later when it formed the AWRU.

Aldred soon realised, however, that the IUDA could only fulfill its revolutionary role if its members held revolutionary ideas. The IUDA needed a propagandist organisation working alongside it, spreading communist ideas among the working class. Aldred therefore began to set up Communist Propaganda Groups to infuse potential IUDA members with communist principles. As it turned out, these propaganda groups outlived the IUDA. Thereafter Aldred consistently put the need for propaganda before the need for organisation, and abandoned dual unionism.

Debating the issue of industrial unionism in 1919 Aldred argued: 'The workers functioned under capitalist society as so much commodities . . . and though they had an industrial union, their position remained the same.' Industrial unions could have just as much of a 'palliative purpose' as trade unions.[71] There was no such thing as an inherently revolutionary form of organisation. Organisations merely reflected the consciousness of their members, and could only function in a revolutionary manner if their members were revolutionaries. The most direct route to revolution, therefore, would be through propaganda aimed at developing communist ideas among the working class. Aldred's method was 'to make Socialists first in order to bring about Socialism. But industrial unionism aimed at organising the workers without making them Socialists.'[72] It was only possible to work for dual unionism 'by postponing Socialism and side-tracking Socialist propaganda'.[73] Thus Aldred summed up his attitude as follows: 'Industrial unionism was a question of machinery and method. It was never one of principle or philosophy . . . It ignored the reality of Socialism, the need for Idealism, and so promoted confusion.'[74]

Aldred's comrades shared this point of view. An article in the *Spur* in 1917 stated that

> the great mass of the workers . . . are an easy prey to the wiles of the Capitalist class, and what is worse, to the ineptitude of their

self-appointed leaders. We must aim at securing an intelligent class-conscious rank and file. In order to achieve this the paramount need is knowledge. Educate! Educate! Educate! must be our first work. Then we can discuss the question of organisation.[75]

Rose Witcop agreed with these priorities. Replying to a letter complaining about the lack of 'constructive details' in the *Spur*, Witcop wrote: 'We believe that it is enough at present to point out the many evils from which we suffer today; whilst in discussing freely first principles we are helping along a mental reconstruction which is preparing us for the social change.'[76]

When workers were conscious of the need for communism they would create whatever form of organisation they required in the course of the revolution itself, but these organisations could not be established in embryo before their hour of need. Thus Aldred did not share the *Dreadnought* group's attachment to the formation of a prefigurative organisation. In June 1923, when Aldred and Pankhurst opposed each other in a public debate on the question 'Is industrial organisation necessary before the social revolution?', Pankhurst affirmed this necessity and Aldred denied it.[77] The APCF also disagreed with the KAPD's view that workers should desert the existing trade unions and form revolutionary factory organisations such as the AAUD. In 1925 the *Commune* stated: 'The Anti-Parliamentary Communist Federation does not believe in, and cannot understand either the need for or the possibility of factory organisation. On this point the APCF differs from the KAPD.'[78]

In contrast to the *Dreadnought* group and the KAPD, Aldred advocated 'Spontaneous Social Revolution'.[79] The organisations that had carried out the Russian revolution, for example, had not been set up in advance by any small group of leaders, nor had they developed from any previously-existing organisations; they had been thrown up by the revolutionary struggle itself – that is, 'spontaneously'.[80] The soviets, Aldred and his comrades argued, would not emerge until the hour of the revolution had arrived. Thus in October 1920 the Glasgow Communist Group stated that while it disagreed 'emphatically' with 'the idea of supporting or working for workers' committees as at present existing', it 'heartily' supported 'the Soviet or Revolutionary Workers' Council System as it will be developed during the transition stage and after the Revolution'.[81]

After 1920, therefore, there seems to have been little common ground between the *Dreadnought* group and Aldred and his comrades with regard to the issue of industrial organisation. Both groups held more or less the same critique of the existing trade unions, but disagreed over what, if anything, should take their place.

Things can be said in support of both sides in the argument. Aldred's groups were right to point out that mass revolutionary organisations could not be expected to emerge except during the revolutionary struggle itself, and that attempts to set up or sustain such organisations in a period of declining class struggle would not succeed. During such periods *mass* organisations could exist only on a reformist basis; *revolutionary* organisations could maintain their communist principles, but not hope to preserve or attract mass support.

It was one of anti-parliamentarism's basic tenets that certain forms of organisation were inherently reactionary, because they did not allow the mass of the working class to participate actively in their own struggles. This did not necessarily mean, however, that there could be forms of organisation which were inherently revolutionary. Thus Aldred and his comrades were right to stress the importance of propaganda for communism, the goal which the supposedly revolutionary organisational forms were intended to achieve. Yet here the argument becomes more complex. Trade unionism could be said to hinder workers' struggles in two senses. First, it embodies particular notions which condition the way workers set about organising and conducting their struggles, and the aims to which they think they can aspire. In this sense revolutionaries had to oppose trade unionist ideology with another set of ideas: the socialist critique of capitalism, and propaganda for the communist alternative.

However, revolutions do not break out overnight when workers are suddenly converted to a new vision of society. They develop out of the most mundane of struggles. And it is here that workers confront trade unionism in its *material* form: its rule books, its divisiveness, its bureaucracy and so on. Now the argument shifts in favour of the *Dreadnought* group. On its own, a rejection of the trade unions, and the development of new forms of organisation designed to facilitate the active participation of all workers, would not have been a sufficient condition for the success of the revolution. But what is equally certain is that capitalism could not be overthrown *without* the self-organisation and mass activity which the forms of organisation proposed by the *Dreadnought* group were intended to foster.

In one sense the ideas of the two groups after 1920 can be seen as polar opposites. In another, more fruitful sense, they can be seen as representing two sides of a dilemma that was impossible to resolve in the circumstances of the time. Revolutionaries can be torn between two impulses: on the one hand their commitment to the struggles of the working class and their desire to do something *now*, and on the other hand their commitment to the final goal of communism. In periods of radical class struggle the conflict between these two impulses disappears, because immediate actions appear to have a direct bearing on whether or not the final goal is achieved. In non-revolutionary periods, however it is far more difficult to effectively reconcile these two impulses, because it appears as if one can only be pursued at the expense of the other.

The *Dreadnought* group's attempt to set up the AWRU was an effort to intervene in order to precipitate events; by opting to concentrate on propaganda for communism Aldred's group took a longer-term view. Each group's actions lacked the dimensions of the other. Not until the period of the Spanish Civil War, but more so the period of the Second World War, would the anti-parliamentary communists once again be able to relate their everyday interventions in the class struggle to their basic principles and final goal. In the meantime, they faced the dilemma of being revolutionaries in a non-revolutionary period. Part II, covering the years 1925–35, looks at how the anti-parliamentary communists faced up to the problems this posed.

Part II

Continuity and Change 1925–35

5 The Late Twenties and Early Thirties

THE DISAPPEARANCE OF THE WORKERS' DREADNOUGHT

After the issue dated 14 June 1924, the *Workers' Dreadnought* ceased to appear. For several years this weekly newspaper had kept its readers in touch with worldwide political developments and had published the views of the most radical international communist groups. In July 1921, after Sylvia Pankhurst had been censured by the CPGB for publicly criticising the conduct of party members belonging to the Poplar Board of Guardians, she defended her actions by arguing that 'only by criticism and discussion can a knowledge and understanding of Communist tactics be hammered out by the Communist Party and communicated to the masses'.[1] It was in this same spirit that after Pankhurst's expulsion from the CPGB the *Dreadnought* continued to publish information, analyses and debates about which most workers would have remained unaware had they relied on the pro-Comintern publications for enlightenment. At the same time the *Dreadnought* group's political views were thoroughly radicalised by the impact of the political events that it reported, and by its contacts with revolutionary groups in other countries. In short, during the period of its greatest intellectual vitality and creativity the *Dreadnought* group was alive to, and sustained by, the controversies of the international communist movement and an unprecedentedly high level of class struggle. The disappearance of the *Workers' Dreadnought* was, therefore, both a sign and a consequence of the ebbing of the great wave of radical actions and ideas which swept over most of Europe after the 1917 Russian revolution.

By 1921 most revolutionaries had reluctantly begun to acknowledge that their confident expectations of widespread revolutions, fuelled by 1917 and its aftermath, were not going to be fulfilled in the immediate future after all. When the Glasgow Communist Group brought out the first (and only) issue of the *Red Commune* in February 1921, for example, it remarked: 'Some will think that we could not have chosen a more inopportune moment . . . Unemployment is spreading throughout the country. Misery, sorrow, poverty, inability to sustain the propaganda exists everywhere. The Communist movement is divided into factions and fractions.'[2] During the same month the *Workers' Dreadnought* made a similarly pessimistic assessment of the situation when it warned that 'it would be folly to pretend that the hour is fully revolutionary'.[3] Nor were the British anti-parliamentarians' comrades abroad any more sanguine. In the summer of 1922 the Russian anti-parliamentarians expressed the view that 'the situation of the Proletariat throughout the world is at present an extremely difficult one',[4] while the KAPD at its Fifth Special Conference also concluded that 'the revolution for the time being is at a standstill'.[5]

The fading prospects of revolution naturally caused a steady haemorrhage of members from the anti-parliamentary communist groups in Britain. In the first six months of its existence (that is, between June and December 1920) the CB(BSTI) had attracted a membership of around 600, organised in more than 30 separate branches, two-thirds of them located outside London. When the *Dreadnought* group tried to set up the Communist Workers' Party in February 1922, however, it managed to established only three branches outside London, in Sheffield, Plymouth and Portsmouth. This illustrates the drastic loss of support suffered by the *Dreadnought* group in the space of less than two years.

The anti-parliamentarians aligned with Guy Aldred and the *Spur* were similarly few in number. When the Glasgow Communist Group's headquarters were raided following the publication of the 'seditious' *Red Commune* in February 1921, the police 'took possession of 51 membership cards, some bearing the name of Glasgow Anarchist Group and some Glasgow Communist Group' (the two groups had united at the end of 1916).[6] This figure ties in with John McGovern's recollection that in 1921 'a number of us in Shettleston formed a branch of the Anti-Parliamentary Communist Federation . . . We started off with between fifty and sixty members'.[7] From the outset the APCF's strength lay where it would always reside: in Glasgow and the surrounding areas. However, it would not be unreasonable to reckon that the APCF, like the *Dreadnought* group, also suffered a steady loss of membership after the start of the 1920s.

When the *Workers' Dreadnought* ceased to appear after mid-1924, therefore, it was because Sylvia Pankhurst and her comrades had finally succumbed to the intense pressures imposed by trying to sustain communist propaganda during a period in which their efforts were receiving practically no encouragement in the form of support from the working class.

SYLVIA PANKHURST'S SUBSEQUENT EVOLUTION

Two historians of the German left communist movement, Authier and Barrot, offer this assessment of Sylvia Pankhurst:

> In her period as a communist, she always based herself on experience. Her radical positions were not based on intellectual reasoning nor on reference to the traditions of the movement, but always relied on her own personal experiences. Her evolution is interesting insofar as it was not at all an intellectual development. She approached communism under the pressure of events and abandoned it when it declined as a practical movement.[8]

Raymond Challinor expresses a similar opinion: Pankhurst 'was never a theoretician, with a firm grasp of Marxism; her significance came from a tremendous courage and dedication, a total commitment to the struggle of working people'.[9] The implication of these observations is that if the struggle of working people declined then Pankhurst's activities would focus on other issues; or that if working-class struggle became less radical, so too would Pankhurst's political views.

This proposition is borne out by the nature of Pankhurst's activities after 1924, when her publications covered subjects as diverse as national independence for India,[10] the adoption of 'Interlingua' as a common world language to promote international understanding and friendship,[11] translations of the work of the Rumanian nationalist poet Mihail Eminescu,[12] and (with the approval of, among others, her one-time enemy Arthur Henderson) a proposal for a universal free maternity service.[13]

After writing historical accounts of *The Suffragette Movement* (1931) and of her activities on *The Home Front* in London's East End during the First World War (1932), opposition to fascism became Panhurst's main political concern. Following the Italian invasion and conquest of Abyssinia in 1935–6, she began publication of a newspaper called the *New Times and Ethiopia News* to champion the Abyssinian cause, and during the Second World War she gave her wholehearted support to the Allies' fight against the Axis powers. Pankhurst's support for the Second World War is evidence of the unbridgeable gulf which by then had separated her both from her own revolutionary past and from the remaining anti-parliamentary communists, who, as we will see in Chapter 8, remained prepared to suffer imprisonment for opposing capitalist war.

CONDITION OF THE BRITISH WORKING CLASS, 1925–35

The disappearance of the *Dreadnought* left the APCF as the sole surviving anti-parliamentary communist organisation in Britain. This chapter is mainly concerned with the APCF's continued propagation and occasional elaboration of the basic elements of anti-parliamentarism developed in the earlier period. To begin with, however, it would be useful to outline the circumstances in which the APCF was active during the years 1925–35.

Several of the trends which had emerged during 1920–1 continued.[14] Wage rates and the cost of living both fell slowly but steadily until the end of 1933, when they gradually began to rise again. This meant that on average living standards rose *for those in full-time employment* – but this is a crucial qualification, since short-time working was widespread and unemployment rates were high: 10.4 per cent of insured workers were unemployed in 1929, 16.1 per cent in 1930, 21.3 per cent in 1931, and 22.1 per cent in 1932.

The debacle of the May 1926 General Strike, and the defeat of the miners' strike in support of which it had been called, had an immediate effect on industrial militancy. In 1927 there were only 308 stoppages of work in all industries (302 in 1928), involving 108 000 workers (124 000 in 1928) with 1.7 million days 'lost' (1.38 million in 1928).

Briefly, this was a period characterised by advantage being taken of the weakened state of 'organised labour' (there was a steady fall in trade union membership), with the introduction of the Trades Disputes Act and the principle of contracting-in for the trade union political levy in 1927; a growth in 'class-collaborationist' ideas, with the 1928 Mond-Turner talks between members of the TUC General Council and leading employers about 'industrial peace', the growth of company unionism in the mining industry, and a right-wing attack on the CPGB-dominated National Minority Movement within trade unions and trades councils; and a turn away from industrial to political action, culminating in the return of a second minority Labour government in 1929.

The world capitalist crisis (1929—33), which covers most of the second half of the period under consideration here, saw a revival of industrial militancy relative to the level to which it had fallen after the General Strike, but this recovery came nowhere near to regaining the levels of the pre-1921 period, and it would be hard to over-emphasise the differences in circumstances between these two periods.

Of these changed circumstances two in particular should be stressed. One concerns the international context. By the end of the 1920s a generation of militant workers had been physically defeated and ideologically disarmed. In Russia the working class faced a dictatorial regime masquerading under the guise of communism, plus increasingly ruthless exploitation to meet the demands of rapid capital accumulation. In Germany revolutionary workers had been crushed by social democracy and now faced the rising threat of Nazism. In Italy Mussolini's fascists had been in power since 1922; the capitalists had extracted their revenge for the *biennio rosso* ('two red years') of 1919–20. Inspiration from abroad, which – in the form of the Russian revolution – had been so important to the development of the post-war revolutionary movement in Britain, was largely absent in the late 1920s and early 1930s. This was reflected in the anti-parliamentarians' publications. International news and translations of the texts of groups in other countries had been a vital feature of the *Workers' Dreadnought*; by comparison there was a dearth of such material in the APCF's *Commune*. The anti-parliamentary movement's political views became increasingly influenced not by major world-historical events as had been the case in the earlier period, but by essentially local issues such as the Glasgow Green 'free speech fight' in the early 1930s (see Chapter 6). Not until the outbreak of the Civil War in Spain in 1936 did the movement in Britain regain something of its former vitality.

The second difference in circumstances concerns changes in the composition and fortunes of the working class in Britain. In this respect the years 1925–35 were typical of a much longer period in that they saw a steady decline in the numbers employed in 'traditional' working-class occupations (such as mining, engineering and shipbuilding) and a rise in the number of workers employed in service industries and 'white-collar' office jobs (such as distributive trades, commerce, banking, insurance and finance, and local government service). At the same time, industries such as mining, engineering and shipbuilding experienced rates of unemployment which were for the most part far above the national average.

Table 5.1 Percentage of workers unemployed (yearly mean), 1925–35

	All workers	*Coalminers*	*Engineers*	*Shipbuilders*
1925	11.3	11.5	13.3	33.5
1926	12.5	9.5	15.1	39.5
1927	9.7	19.0	11.8	29.7
1928	10.8	23.6	9.8	24.5
1929	10.4	19.0	9.9	25.3
1930	16.1	20.6	14.2	27.6
1931	21.3	28.4	27.0	51.9
1932	22.1	34.5	29.1	62.0
1933	19.9	33.5	27.4	61.7
1934	16.7	29.7	18.4	51.2
1935	15.5	27.2	13.6	44.4

Source: Department of Employment and Productivity, 1971.

Thus previously militant sections of the working class, and the geographical areas in which they had been concentrated, became centres of high unemployment, dire poverty and demoralisation.

RUSSIAN STATE CAPITALISM, THE COMINTERN AND TROTSKY

During 1925–35 the anti-parliamentary communists appear to have had three main theoretical preoccupations: an analysis of the state and economy established in Russia after 1917, opposition to parliamentary action and opposition to the Labour Party and trade unionism. We will now examine the APCF's treatment of each of these issues, beginning with Russia.

During 1925 Guy Aldred's bitter quarrel with Emma Goldman and *Freedom* over the anarchists' criticisms of the Bolshevik regime continued, with Aldred still defending the Bolsheviks. In May 1925, for example, the APCF stated: 'we take our stand by the Soviet Union', and called on the Third International to abandon its opposition to left communism ('a grave error of judgement') so that 'unity of association' between the APCF and the Comintern could be re-established.[15]

In November 1925, however, on the occasion of the eighth anniversary of the Russian revolution, the APCF suddenly announced a profound change of view. It denounced the commemoration of the anniversary as a celebration of 'counter-revolution', in which the APCF would not be participating. Instead, it would be thinking of 'our persecuted comrades in Russia' and 'our comrades rotting in Soviet prisons'.[16] The reasons behind this bolt from the blue were never explained at the time, but a clue can be found in a pamphlet written by Guy Aldred 20 years later. Recalling that during his quarrel with Goldman and *Freedom* he had been 'unwilling to believe the allegations of despotism and imprisonments of revolutionists', Aldred admitted that, in retrospect, 'this scepticism was most unjust to the imprisoned and persecuted comrades in Soviet Russia'.[17] In the same passage he referred to a book published in America in 1925 by the International Committee for Political Prisoners. This had been reviewed in *Freedom* after its publication in England in 1926. Endorsed by a score of well-known intellectual sympathisers and fellow-travellers of the Russian regime, it brought to light detailed documentation of the persecution and imprisonment of hundreds of revolutionaries by the Bolsheviks during 1923–4 alone.[18] Thus the most likely explanation for the APCF's change of view would appear to be that the amount of trustworthy evidence which had accumulated in corroboration of the anarchists' claims had finally become too great for the anti-parliamentarians to ignore or dispute.

With a zeal typical of converts to a new-found point of view the APCF began to publicise the plight of persecuted revolutionaries in Russia, giving particular attention to the case of Workers' Group member Gabriel Miasnikov, whose cause had first been championed by the *Workers' Dreadnought* in December 1923.[19]

The first signs of the APCF's adoption of the *Dreadnought*'s view that capitalism existed in Russia also began to appear. In the November 1925 *Commune* the Communist Party of Great Britain was said to stand not for 'the emancipation of the proletariat either in Russia or in Britain, but for bureaucracy, capitalism and militarism'. The CPGB's conception of the dictatorship of the proletariat really meant 'the rise to authority of a new ruling class, and not the end of class society'. The APCF's conclusion as that 'not Communism, not Socialism, but capitalism and militarism, exactly as in Britain, now exists in Russia'.[20] The same point of view was repeated two months later. Warning the working class that 'The Communist Party . . . has nothing in common with Communism or the working-class struggle', the *Commune* predicted that before long the 'Moscow Janus' would be 'dismissed with scorn and loathing from its place of proletarian honour by the enraged and enlightened workers of the world'.[21]

The APCF's explanations of how capitalism had emerged from a revolution originally hailed as the inauguration of communism echoed the Fourth International's analysis of 1917 as a dual revolution – part proletarian-communist, part peasant–bourgeois – in which peasant interests had eventually triumphed. In 1926 the *Commune* argued:

> Lenin sought to found the Communist order not on the interests of the industrial proletariat, but on an attempted combination of these interests with those of the peasants. This policy gave birth to the question how far, politically and economically, one could meet the demands of the peasants without deviating from the real aim of Socialism or Communism, without estranging the workers, the real power of Sovietism. The Anti-Parliamentary answer is that the interests of the peasants cannot be reconciled with those of the industrial proletariat.[22]

References in the APCF's press to the Bolsheviks' 'abandonment of Communism in 1921'[23] (the date that the NEP was introduced) followed on from this analysis.

In 1934 the first part of a revised edition of Aldred's 1920 pamphlet on Bakunin was published by comrades of Aldred in France. In this work Aldred referred to 'the counter-revolutionary fallacy that an agrarian country can build a socialist state surrounded by capitalist nations',[24] thus echoing two explanations previously put forward by the *Dreadnought*: that the material preconditions for socialism in terms of the development of the productive forces had been absent in Russia ('an agrarian country'), and that the Bolsheviks had been forced to compromise with capitalism because of the absence of successful working-class uprisings elsewhere in the world.

Further light on Aldred's explanation of the 'reversion to capitalism' in Russia was shed by one of the crucial differences between the original and revised texts. In the 1920 version Aldred had argued forcefully in favour of the need for working-class dictatorship during the post-revolutionary transitional period. In the 1934 version, however, Aldred added a significant caveat: the workers' dictatorship had to be 'the living power of action of life in revolt; not the dead power of decrees and a new state authority'. In Russia this living power of action of life in revolt – in other words the working class's autonomous activity – had been overpowered and defeated by the

Bolsheviks, and 'a dictatorship established on the basis of [the workers'] surrender to an external central bureaucracy'.[25] The Bolshevik-controlled state, rather than the Russian workers themselves, had established its own direction and dictatorship over all economic, political and social activity.

As a corollary of this point of view the APCF developed an analysis of Russia as a state-directed capitalist economy. In 1928 it was pointed out in the *Commune* that 'The State of Labourers and Farmers, the Workers' and Peasants' Republic, owns the means of production *in opposition to* the workers *themselves*'. Thus socialism did not exist in Russia, since the fundamental categories of capitalism had not been superseded: 'The Soviet state-labourer remains a wage-labourer. Industry brought to the State is based on surplus value robbery, the extortion of labour-energy, and liquidation of industrial power. The State Communist Party of Russia has destroyed Sovietism and prepared the way for private capitalistic production.'[26]

The APCF also reassessed its view of the Third International. In 1927 the *Commune* published a leaflet written by the Group of International Communists (GIC) in Holland about a recent agreement between the German and Russian governments, under which Germany was allowed to manufacture aeroplanes, munitions and poison gas on Russian territory. Observing that the German Communist Party's Reichstag deputies had supported the agreement, the Dutch group's leaflet concluded: 'The Third International is only a weapon in the hands of the new Russian capitalist class . . . under the mask of Communism, the interests of RUSSIAN CAPITALISM are being advanced and protected.' The *Commune* commented: 'We endorse every word of this manifesto of our Dutch Anti-Parliamentarian comrades. The Third International represents the counter-Revolution, and the Moscow "Communists" stand for anti-Socialism, *pure and simple*.'[27]

Thus the APCF had adopted a critique of Russia and the Third International closely resembling that pioneered by the *Dreadnought* group. Both saw the introduction of the New Economic Policy in 1921 as the decisive turning-point in the fortunes of the revolution, after which Russia had become a state capitalist regime. Both explained the failure to establish communism in Russia by reference to the same basic factors: the insufficient development of the productive forces; the predominance of a peasant class intent on acquiring petit-bourgeois property rights; the inability of the working class to establish its own control over all aspects of the economy, politics and society; the self-seeking ambitions of the Bolshevik party, which had acted in opposition to the working class; and the fatal isolation of the revolution within Russia's boundaries. Finally, both groups came to regard the Third International as the tool of the Russian capitalist state's counter-revolutionary foreign policy.

Despite criticising the Comintern in such terms the APCF's federalist inclinations in organisational matters, along with the international decline of the revolutionary movement, caused the group to take no part in trying to build a new International. The *Commune* talked of 'the relative non-importance and non-usefulness of International Congresses'; it supported the idea of forming a new International 'for propaganda purposes . . . but not as a practical organisation of action, issuing decrees, and passing binding resolutions'.[28] In 1927 some of the surviving left communist groups in Germany and Holland made renewed contact with the APCF and tried to forge closer links, but to no avail. In 1933 the secretary of the Fourth (Communist Workers') International complained that 'the British groups have not made any effort to come into closer contact with the comrades here. Although I fully agree that things should not be precipitated, I don't see why international linking should be neglected so obstinately as your groups do.'[29]

This section on Russia can be concluded with some remarks about the APCF's attitude towards Trotsky. When the Trotskyist Left Opposition within the Bolshevik party first came to its attention, the APCF described it as a 'worthless sham', since Trotsky had no intention of forming a new organisation to oppose the 'Stalin party of Thermidor', and also because Trotsky had declared his ultimate loyalty to Russia as the 'proletarian fatherland':

> This Trotsky Opposition stands, therefore, on the same platform as Stalin, the delivery of shells to the German bourgeoisie, the forming of blocks with the bourgeois States, and the forcing of the toilers of those States to *fight with and under the banner of their bourgeoisie*, at the instruction of the Third International and the request of the Soviet Union.[30]

Trotsky's opposition to Stalin was regarded as a power struggle within the ruling class of a capitalist state, while the Trotskyist Opposition's persecution by a state apparatus it had helped to create evoked irony rather than sympathy. The Trotskyists were being hoist by their own petard.[31]

Nevertheless, when Trotsky was eventually exiled from Russia and forced to move from country to country to avoid offending reluctant hosts or being silenced for ever by Stalin's hired assassins, Guy Aldred stated his support for Trotsky's right to engage in political agitation wherever he chose, and for his right to return to Russia by virtue of his heroic role in the revolution.[32] Some anti-parliamentarians also helped to distribute *Militant*, the newspaper of the Trotskyist Left Opposition in the USA,[33] and in the 1930s there were occasional moves towards co-operation between the anti-parliamentarians and Trotskyist groups in Britain and America. More often than not, however, such contacts were based on a misunderstanding of Trotsky's views. In 1932, for example, Aldred wrote that the APCF agreed with Trotsky's analysis of Russia, which as they understood it was that 'Socialism does not exist in Russia, and cannot exist there because of the peasant problem within the USSR, and the dictates of the surrounding capitalist nations, with whom the Soviet Union has to trade.'[34] The APCF inferred from this that Trotsky regarded Russia as state capitalist. Yet in *The Revolution Betrayed*, written in 1936, Trotsky stated: 'The attempt to represent the Soviet bureaucracy as a class of "state capitalists" will obviously not withstand criticism.' In his view, 'the nature of the Soviet Union as a proletarian state' remained 'basically defined' by 'the nationalisation of the land, the means of industrial production, transport and exchange, together with the monopoly of foreign trade'.[35] Despite what they may have thought, therefore, the anti-parliamentary communists' view of Russia was completely different from Trotsky's.

THE CASE AGAINST PARLIAMENTARISM

Whilst it was falling into line with the critique of Russia formulated earlier by the *Dreadnought* group, the APCF carried on with the task of propagating the basic principles of anti-parliamentary communism that have been discussed in Part I.

The case against parliamentary action continued to be argued along the lines sketched out previously. According to the APCF, Parliament, as an integral part of the capitalist state, served no interests except those of the ruling class. Its 'only function' was to 'conserve the private appropriation by the few of the wealth produced by the many . . . No government can sit and talk at Westminster except it serve the interests of its master, High Finance'.[36]

This capitalist institution could not serve the cause of working-class self-emancipation. As Guy Aldred argued in 1926: 'Parliamentarism . . . can never secure to the wealth-producers the ownership by themselves of the means of production and distribution. Access to the means of life proceeds from direct action. A class-conscious proletariat will emancipate itself by spontaneous action.'[37] During the course of its 'spontaneous' revolutionary actions the working class would have to uproot and destroy all the existing institutions of the capitalist state – such as Parliament – and create new institutions – the councils or soviets – to express its own authority over the rest of society.

The APCF also continued to warn of the reformist, careerist and opportunist snares which would inevitably entrap anyone who participated in parliamentary politics. 'The parliamentary runner seeks not to emancipate the workers but to elevate himself', stated the *Commune*,[38] while Guy Aldred likewise argued: 'A parliamentarian has no principles, and but one purpose: to oust from fame and office another parliamentarian, and so attain place and distinction.'[39]

Parliamentarism was also rejected as a diversion from the essential tasks of the working class and its revolutionary minorities. This particular argument was summed up most succinctly by a *Commune* statement: 'A Socialist Proletariat is more important than a Labour House of Commons.'[40] Parliamentarism engaged the working class in 'the impossible task of discovering honest representatives to play at capitalist legislation, instead of addressing itself to the Socialist education of the masses'.[41]

The view that socialist education and propaganda was a vital precondition of social change revealed the essential difference between parliamentarism and anti-parliamentarism. 'Parliamentarism' was a synonym for any sort of political activity that 'makes the task dependent on the ability of leaders'; 'anti-parliamentarism' encompassed all political activity which 'makes the struggle the task of the workers themselves'.[42] Parliamentarism 'empties the proletariat of all power, all authority, all initiative'[43] and so had to be opposed, since the working class needed all the power, authority and initiative it could muster if it was to achieve its own liberation. This *self*-emancipatory aspect of working-class revolution was constantly stressed in the APCF's writings, for example by Guy Aldred in his 1929 pamphlet *At Grips With War*: 'No parliamentary discussion can end war. Only the direct thought and action of the common people can stop war . . . The one hope of world peace is the direct social and individual self-emancipation of the working class from the thraldom, economic and therefore mental and moral of class society.'[44] In 1928 Aldred criticised the Socialist Party of Great Britain's view that the working class could use the parliamentary apparatus of the capitalist state for revolutionary purposes, and its apparent reduction of the working class's role in the revolution to the passive act of marking a ballot paper. Aldred reasserted his view: '*The only way to secure the emancipation of the workers is for the workers to take control of the machinery of production and distribution, the economic organisation of life*.'[45] This would not be achieved if the working class relied on leaving everything to the few individuals who stood for or were elected to Parliament. The great mass of the working class had to actively take matters into its own hands where the source of its greatest potential power lay – on the economic field.

To a large extent this view dictated where the most effective arena for revolutionary activity was thought to lie; hence another of the APCF's reasons for rejecting participation in elections and Parliament: 'It withdraws to the parliamentary arena men and women who should be working and agitating directly amongst the workers on the field of production, spreading the gospel at the street corners, in the lecture-hall, and wherever the workers assemble to consider and discuss.'[46]

THE LABOUR PARTY, NATIONALISATION AND TRADE UNIONISM

In the APCF's view the counter-revolutionary consequences of parliamentarism were perpetuated by *all* parties which participated in parliamentary politics: 'Whatever party persuades the workers to accept the political machinery of capitalism deprives the workers of their consciousness of revolutionary political power on the industrial field, and so betrays the interests of the workers.'[47] This was one of the angles from which the APCF attacked the Labour Party during this period, just as the anti-parliamentarians had done in earlier years.

A new development in the anti-parliamentary attack on the Labour Party was the formulation of a detailed critique of the 1924 Labour government. In the October 1926 *Commune* the APCF published its first full-length assessment of Ramsay MacDonald's administration, indicting its record under such headings as Reparations, Disarmament, Empire Administration, Nationalisation of Industry,

Unemployment Relief, Housing and Education. This article was also published in pamphlet form in 1926 and 1928 – the latter edition including an added passage on Military Strike Breaking.

The thrust of the APCF's argument was that the Labour government had 'functioned no differently from any other Capitalist Government'[48] and that 'Labour Parliamentarism does not menace, but on the contrary serves to preserve, the business interests of capitalist society'.[49] In its remarks on Military Strike Breaking, for example, the APCF alleged that 'the MacDonald Government rejoiced in recruiting cannon-fodder and strike-breaking military material, under the specious pretence of patriotic efficiency, in order to prove that *Labour* could *govern* capitalist society in capitalism's interests'.[50]

The Labour government's basically capitalist nature was also brought out in the APCF's comments on Nationalisation of Industry:

> Government ownership, or nationalisation of industry, is not Socialism. Capitalist necessity may dictate the transfer of industries to state ownership and of certain services to municipal ownership. It remains joint-stock administration just the same. Anti-Socialists have nationalised railways and coalmines without benefitting the workers. Strikes have been ruthlessly repressed, under Briand, on the State Railways of France. The same thing has occurred on the State Railways of Canada. Sweated conditions exist in the Post Office and the Mint. Municipal employees have been victimised. There is nothing radical, nothing essentially Labour, nothing fundamentally serviceable to the workers, in municipalisation and nationalisation. Socialisation, involving complete change of industrial administration, and a Labour Democracy only, is the only solution of the poverty problem. But the Labour Party, confusing the workers' mind with the parody of nationalisation for socialisation, stood for nationalisation.[51]

The APCF's attack on the equation of nationalisation with socialism represented one of its strengths in comparison with the *Dreadnought* group. During 1914–18 the demands of organising and sustaining the economy on a war footing had forced the British state into exercising direct control over many sectors of the economy. Some revolutionaries saw state intervention of this sort as leading towards a state capitalism more thoroughly repressive than private capitalism. In October 1917, for example, Sylvia Pankhurst wrote that

Under the pre-war system of nationalisation, which we see in such departments as the Post Office, the workers are scarcely better off on the whole, and in some respects even worse off, than in private employment. The system of State control of munitions factories, railways and mines which has grown up during the War, has preserved capitalism and the capitalist, whilst rendering still more rigorous the conditions under which the workers are employed.[52]

However, the *Dreadnought's* opposition to pre-war and wartime nationalisation represented only one aspect of its attitude towards nationalisation. In March 1917 Sylvia Pankhurst criticised government intervention as 'not State Socialism, but state-aided capitalism'.[53] While Pankhurst opposed 'state-aided capitalism' – meaning industries being taken over and run by a capitalist government – she was in favour of 'State socialism' – that is, industries being taken over and run by a 'socialist' government. This distinction enabled Pankhurst to describe as 'both just and practical' the demand 'that industry shall be nationalised, and that all workers in it shall combine in its management',[54] and she herself put forward detailed proposals for the implementation of this demand. In May 1917, for example, Pankhurst outlined a 'scheme of nationalisation extending from the farmer and the importer to the consumer' under which the government would buy, produce, ration and distribute food for the nation's population as a way of overcoming wartime food shortages.[55] These proposals were shortly afterwards adopted by the WSF at its 1917 Annual Conference.[56]

When workers in industries such as mining and the railways put forward demands for nationalisation at the end of the First World War, one aspect of the *Dreadnought*'s response was its argument that 'nationalisation of the mines, so long as the capitalist system exists, will not end the exploitation of the mine-workers'.[57] This was similar to what Guy Aldred and his comrades were arguing at that time: 'To nationalise the mines would be to give them to the State: but the State represents the non-producing class: therefore the miners have nothing to gain from the nationalisation of the mines.'[58]

The *Dreadnought* also argued, however, that 'unless the workers are strong enough to control the Government, the capitalists who are behind the Government will never allow the workers to maintain control of the mines'.[59] In view of the group's previous support for 'State socialism', this statement can be interpreted as implying a distinction between nationalisation carried out by a state controlled by private capitalists and nationalisation carried out by a 'workers' government'. Thus when Sylvia Pankhurst reviewed a South Wales Socialist Society pamphlet titled *Industrial Democracy for Miners: A Plea for the Democratic Control of the Mining Industry*, she agreed with the authors' argument that nationalisation under the control of a Minister responsible to Parliament would involve only a 'minute' change from being exploited by the existing mine owners, and approved of the pamphlet's proposals for nationalisation under the administration of the Miners' Federation of Great Britain.[60] Pankhurst also put forward proposals for nationalising the railways, which included equal wages for all rail workers, no share dividends, a pension equal to a wage for those unable to work, and control of the railways by the railway workers.[61]

It was the *Dreadnought*'s analysis of Russia as a state capitalist regime which eventually forced the group to recognise that widespread state ownership, even by a so-called 'workers' government', would not change the basically capitalist nature of the economy after all. In August 1923, for example, Sylvia Pankhurst argued that 'State Socialism, with its wages and salaries, its money system, banks and bureaucracy, is not really Socialism at all, but State Capitalism'.[62] At the same time, the *Dreadnought* group also sustained its opposition to ownership by capitalist governments. In January 1923 Pankhurst's view of state-owned enterprises was that

> The bulk of the work is done by hired servants whose status, in essentials, does not differ from those employed in Capitalist enterprises. They have no stake in the concern, no security of tenure, no voice in the management, no power to choose their work or the persons who are appointed to direct it.
>
> It is not thus that the socialised industries will be administered when Capitalism disappears.[63]

Yet even despite such statements the *Dreadnought* group's attitude remained inconsistent. As we saw in Chapter 3, for example, in January 1924 the *Dreadnought* demanded that the Labour government should nationalise the railways. Thus the APCF's unambiguous opposition to nationalisation in the period after the disappearance of the *Dreadnought* group represented an important advance in the clarity and consistency of the anti-parliamentarians' attitude towards an issue which remains to this day a source of widespread confusion.

Besides criticising the Labour Party's capitalist policies – such as nationalisation – the APCF also continued its well-documented attacks on prominent Labour individuals. In August 1925, for example, a 'Special "Empire Socialism" Exposure Issue' of the *Commune* was devoted to attacking J. H. Thomas, Secretary of State for the Colonies in the 1924 Labour government. A month later the APCF poured scorn on proposals to commemorate the sixty-fifth birthday of the old dockers' union leader Ben Tillett, a notorious jingoist who had touted war-recruitment speeches around music halls during the First World War. The mere fact that people were actually planning to *honour* 'this lying knave whose speeches sent thousands to their graves' simply illustrated the urgency of the need to 'destroy the existing so-called "Labour movement" and on its ruins rear a genuine Socialist movement'.[64] The October 1925 *Commune* contained the first in a long line of articles criticising the 'renegade' John S. Clarke, an ex-member of the SLP who had abandoned anti-parliamentarism to stand as a Parliamentary candidate for Labour. In the May 1927 *Commune* Clarke was criticised for having been among the minority of Labour councillors in Glasgow opposed to boycotting a forthcoming royal visit to the city.

Other targets included miners' union leader A. J. Cook, who shortly after criticising socialists who wrote for the capitalist press had contributed 'a pure and simple capitalist essay' to *John Bull*,[65] and Ramsay MacDonald, who had dined with the Governor of Boston responsible for decreeing the judicial murder of the anarchists Sacco and Vanzetti.[66] After Arthur Henderson had been billed to speak at a public meeting in Shettleston in January 1929, the APCF published a special 'Henderson Visit Outrage' issue of the *Commune Anti-Parliamentary Communist Gazette*, calling for Henderson's expulsion from the labour movement on account of his complicity in the anti-working class actions of the wartime government (see Chapter 3).[67] There were seventeen arrests for 'disorderly conduct' when Henderson's revolutionary opponents disrupted the Shettleston meeting, but this did not deter the APCF from publishing a second edition of the *Gazette* when Henderson went on to speak at Clydebank. In addition to repeating the charges against Henderson, this issue also called for John Wheatley and David Kirkwood to be ostracised on account of their willingness to associate with Henderson.

In terms of method and content these attacks were typical of the way the APCF criticised trade union leaders and labour parliamentarians. Aldred described this method as 'not just so much deductive reasoning from theory as inductive reasoning from experience'.[68] By sheer weight of empirical evidence the APCF sought to prove beyond doubt the truth of two key anti-parliamentary assertions: that the rise 'from the gutter' to 'place in class society' was invariably accompanied by a rightwards shift in political outlook, and that no matter what their initial intentions might be, those who participated in the parliamentary circus always ended up administering the capitalist system against working-class interests.

The APCF's view that 'there exists as much Socialism in the constitution and the activity of the Parliamentary Labour Party as there is divinity in the priesthood'[69] also led it to attack the CPGB, since the Communist Party was still seeking to affiliate to the Labour Party, and (until 1929) was still peddling the United Front tactic. As it had done previously, the APCF refused to have anything to do with affiliation, on these grounds: 'If the Labour Party WERE a Socialist Party, every Communist should be inside. It is precisely because it is an Anti-Socialist party that no communist should associate with it.'[70] The APCF also continued to oppose the United Front – a tactic which it considered could only profit the careerist aspirations of Labour politicians and assist to power such anti-working class administrations as the 1924 Labour government.

From August 1924, with the formation of the National Minority Movement, the CPGB's efforts to put the United Front tactic into practice focused mainly on attempting to build rank and file movements within the trade unions and on forging alliances with left wing union leaders. The APCF rejected the Minority Movement's arguments that a United Front within the unions could be an effective way of resisting attacks on working-class living standards, since the tactic offered no prospect of a *permanent* solution to the working class's problems. 'Coming together for the social revolution' remained 'the only logical and the only effectual resistance to capitalist aggression'.[71] When the National Minority Movement drew up a list of demands which included calls for a 44 hour working week and a £4 per week minimum wage, the *Commune* responded by publishing an article written by the anarchist Albert Parsons at the time of the Eight Hour Day agitation in America in the 1880s. Parsons opposed this demand on the grounds that the capitalists had no 'right' to *any* amount of the working class's labour, and because workers could never dictate their conditions of labour so long as the capitalists controlled the means of production. Commenting on this the *Commune* stated: 'The position adopted by Parsons in 1885 is that adopted by the Anti-Parliamentary Communist movement in 1926. It defines our opposition to . . . the Minority Movement.'[72]

This section can be concluded with a brief look at the APCF's attitude towards the labour movement's industrial wing. In May 1926 the APCF published a General Strike issue of the *Commune Special Anti-Parliamentary Communist Gazette*. Against the CPGB's slogan of 'All Power To The General Council' (of the TUC), the APCF called for 'NO Power to the General Council' and 'ALL POWER to Labour through its Strike Committees and Mass Meetings'.[73] It was a sign of the anti-parliamentary communist movement's decline, however, that the APCF did not manage to publish its General Strike *Gazette* until four days *after* the strike had been called off by the TUC. In its post-mortem on the strike in the July *Commune*, the APCF repeated its demand for industrial action to be conducted on the following basis: 'All Power to THE WORKERS THEMSELVES, through their mass meetings, their DIRECTLY controlled strike committees, and the federation of their districts for power and action.' Mass struggle of this sort would abolish 'centralised negotiation' and thus defeat the power of the 'self-seeking treacherous bureaucrats, who crawl and squirm like worms in the hour of crisis'.[74] The 'eternally infamous' conduct of trade union leaders – right wing and left wing – during the General Strike 'debacle' strengthened the APCF's view that trade unions had become 'part of the machinery of the Capitalist State for facilitating the exploitation of the Working Class and keeping it in subjection'.[75]

CONCLUSION

As far as the history of anti-parliamentary communism in Britain is concerned, the differences between the years before and after 1924 can be summed up as follows. The earlier period was characterised by intellectual ferment and high hopes of revolution, the later period by intellectual stability and dwindling expectations of revolution.

Between 1917 and 1924 the *Dreadnought* group evolved from a federation of suffragist reformists into a party of revolutionary anti-parliamentary communists; from working within the Labour Party and trade unions to standing outside and against them; and from enthusiastic supporters of the new Bolshevik state to pioneering critics of its state capitalist nature. These rapid changes in political outlook all took place in the context of the firm belief that the world revolution lay just around the corner.

By contrast, the years after 1924 saw the anti-parliamentarians consolidating the intellectual advances won previously. The anti-parliamentarians' views on the Labour Party and the trade unions were tested by the 1924 Labour government and the 1926 General Strike, and found to be correct. What was remarkable about the APCF's maintenance of anti-parliamentary communist positions after the disappearance of the *Dreadnought* group was that they upheld these views during a period when the prospects of revolution had suffered a series of seemingly decisive defeats.

Towards the end of 1923 one of the *Commune*'s correspondents wrote:

> The recent history of the working class since 1918 has been a record of steady misfortune from the time of the miners' lock-out [1921] . . . Very many comrades have lost heart in the losing fight and have fallen out of the struggle. The high hopes of 1918 have vanished and now the lament is 'Not in our day; we will not see the Revolution; perhaps in 50 years' time . . . '[76]

As members of the working class themselves, no doubt the revolutionaries who belonged to the APCF could not help feeling down-hearted by the defeats of their class. To their credit, however, they did not become disillusioned and drop out of the struggle. To the best of their abilities they carried out the essential tasks of keeping the idea of communism alive, and nurturing the basic principles borne from previous periods of struggle.

Thus the anti-parliamentary communist movement's numerical decline during the 1920s did not result in any weakening in terms of theoretical clarity. Since the forerunners of the APCF had been organised on the basis of a revolutionary political programme long before the post-war revolutionary wave, their existence as a revolutionary group did not tail-end the ups and downs of the class struggle to anything like the same extent that the *Dreadnought* group's existence did. Therefore they were far less likely to disappear when the level of class struggle declined. The communists who remained loyal to anti-parliamentarism during these bleak years had to be the hard core of the movement simply in order to keep going, and so were the best suited to carrying out the tasks appropriate to the period.

The stagnation in the class struggle also had the effect of giving the APCF's existence some stability. Undisturbed by having to come to grips with any new developments, it could peacefully propagate the lessons of the earlier period. But this period of calm would not last for long. By 1933 the anti-parliamentary communists had become divided amongst themselves. Typically, this was a rupture provoked by differing responses to new events which cast doubts on the relevance of established ideas. It is to an account of this split and its aftermath that we now turn.

6 The Split in the APCF and Formation of the USM

TOWARDS THE SPLIT IN THE APCF

At the begining of the 1930s an irreparable split among the anti-parliamentary communists in Britain was caused by a combination of two separate sets of events.

The first of these concerned the world economic crisis which began in 1929, and the consequent political crisis in Britain which resulted in the formation of a national coalition government in 1931. The anti-parliamentary communists interpreted these events in apocalyptic terms. The long-prophesied collapse of capitalism was at last nigh. The obviously bankrupt system had nothing left to offer the working class except increasing misery, unemployment and war: 'The existing social order, operating through the chaos of its economic forces, imposes upon the working-class nothing but: *A tendency towards Poverty and Corruption*.'[1] Sheer economic necessity would compel the working class to revolt; as Guy Aldred wrote on May Day 1929, 'the economic incentive to revolution is with us as it was on no previous May-Day'.[2]

The economic crisis had also destroyed the material basis of reformism: 'In place of palliation of poverty, the world is witnessing the poverty of palliation.'[3] This was bound to have fatal implications for parliamentarism. As APCF member William McGurn pointed out in 1932, 'there remains nothing to palliate. Seeming security for the great majority has passed away for ever. This fact has emptied the political programmes. Politicians have no careers because they can promise nothing.'[4] Since anti-parliamentarians had always said that all parliamentarism was reformism, it followed that if reformism was bankrupt, so too was parliamentarism. In 1929 Guy Aldred had predicted that 'MacDonaldism' (the Labour Party) and 'Baldwinism' (the Tories) would converge;[5] the formation of the National government in October 1931, with MacDonald as Prime Minister and Baldwin as Lord President of the Council, seemingly vindicated everything the anti-parliamentarians had ever said about Labour parliamentarism. MacDonald's decision to join forces with Conservatives and Liberals was surely the ultimate betrayal of the working class, the last word in parliamentary careerism, opportunism and corruption. In triumph Aldred declared: 'Anti-Parliamentarism has arrived.'[6]

This partly explains why, in February 1933, Aldred announced his resignation from the APCF. As his comrade John Caldwell would explain later, 'the betrayal of MacDonald and the general collapse of the Labour Party . . . made it so clear to the workers that Parliament was not the way to Socialism that Anti-Parliamentary propaganda seemed superfluous'.[7] In Aldred's opinion it was 'no longer necessary to pioneer Anti-Parliamentarism, because Anti-Parliamentarism has conquered. Parliamentarism has collapsed. Our task is to define Anti-Parliamentarism in living terms of action.'[8]

Exactly what these 'living terms of action' would be became clear in the light of the second set of events which contributed towards the split in the APCF: namely, the fight for free speech on Glasgow Green at the beginning of the 1930s. During the First World War Glasgow Corporation had passed a by-law which made open-air public meetings illegal unless the organisers had obtained a permit from the authorities. In 1931 a number of organisations began a campaign of direct action to re-establish free assembly and free speech on the popular speaking pitches at Glasgow Green.[9] As far as the split in the APCF is concerned the significance of the free speech fight lay in the manner in which it was conducted. Representatives from a wide range of organisations collaborated in the formation of a Free Speech Committee. This seems to have filled Guy Aldred with enthusiasm for lasting unity among the various groups. At a conference in Glasgow in September 1931, the Free Speech Committee transformed itself into a permanent workers' Council of Action, so that the co-operation achieved during the free speech fight could be sustained and extended into unity based on a much wider set of issues.[10] The founding conference was attended by 200 delegates. However, this initial support soon declined, so that the Council of Action became in effect the APCF under another name, along with some participation from members of the ILP. The monthly *Council*, edited by Guy Aldred, was started as the organisation's unofficial mouthpiece.

Having been struck by 'the value of the unity attained in the fight for freedom of speech on Glasgow Green', the delegates to the September conference agreed that 'the vital need of the moment' was 'a united movement composed of all the organisations of the working-class and of the organised unemployed to concentrate upon a mass agitation to defeat the ends of the capitalist class and to oppose immediately the attacks upon all wages and unemployment benefits under the plea of economy'. (September 1931 had seen the 'Economy Cut' of 10 per cent in the level of unemployment benefit.) Beyond this immediate aim the conference also proclaimed its intention to 'promote the transfer in every district of all power of political action and all social authority to representative Councils of Action, properly delegated and established'.[11] To further its programme the Council of Action aimed to end all inter-party sectarianism and bring about 'the complete re-organisation of workers, through delegation from all factions, in one movement of action'.[12] The Councils would 'include all factions without impeaching the integrity of any'.[13] Participating groups would be bound by all Council decisions which had been properly discussed and put to a vote.[14] 'All political sectarianism must vanish . . . Above our respective groups and factions, our supreme loyalty must be to the Council of Action as the instrument of working-class struggle and achievement.'[15]

Guy Aldred saw the Council of Action as the means by which the political conclusions he had drawn from the capitalist crisis and the formation of the National government could be put into practice: 'Instead of continuing to criticise the parliamentarians, we advance to building the *Workers' Council Movement*'.[16] However, not all APCF members drew the same conclusion. In June 1932 William McGurn expressed grave reservations about Aldred's enthusiasm for the Council of Action:

> There is an Anti-Parliamentary criticism, which arises consistently from our past propaganda. This criticism objects: such Councils will arise, and can arise only, at the moment of crisis. They will arise spontaneously, because they must arise to administer production when the system collapses. Meantime, Councils of Action must fall into two groups: one grouping the Anti-Parliamentarians can support; the other, they must oppose. These groups are as follows:-
>
> (1) Councils of Action can act as propaganda bodies;
>
> or
>
> (2) they can act as bodies, agitating for, or advocating reforms.
>
> Anti-Parliamentarians can support propaganda centres, but they cannot support reformist activity. They are not opposed to

> the idea of the Council of Action. But they are opposed to Councils of Action, in their present form.[17]

McGurn concluded by conceding that Councils of Action could be supported if their activities did not make use of capitalist political institutions nor assist the careerism of aspiring professional politicians, and provided their activities were aimed at destroying the capitalist state (he cited rent strikes as an example of action which satisfied these conditions). Nevertheless, McGurn's criticisms were serious enough to place him among those members of the APCF who chose not to follow Aldred's example in resigning from the group.

Aldred and the APCF did not part company on amicable terms. The 1933 split sowed the seeds of personal antagonisms which bedevilled relations between the disunited anti-parliamentary groups for the rest of the period covered in this book. At the same time, the genealogy of the anti-parliamentary tradition became a matter to be squabbled over by belittling any other group which posed as the rightful heir. In 1935, for example, Guy Aldred claimed that the APCF had been in decline since February 1933 – that is, since his own resignation![18] Likewise, in 1942 he stated that 'As a virile organisation, the APCF ceased to exist in 1933', and claimed that the group to which he then belonged – the United Socialist Movement – was the APCF's 'direct successor'.[19] Two years later USM member John Caldwell expounded a similar version of the APCF's history when he wrote that after Aldred's resignation the APCF had 'declined and died a few years later'.[20]

These reports of the APCF's death were somewhat exaggerated. In April 1934 Aldred told a London comrade: 'I don't think the Anty-Panty Group [a popular dimunitive of 'Anti-Parliamentary'] is doing very much here . . . it does not seem to be very active.'[21] This was, however, no more than a temporary lull. In 1935 the APCF resumed its activity, publishing two pamphlets which will be discussed in due course. Meanwhile, important developments had taken place among those who had split away from the APCF.

THE FORMATION OF THE USM

In August 1933 a new body called the Workers' Open Forum was formed on the initiative of newly-resigned ex-members of the

APCF – such as Aldred, Ethel MacDonald and Leigh Fisher – along with 'outsiders' such as William Dick of the Glasgow Townhead branch of the ILP. The Workers' Open Forum met regularly for political discussion and to organise propaganda.[22]

At the end of 1933 Aldred published the first issue of a newspaper called the *New Spur*. The title recalled the 'old' *Spur* – so called 'Because The Workers Need A Spur' – which had appeared from 1914–21. The name was revived 'Because The Workers Need A Spur More Than Ever'. Since Aldred's own 'Bakunin Press' was by now defunct, the *New Spur* was printed by Aldred's comrade André Prudhommeaux in Nîmes. Running to five monthly issues, the paper was filled mainly by historical essays on 'Pioneers Of Anti-Parliamentarism' such as Bakunin and Malatesta; its topical content was limited due to the early deadlines imposed by having each issue printed in the south of France. One issue was devoted to commemorating the anti-parliamentarian Reichstag arsonist Marinus van der Lubbe,[23] while another article, spread over two issues, criticised moves towards a united front between the ILP and CPGB.[24]

Aldred had more than a passing interest in the latter topic, for in January 1934 he had requested to join the ILP. He explained his application for membership in the following terms:

> I have before me this choice. Either I must remain a strict anti-Parliamentarian, practically futile in my activity because standing apart from my fellow socialists in the struggle, or I must pool my abilities and help to build a genuine all-in revolutionary movement.
>
> The situation today is such that I must either join up with some existing Socialist organisation or else remain forever outside the main historic events of our time.[25]

It was the rise of fascism in Europe which had presented Aldred with these choices: 'It is obvious that no anti-Parliamentary movement exists in the country and that Fascism grows daily a greater menace. Under these circumstances, it is imperative to build, to the best of our ability, a united revolutionary movement . . . Parliamentarism versus anti-Parliamentarism is not the immediate issue.'[26]

Aldred elaborated these remarks, and related them to his train of thought since the end of 1931, in his 1934 *Socialist May Special*, and in a new edition of *Socialism and Parliament* published later the same year. Aldred repeated his view that anti-parliamentarism had been completely vindicated by recent events: 'No longer should we cry: "*Parliamentarism Is Illusion*", because that issue has been settled beyond dispute.'[27] But now another reason for abandoning outright attacks on parliamentarism had arisen; recent events on the continent of Europe had thrown up a new anti-parliamentarism more threatening than parliamentarism itself. This was not the 'Anti-Parliamentarism of the new Social Order' (that is, communism), but the 'Anti-Parliamentarism of Fascism'.[28] In these circumstances, Aldred argued, 'the attack on Parliamentarism must give place to the attack on the Anti-Parliamentary product of Parliamentarism: Fascism! . . . Today, our cry must be: "*Division is Dangerous*" '.[29] Overthrowing views he had held for nearly 30 years, Aldred argued that anti-parliamentarism was no longer synonymous with communism – since fascism was also opposed to parliamentary democracy – and that communism was no longer synonymous with anti-parliamentarism – since many parliamentary socialists were as genuine in their desire for revolution as the anti-parliamentary communists. Aldred thus appealed to all 'socialists', parliamentary and anti-parliamentary , to unite against the immediate danger of fascism, and advanced the slogan: 'THE PROLETARIAT PARLIAMENTARY or the PROLETARIAT ANTI-PARLIAMENTARY but THE PROLETARIAT UNITED.'[30]

When applying to join the ILP Aldred had stated that he remained 'convinced of the accuracy of my anti-Parliamentarian conceptions'.[31] The 1934 edition of *Socialism and Parliament* was no different from its two predecessors in arguing that parliamentarism could 'never secure to the wealth-producers the ownership by themselves of the means of production and distribution'.[32] In *Socialism and the Pope* (also published in 1934), Aldred still maintained that the future of working-class struggle lay with the Council of Action form of organisation.[33] However, these ideas were now set aside; the issue of parliamentarism versus anti-parliamentarism had become 'subsidiary to the interests of the working class as a whole'.[34] Working-class unity against fascism took precedence over anti-parliamentary principles.

Aldred's initial application to join the ILP was accepted and he became a member of the Townhead branch in February 1934, but soon afterwards he ran into difficulties. He was asked to appear before the Management Committee of the ILP's Glasgow Federation to be interviewed about his membership, but the Townhead branch was not in favour of him attending since it resented the federal body's interference in local branch affairs. After failing to attend the Management Committee Aldred and William Dick were suspended from membership.[35] In response to these expulsions the Townhead branch resigned from the Glasgow Federation and united with the Workers' Open Forum in July 1934 to form the United Socialist Movement.[36] During the same month Aldred visited Leeds on a speaking tour and persuaded the Leeds Anarchist Group to affiliate to the USM. The new group also had some support in London among old adherents of the APCF and of the long-defunct Hammersmith Socialist Society (1911–16).[37]

In July 1931, at the height of the Glasgow Green free speech fight, Aldred had advocated electoral action 'to sweep from the Council every councillor standing for the suppression of free speech and the present iniquitous by-laws'.[38] This ambition had been thwarted by the rest of the APCF's refusal to support any ballot box activity.[39] However, since the free speech fight had not succeeded in completely abolishing speaking permits, in October 1934 the USM decided to nominate Aldred as a free speech candidate in all 37 wards in the forthcoming Glasgow municipal elections.[40]

In his election address Aldred stated that he stood for

> the total abolition of the existing Parliamentary and Municipal system, which merely reflects the interests of Capitalism. I desire to see established a Workers' Industrial Soviet Republic. Meanwhile, I am living under the present system, and, with my comrades of the United Socialist Movement, I believe in the inviolate right of Free Speech.

The main demand of the address was for complete freedom of assembly and public speaking. The voters were urged to 'Treat the election as a referendum on this great public issue . . . The desire of the United Socialist Movement is not to secure the return of a representative to the Town Council . . . It simply wishes to ask the electors to think and to direct their attention to the fundamental issue of Free Speech'.[41] In the elections, on 6 November 1934, Aldred came bottom of the poll by a long way in all fourteen wards for which he had been nominated. When he stood for a second time in the Exchange Ward on an identical platform[42] in a municipal by-election the following month the result was typical of his efforts first time around: W. Unkles ('Socialist') 1881 votes; A. Holmes (Independent) 1767; G. Aldred (Communist) 22.

RUSSIA: 'WORKERS' STATE' AND 'BOURGEOIS REVOLUTION'

During Aldred's brief period of membership the Townhead branch had sent William Dick as its delegate to the 1934 Annual Conference of the ILP, briefed with 'revolutionary and anti-parliamentary' amendments to conference motions. One of these amendments, concerning a motion on 'The Struggle Against Fascism', proposed to delete a reference to unity with 'the workers of Soviet Russia' on the grounds that this phrase had become synonymous with

> the present Stalin regime and what many of us have come to regard as the Soviet Bureaucracy. To some of us this bureaucracy is not developing Socialism, but is compelled, even though it may destroy itself, to retreat to Capitalism. This retreat is described as the building of Socialism in one nation. The Townhead Branch holds to the theory of permanent revolution and maintains that Socialism cannot be built in Russia until a definite proletarian revolutionary struggle is moving towards triumph in the Capitalist nations of the West.[43]

The Trotskyist phraseology of this amendment suggests that Aldred had played a significant part in drafting it. In *Towards The Social Revolution?*, a pamphlet explaining his reasons for wanting to join the ILP, Aldred had appended two articles about the ILP written by Trotsky. In March 1934 Aldred approached Frank Leech of the APCF with a proposal to produce a reply to William Gallacher's pamphlet *Pensioners of Capitalism: An Exposure of Trotsky and the Social Democrats*.[44] When Leech declined to co-operate Aldred proceeded with the project on his own, publishing two essays by Trotsky as a pamphlet titled *The Soviet Union and the Fourth International*. Aldred's foreword to this pamphlet was remarkable for its endorsement of Trotsky's views about the nature of the Russian state and economy:

> [Trotsky's] point that the Soviet bureaucracy is not an independent class but only an excrescence upon the proletariat makes clear exactly what attitude the genuine and intelligent working class revolutionaries must adopt towards the USSR . . .
>
> The tendency of the bureaucratic dictatorship over the proletariat is towards the collapse of the Soviet regime. But until this

> tendency results in the end of the bureaucratic domination as well as of the workers' republic, the necessity is for the reform, however violent, of the Soviet regime, but not for the overturn of its property relations, i.e., a new social revolution.[45]

This represented a radical departure from the established anti-parliamentary position. Since 1925 the APCF had argued that Russia was *not* in any sense a 'workers' state', that the dictatorship of the party bureaucracy *was* the dictatorship of a new ruling *class*, and that capitalist property relations (and hence the need for a *social revolution*) *did* exist in Russia. However, Aldred's apparent conversion to Trotskyist views was short-lived. Only seven months after publishing the Trotsky pamphlet he was once again expressing the view that 'to pretend that Russian Capitalism is some kind of Socialism is ridiculous. Russian industry is entirely capitalistic; and we have in Russia today a propertyless class of wage earners, a class of capitalist investors, and concessions worked by foreign capitalists.'[46]

Aldred clarified his views in *For Communism* (1935), a pamphlet containing a lengthy appraisal of Russia's post-revolutionary history. Here Aldred rejected Trotskyist ideas as insufficiently thorough in tracing the origins of the defeat of the revolution: 'The destruction of Soviet Russia as the land of Sovietism and the temporary stabilisation of capitalism is said by the Trotskyists to date from the death of Lenin . . . Trotsky is quite wrong to make Stalin solely responsible . . . as regards the collapse of Socialism in Russia, Stalin merely continued the work that Lenin began.'[47] Aldred's argument that Russia's 'economic opportunism' began 'with Lenin and goes back to 1921 and the NEP'[48] was a further reaffirmation of the established anti-parliamentary position. Distancing himself still further from Trotskyism, Aldred also argued that 'the Soviet Union is not a Workers' State' and that 'fundamentally [Russia] is a capitalist country'.[49]

It is curious to note that while Aldred was engaged in reiterating the accepted anti-parliamentary communist analysis of Russia, the APCF had just published a pamphlet on the same subject which departed from the usual anti-parliamentary viewpoint in several crucial aspects. This pamphlet was the work of the Dutch-based Group of International Communists (GIC) and had first appeared as 'Theses On Bolshevism' in the German council communist publication *Ratekorrespondenz*. It had then been translated into English and published in the December 1934 issue of *International Council*

Correspondence, a journal edited by Paul Mattick in Chicago. The APCF published the text exactly as it had appeared in *International Council Correspondence*, save for retitling it *The Bourgeois Role of Bolshevism*.

As this new title suggested, the GIC's text challenged the anti-parliamentarians' view of the Russian revolution by arguing that it had been a 'bourgeois' revolution from the very beginning. Before 1917, the pamphlet argued, the dominant agricultural sector of the Russian economy had been 'a feudal economy sprinkled with capitalistic elements', while its industrial sector had been 'a system of capitalist production interspersed with feudal elements'. The historic tasks of the revolution had therefore been:

> first, the setting aside of the concealed agrarian feudalism and its continued exploitation of the peasants as serfs, together with the industrialisation of agriculture, placing it on the plane of modern commodity production; secondly, to make possible the unrestricted creation of a class of really 'free labourers', liberating the industrial development from all its feudal fetters. Essentially, the tasks of the bourgeois revolution.[50]

The period from the collapse of Tsarism in February 1917 to the success of the Bolshevik insurrection in October had been 'a quite unitary social process of transformation'; it was an 'absurdity' to regard the February Revolution as bourgeois and the October Revolution as working class, since Russia had only just entered the era of capitalism and could not have created 'the economic and social presuppositions for a proletarian revolution' in the space of only seven months.[51]

The Bolsheviks had seized power by welding the mass insurrection of 'the peasant masses fighting for private property and the proletariat fighting for communism' into an alliance which overthrew the 'feudal' state.[52] Then,

> Just as the state apparatus of Czarism ruled independently over the two possessing classes [nobility and bourgeoisie], so the new Bolshevik state apparatus began to make itself independent of its double class basis.
>
> Its existence as an independent state power depends on its success

in maintaining an equilibrium between the dominated working class and peasantry.[53]

It is obvious even from such a brief outline that several elements of the anti-parliamentary critique of the Russian revolution were also expressed in the GIC's text, such as the theory of stages of development, the incompatibility of the aims and interests of the working class and peasantry, and the overriding dominance of the Bolshevik party. The crucial difference was that the GIC did something that anti-parliamentary communists in Britain had resisted: it rejected the idea of 1921 as a turning point and applied its critique to the period in Russia's history between 1917 and 1920. Central to the GIC's assessment of the revolution as bourgeois was its portrayal of the Bolsheviks as a party with a capitalist programme: even before 1917 the Bolsheviks' plans for 'socialisation of production' had been conceived in terms of 'nothing but a capitalist economy taken over by the State and directed from the outside and from above by its bureaucracy. The Bolshevik socialism is state-organised capitalism'.[54]

The anti-parliamentary communists in Britain had hitherto regarded the Bolsheviks as revolutionaries who had been more or less forced by circumstances beyond their control to set Russia on the road of capitalist development. Furthermore, it had always been an article of faith among the anti-parliamentarians that 1917 had been a working-class revolution. Thus the GIC's claims that 1917 had been a bourgeois revolution, and that the Bolsheviks had always been a capitalist grouping, were views which one would have expected the APCF to address, either reaffirming their old ideas or else intimating that they now endorsed the GIC's standpoint. However, the APCF's foreword to *The Bourgeois Role of Bolshevism* was non-committal on these issues, and gave the impression that the text was being published to add weight to the argument that Russia was fully capitalist *now*, regardless of the precise origins of this development.

DICTATORSHIP OF THE PARTY OR DICTATORSHIP OF THE WORKING CLASS

Besides the issue of the nature of the Russian state and economy, another subject discussed in the publications of the APCF and USM after 1933 was the relationship between communist organisations and the rest of the working class during revolutionary periods. This question was related to an analysis of the failure of the Russian revolution, from which the anti-parliamentarians drew lessons intended to guarantee the success of any future revolutions.

In two articles about the revolutionary role of workers' councils published in the USM journal, *Attack*, in 1936, Guy Aldred argued that 'a revolutionary class dictatorship' would be 'indispensable' during the immediate aftermath of the revolution, whilst repeating what he had said in his revised work on Bakunin (1934) about the need for this dictatorship to be based on working-class self-activity. The transitional dictatorship, Aldred stated, 'must be the work of a class: not of a small minority in the name of a class; that is it must proceed at each step with the active participation of the masses, be subject to their direct influence, stand under the control of unlimited public opinion, proceed from the growing political education of the masses'. By stressing these principles, Aldred once again rejected the substitutionism of political parties taking power on behalf of the workers: the dictatorship should be exercised by 'no single revolutionary group, no party or outstanding selection of revolutionists', nor should it be 'the dictatorship of a Marxist party executive whose power extends over that of the Soviets'. Party dictatorship, Aldred warned, 'paves the road for class oppressions, leads to new forms of exploitation and revives the evils that had been swept away with the revolution'.[55] In *For Communism* Aldred had derived the same point of view from his analysis of the fate of the Russian revolution:

> Lenin erred in regarding the Soviets merely as organs of insurrection and civil war, which they are, and not as organs of administration, which is their final and higher function if democracy is to be established . . . To recognise this fact is to liquidate the political party in the course of the struggle, and to conceive of the party as being subsidiary to the working class. Lenin lacked the ability to realise this simple truth . . . to him the party was more important than the workers.[56]

The relationship between revolutionary groups and the working class was also the subject of the second pamphlet published by the APCF in 1935. This consisted of two texts by Rosa Luxemburg: 'Organisational Questions of the Russian Social Democracy' (1904) and 'The Problem of Dictatorship' (1918). After they had appeared in the February 1935 issue of *International Council Correspondence*, the APCF published them together under the title *Leninism or Marxism*.

The 1904 text was a reply to Lenin's case for centralised organisation, as a safeguard against opportunism, within the Russian Social Democratic Party and in the party's relations with the working class. Luxemburg observed that in all of the Russian working class's 'most important and fruitful' actions of the previous decade, 'the initiative and conscious leadership of the social-democratic organisations played an exceedingly small role'. The St Petersburg textile workers' strike of 1896, the political demonstrations in St Petersburg in 1901, and the Rostov-on-Don general strike of 1902, had been 'things of which the boldest blusterer among the Social Democrats would not have ventured to think a few years earlier'. The tactics adopted in these actions 'were in each case the spontaneous product of the unbound movement itself'. This applied to other countries besides Russia:

> the small part played by the conscious initiative of the party leadership . . . is still more observable in Germany and elsewhere. The fighting tactics of the Social Democracy, at least as regards its main features, is absolutely not 'invented', but is the result of a progressive series of great creative acts in the course of the experimenting and often elemental class struggle.[57]

Luxemburg also opposed centralisation within the party. In her view, the only sure guarantee against 'opportunistic abuses on the part of an ambitious intelligentsia' was 'the revolutionary self-activation of the working masses, the intensification of their feeling of political responsibility'.[58] Luxemburg concluded with a warning that subsequent events would make famous: 'Mistakes which a truly revolutionary labour movement commits are, in historical perspective, immeasurably more fruitful and valuable than the infallibility of the very best "central committee".'[59]

The 1918 text also emphasised mass action by the entire working class as indispensable in overthrowing capitalism. There was no 'ready-made recipe' for revolution 'in the pocket of the revolutionary party'. Party programmes contained only 'a few big sign-posts'; the 'thousand concrete practical matters to be dealt with' in the course of establishing communism were ones in which 'the whole mass of the people must participate': 'Only unrestrictedly flowing life hits upon a thousand new forms, makes improvisations, contains creative power, itself corrects all blunders.'[60] Luxemburg ended by supporting the need for proletarian dictatorship after the overthrow of capitalism, but on these conditions:

> This dictatorship must be the work of the class, and not of a small minority in the name of the class; that is it must proceed at each step with the active participation of the masses, be subject to their direct influence, stand under the control of unlimited public opinion, proceed from the growing political education of the masses.[61]

These were precisely the words in which Guy Aldred, without acknowledging Luxemburg as their author, expressed his own support for working-class dictatorship the year after Luxemburg's texts had been published by the APCF.

The APCF's own introduction to *Leninism or Marxism* observed that Lenin had 'consistently denied that the working class could be active and conscious agents of revolutionary change . .. his works teem with arguments that a revolutionary policy could only be thought out and imposed upon the working class by the "intellectuals"'. As such, Leninism remained 'a strong tradition in the working class movement, delaying the development of revolutionary working class understanding. To destroy this tradition . . . is the immediate and urgent task of the Communist movement.'[62] Hence the publication of Luxemburg's texts, as a contribution to the destruction of the 'Leninist tradition' in this sense.

PROBLEMS OF REGROUPMENT

Throughout the 1930s the APCF and USM made occasional attempts to co-operate between themselves and with other like-minded political groups. While he was writing *For Communism*, Guy Aldred came into contact with various groups and individuals overseas, including the French anarchist André Prudhommeaux, Lopez Cardoza (secretary of the Communist Workers' International in Amsterdam), Paul Mattick (an ex-member of the KAPD who had helped to form the United Workers' Party in Chicago and was now editor of *International Council Correspondence*) and Albert Weisbord (a leading member of the Trotskyist Communist League of Struggle in New

York). Aldred argued: 'If we are to build up a revolutionary movement we must throw down the sectarian barriers and affiliate our groupings.'[63] His ambition was the formation of a new anti-parliamentary International, involving the above groups and individuals plus any others which might be persuaded to join. However, Aldred's appeal fell on stony ground. The United Workers' Party rejected the suggestion of uniting with the Communist League of Struggle, criticised Aldred for being 'incapable of seeing the real differences between these groups', and firmly declared that it wanted 'nothing to do with people of Aldred's stamp'.[64] Thereafter, the *International Council Correspondence* Group's links with communists in Britain were maintained solely through the APCF.

Despite the UWP's rebuff Aldred had high hopes that the Communist League of Struggle was evolving in a positive direction, having expressed the opinion in *For Communism* that its history was one of 'slow approach to the real Anti-Parliamentarian conclusion'.[65] In May 1935 Vera Buch Weisbord of the CLS arrived in Glasgow at the invitation of the USM, and during her visit she spoke of 'the vital need for an International Conference of the various Left Wing Communist groups, to discuss points of difference with a view to forming a 4th International'.[66] Her departure was soon followed, however, by an acrimonious exchange of correspondence with Guy Aldred over financial arrangements and political disagreements, and relations were severed.[67]

Aldred's strategy for unity in Britain – which was that anti-parliamentarians should either build up the USM or join the APCF with the aim of uniting it to the USM – was equally unfruitful. Vera Buch Weisbord's visit encouraged the USM to resolve to 'meet the Anti-Parliamentarian Group in mutual discussion with an endeavour to find a basis of agreement for calling an International Conference of Left wing Communist Groups with a view of forming a 4th International',[68] but nothing concrete resulted from this decision. The USM itself only managed to establish affiliated groups outside Glasgow and its environs in Leeds (1934) and in London, where a United Socialist Movement Anti-Parliamentary Group was formed in 1938. Aldred edited and published one issue of a paper called *Hyde Park* for the London group in September 1938.

During the Spanish Civil War years contact between the APCF and USM increased, and these relations will be discussed in the following chapter. Before leaving this topic, however, one other attempt at co-operation between the two groups is worth mentioning.

One of the USM's main concerns during the 1930s was with the 'Stalinist Terror' in Russia, as manifested in events such as the Moscow Show Trials. The USM's comments on this issue sought to emphasise that there was nothing new about such events. A letter sent to the Russian Ambassador in August 1936 by Ethel MacDonald on behalf of the USM pointed out that 'this horror is merely the culmination of the imprisonments and persecutions of Socialists that has been continuous in the USSR since 1920'.[69] The USM's attitude was the same as it had been during Trotsky's persecution and exile: the former leading Bolsheviks now standing trial had been 'parties to these outrages' in the past and were now paying 'the penalty of acquiescence'.[70] As Guy Aldred pointed out in May 1938, 'the Stalinist conspiracies are but the continuation of methods which prevailed in Trotsky's time. Zinoviev, and those who were parties to the Kronstadt massacre, reaped what they helped to sow.'[71]

Nevertheless, when a Socialist Anti-Terror Committee was formed in Glasgow at the end of 1937, the USM felt prompted to participate, along with members of the APCF, ILP and the Revolutionary Socialist Party (a group which had evolved towards Trotskyism from De Leonist origins). In March 1938 Guy Aldred wrote a pamphlet for the SATC titled *Against Terrorism in the Workers' Struggle*, in which he argued that 'the perpetuation of persecution, firing squads, and the supremacy of the State' were alien to the socialist philosophy of freedom and liberty, and that 'those who call themselves Socialists must rally against this terrorism and denounce it in the name of Socialism and the workers' struggle'. The pamphlet accused the Stalinist Communist Parties of 'three crimes against the workers' struggle: (1) terrorism; (2) imperialist opportunism and counter-revolution; (3) corrupt destruction of working class propaganda throughout the world', and called on the working class to 'organise to destroy Communist Party and Stalin Terrorism, and to rank it with Fascism and all other terrorism'.[72]

Soon after co-operating to publish this pamphlet the organisations involved in the SATC again went their separate ways. Guy Aldred claimed that the Committee had been illicitly sabotaged by the ILP participants, who had wanted to give the impression that it was impossible for anyone else to work in organisations in which Aldred was involved.[73] Certainly, accusations concerning Aldred's domineering personality were always plentiful, and were made by friend and foe alike. In June 1935, for example, B. Meehan resigned from the USM because of Aldred's inclination to 'ignore organisations and work on his own initiative'. Such behaviour discouraged other USM members from developing their own ideas and abilities: 'the majority of the Comrades that at present are members of the USM are members because Comrade Aldred is a member; if Comrade Aldred left they would also leave, because they can only think and act through the medium of Comrade Aldred'.[74] When these allegations were discussed by the USM William Dick moved that Meehan's criticisms should be acknowledged as correct. When this motion was defeated Dick tendered his own resignation.[75] He was later readmitted to membership, but after the group barred him from speaking on its public platform he resigned for a second time, 'stressing the point that he was sick of the Socialist movement'.[76] Soon afterwards Dick joined the APCF, so it was clearly the *United* Socialist Movement with which he was disenchanted, rather than 'the Socialist movement' as a whole.

It would be too simple, however, to view these acrimonious clashes as merely the inevitable product of Guy Aldred's supposed egomania. Aldred's attempts to unite the various small groups in a new International had come to nothing. In terms of numbers and their ability to influence events the USM and APCF remained pathetically weak. As such they were forced to live what Serge Bricianer, referring to the German council communists during roughly the same period and in similar circumstances, has called a 'group-centred life': 'unable to direct one's aggression effectively against the world, one directed it against the nearest group, and, through lack of numbers, one saw discussions about principles in terms of personal antagonisms'.[77]

The isolation Bricianer describes was felt keenly by all the anti-parliamentarians. In 1935, for example, Guy Aldred expressed profound pessimism about the prospects for revolution in Asia or continental Europe. In his view only the workers of the English-speaking countries – primarily Britain and America – remained likely instigators of the world revolution.[78] Yet even in those countries the outlook was bleak. In his vision of Britain in 1936, Aldred saw only 'the poverty and apathy of the working class; its exhaustion by despair and charlatanism; the menace of war . . . this massed confusion of misery and error'.[79] In such circumstances, however, Aldred did not admit defeat. In May 1936 he launched the first issue of a new paper, called *Attack*, precisely because this bleak outlook made it 'imperative that Anti-Parliamentarism should be heard again in the land'.[80] However, the response to this initiative was insufficient to sustain the *Attack* beyond its first and only issue.

It was the same for the APCF. In the May 1936 issue of the APCF paper *Advance*, R. Bunton wrote: 'Today, an atmosphere of despair envelops the working class.' The same atmosphere that surrounded the working class as a whole was also felt by the anti-parliamentary groups in particular. The fascists had taken power in Germany; the Italian invasion of Abyssinia in October 1935 made the threat of another world war loom large (in August 1935 Guy Aldred wrote that 'there can be no doubt that war is inevitable');[81] Britain was only just beginning to recover from the effects of the greatest ever crisis of the world capitalist system. The anti-parliamentarians were powerless to influence the working class's response to any of these events. All they could do was analyse and comment from the sidelines. It is hardly surprising that such circumstances gave rise to tension and frustration, and that when these feelings did burst forth they were often expressed on a personal level.

THE CRISIS OF CAPITALISM

The APCF's contribution, in the mid-1930s, towards the development of anti-parliamentary theory in the area of capitalist economic crisis, provides a good example of the way in which the anti-parliamentarians were restricted to commenting from the sidelines about events which they were in no position to influence.

Previously, a lack of serious study and comment on the dynamics of world capitalism had distinguished anti-parliamentary communists in Britain from their comrades in other countries, notably the Dutch and German council communists, among whom such work was undertaken in order to give a 'scientific' underpinning to their view of parliamentarism, trade unions, the revolutionary party, and so on. During the 1930s *International Council Correspondence* (later known as *Living Marxism* and *New Essays*) was the main forum for the debate on economics among the council communists. The editor, Paul Mattick, recalled that it had shown

> a great concern with the inherent contradictions of the capitalist system and their unfolding in the course of its development. The nature of the capitalist crisis was more intensely discussed, and on a higher theoretical level, than is generally the rule in labour publications, encompassing as it did the most recent interpreta-

tions of Marxist economic theory and its application to the prevailing conditions.[82]

The contributors to these debates developed a general line of argument known now as the theory of 'capitalist decadence'. The starting-point of this theory was Marx's argument that

> At a certain stage of their development, the material productive forces of society come in conflict with the existing relations of production . . . From forms of development of the productive forces these relations turn into their fetters. Then begins an epoch of social revolution . . . No social order ever perishes before all the productive forces for which there is room in it have developed.[83]

Decadence theory was an attempt to establish *when* the epoch of social revolution began, and *why* the relations of production fettered the development of the productive forces.

According to decadence theory, during capitalism's early period of development crises were the growing pains of an ascendant mode of production which was integrating the whole world into a single economy and raising the productive forces to great heights: 'depressions could be regarded as a "healing process" of a sick economic body . . . leading to a new prosperity enjoying a new level of productivity which the depression itself established'.[84] So long as this progressive phase continued, the main task on the working class's agenda was to organise itself in trade unions and parliamentary parties to win the economic and political reforms which capitalism could afford to grant.

As Marx had pointed out, however, capitalism's ascendant era would not last for ever. Among the council communists there was disagreement over precisely why the relations of production should become fetters on the development of the productive forces – that is, over the fundamental causes of capitalist crisis. While Mattick and Henryk Grossman based their analyses on the 'falling rate of profit' theory, other contributors took up the position adopted by Rosa Luxemburg, who had argued that crises were caused by 'overproduction', the saturation of markets, and the capitalists' inability to realise the profits derived from the exploitation of labour power. Here we will concentrate on the Luxemburgists' ideas, since these were the ones taken up by anti-parliamentarians in Britain.

The Luxemburgist position pointed to imperialist expansion – a source of new markets in which to sell goods – as one way in which capitalism could offset its tendencies towards crisis. However, in 1914 the outbreak of the First World War between the most powerful imperialist rivals signalled that the limits of this outlet had been reached, since there were no unclaimed areas of the world left to conquer. Capitalism's ascendant period had come to an end. In the following period – decadence – further development could take place only at great cost to humanity through a military redivision of markets. Capitalism's cycle of boom and slump now took a different form: 'The question today is only inasmuch as the depression no longer seems to re-establish a basis for prosperity, whether in the same way war no longer can establish a basis for another period of capitalist peace'.[85] In the ascendant period crises had eliminated 'excess' capital, enabling the system to emerge each time on a healthier basis. In the decadent period the only resolution to crises was war, but this merely laid the foundations for a short reconstruction-based boom, before the inevitable emergence of another crisis, and so on.

The onset of economic decadence also affected the political organisation of capitalism. During the ascendant period,

> the capitalists, still fighting against the remnants of feudalism, fighting between themselves and against the workers, at first needed a political democracy in which they could settle their problems within the general competitive struggle. But the more the concentration process of capital became intensified, law and government became less and less the synthesis of numerous political and economic frictions, and instead 'the needs of the whole' were served better through exclusively serving the needs of the few. Government became solely the instrument for suppression within the country and an instrument for imperialistic policies.[86]

The decadent period witnessed a huge increase in state intervention in the economy – in order to carry out 'the economic centralisation and the "rationalisation" which the intensification of international competition on a saturated market imposes on each nation'[87] – accompanied by a widespread emergence of totalitarian forms of political rule. Stalinist state capitalism in Russia, fascist corporatism in Italy, National Socialism in Germany, and the New

Deal in America, were all regarded as evidence of these phenomena.

Capitalism's entry into its period of decadence and permanent crisis destroyed the material basis for the mass reformist movements built up during the era of ascendant capitalism, since according to decadence theory lasting reforms could no longer be granted nor won. 'The workers' organisations could no longer limit themselves to struggling for higher wages. They could no longer see their principal aim as one of acting as parliamentary representatives and extorting improvements for the working class'.[88] In the period of decadence and 'eruption of open revolution', the immediate task of the working class had become nothing less than the smashing of the fetters of profit and market which were restraining the potential development of the productive forces, and the establishment of a worldwide communist society. To do this the working class would have to create new revolutionary organisations, not least in opposition to the 'old' labour movement of social democratic parties and trade unions, which had passed over to become the left wing of the *capitalist* political spectrum.

The council communists' attitudes toward issues such as parliamentarism and trade unionism were firmly rooted in this distinction between capitalism's 'ascendant' and 'decadent' periods. Practically all of the European left or council communists had originally belonged to the pre-First World War mass parliamentary parties of the Second International, and had supported the electoral and trade unionist struggle for political and economic reforms within capitalism. However, these ideas and activities were rapidly rejected once the First World War had signalled the end of capitalism's ascendant period. When the Comintern advocated a continuation of the same old methods of struggle (such as Revolutionary Parliamentarism) *after* the war – that is, when capitalism had entered its decadent period – the European left communists and council communists were the foremost *opponents* of such tactics.

The European left communists thus evolved from very different origins compared to their counterparts in Britain. Possessing no theory of ascendant and decadent periods in capitalism's development, British anti-parliamentarians had been consistently hostile towards parliamentarism, trade unionism and reformism since long *before* the First World War. In the mid-1930s, however, some of the council communists' ideas – transmitted via the APCF's contact with *International Council Correspondence* – began to enter into the thinking of the movement in Britain. For example, whilst opposing parliamentarism on the customary grounds that it led to 'self-seeking', 'desire for office', 'revisionism' and 'betrayal', a statement of 'APCF Aims' published in 1935 also declared that it was 'the permanent crisis of capitalism' that had 'rendered obsolete the official trade and industrial union movements'.[89]

The influence of decadence theory was also evident in the first issue of the APCF paper *Advance*, published in May 1936. In one article, T. L. Anderson (who at that time belonged to the USM) explained Italy's invasion of Abyssinia in a manner consistent with the Luxemburgist analysis which underpinned council communist theories:

> like every other capitalistic country in the world, [Italy] is suffering from a lack of markets . . . Complete bankruptcy stares her in the face. She is now learning by bitter experience what Karl Marx taught about 80 years ago – that the law of capitalist development is expand or collapse. The result is, of course, she decides to expand on Abyssinian territory.[90]

In the same issue an editorial on the class struggle in Spain put forward the standard anti-parliamentary criticism of reformist demands – the working class should use its power 'not to modify the existing regime but to abolish it' – but also criticised reformism on the grounds that 'the economic laws of developing capitalism continually cancel out any immediate gains'.[91]

Most interesting of all was an article by APCF member Willie McDougall, titled 'Capitalism Must Go!', which explained the economic crisis in terms of 'over-production' and also hinted at the concept of decadence. 'Side by side with prolific production and ever increasing potentialities for higher standards of living, the people are driven down to even lower levels.' Starvation and poverty co-existed with the destruction of produce which could not be sold profitably. 'Glutted markets' and over-production had caused unemployment and short-time working, as there was a lack of 'effective' demand for products and thus for the labour power used to make them.

> [Capitalism's] historic mission – the superseding of feudalism – has been accomplished. It has raised the level of production to heights undreamed of by its own pioneers, but its peak point has been reached and decline set in.
>
> Whenever a system becomes a fetter to the expansion or proper

> functioning of the forces of production, a revolution is imminent and it is doomed to make way for a successor. Just as feudalism had to give way to the more productive system of capitalism, so must the latter be swept from the path of human progress to make way for Socialism.[92]

Apart from providing further evidence of *International Council Correspondence*'s influence on anti-parliamentarians in Britain, McDougall's article also typified the anti-parliamentarians' dilemma in the first half of the 1930s. Perceptive in its analysis, hard-hitting in its condemnation of capitalist 'anarchy', and convincing in its case for capitalism's replacement by communism, its impact on the reality it described and criticised was nevertheless nil. To their great credit, the anti-parliamentarians had followed the advice of Channing quoted at the beginning of one of Guy Aldred's autobiographical pamphlets: 'Wait not to be backed by numbers. Wait not till you are sure of an echo from the crowd. The fewer the voices on the side of truth, the more distinct and strong must be your own.'[93] They had continued to state in distinct and strong voices that 'Capitalism Must Go!', but rarely in the years from 1925–35 was there ever an echo from the crowd. As we are about to see, however, this bleak period of isolation came to an end in 1936, with the outbreak of the Spanish Civil War.

Part III

Capitalist War and Class War 1936–45

7 The Civil War in Spain

The Spanish Civil War began in July 1936, when a fascist coup aimed at replacing the left wing Republican government was met across one half of the country by armed resistance from the working class and peasantry. The outbreak of the Civil War, and the mounting wave of class struggle which had preceded and provoked the fascist coup, were greeted by the anti-parliamentary communists in much the same way that Sylvia Pankhurst had welcomed the Russian revolution nearly 20 years earlier. It was like 'the dawn on the horizon after a long and painful night'.[1]

Surveying the violent class struggle which had continued in Spain after the victory of the Popular Front in the elections of February 1936, the APCF commented: 'The recent events in Spain have given the International Proletariat the first welcome news for some time. The drift towards Fascism has been challenged in one European country at least.'[2] At the beginning of August 1936 Guy Aldred described the 'Spanish Struggle' as 'the mighty proletarian movement that Europe needed'.[3] More to the point, the Spanish struggle was the mighty proletarian movement the anti-parliamentarians needed. After several years of decline, the outbreak of the Civil War provided the impetus for a period of sustained and intense activity. Within ten days of the beginning of the Civil War on 19 July 1936, the USM had published the first issue of a foolscap news-sheet called *Regeneracion*. Between then and 7 October another eighteen issues were published and distributed by the thousand. Open-air meetings were also stepped-up. John Caldwell, a member of the USM at that time, has recalled that public meetings soon 'drew bigger crowds than at any time since the general strike',[4] while Willie McDougall of the APCF noted that he was 'never so active in speaking at street corners as . . . during the Spanish crisis'.[5]

The anti-parliamentarians immediately began to use the attempted overthrow of the Republican government as evidence to substantiate their view that parliamentarism was useless as a means of achieving reforms or of bringing about a revolution. In September 1936 the APCF warned: 'Elect a government to bring about genuine reforms . . . and your Bishops, Priests and Ministers, your Churchills, Mosleys, Chamberlains, MacDonalds, etc., will immediately call for a so-called volunteer force to protect the property of the rich.'[6] Twelve months later, APCF member A.S. Knox argued along similar lines: 'The uselessness of parliament should be obvious to all . . . wherever the ruling class decides that parliament fails to express their desires, parliament will be abolished!'.[7] In 1939 a section of the APCF's 'Principles And Tactics', directed against the parliamentary strategy of the SPGB, dismissed the idea that the ruling class would tolerate 'a genuinely revolutionary parliament, elected expressly to dispossess them' with the comment: 'Surely Franco supplies the answer to such a childish notion.'[8]

A final example of the way in which the Civil War was cited as evidence whenever the anti-parliamentary case was put forward could be found in the November 1940–January 1941 issue of the APCF paper *Solidarity*. Arguing against 'the belief in parliamentary action as the road to working class power', the author pointed to 'the recent Spanish tragedy' in which 'the incensed ruling class repudiated even their own bourgeois legality and unleashed the most bloody butchery of the proletariat the world has ever witnessed'. This experience was then used to criticise the Communist Party's demand for a 'Workers' Government' to replace the wartime coalition national government. The British ruling class could not be expected to 'respect their own institution' if 'a Government prepared to accede to the workers' demands' took power: 'At the first threat of resistance to their will, they would immediately establish a military dictatorship and by sheer weight of arms smash any attempt at progressive legislation.'[9]

The APCF had expressed a similar lack of faith in parliamentarism shortly after the elections which had brought the Popular Front government to power in Spain. While admitting that the new government had taken some useful measures, such as the release of '30 000 class war prinsoners', the APCF pointed out: 'It was the mass pressure of the people and not the empty promises of politicians, that gave these comrades their freedom . . . the workers have had to resort to repeated demonstrations and general strikes to force the fulfilment of the amnesty and other promises made.' The Republican government was described as a capitalist administration which would not hesitate to crush the working class and which it was in the workers' interests not to support but to destroy:

> The election pact of the People's Front, while promising the amnesty demanded by the workers, was nevertheless a liberalistic and reformist document from start to finish . . . The People's Block of today leaves Capitalist society intact, and left alone . . . the Spanish capitalist class will repeat what their German confrères did in 1918 . . . there is ample reason for the Spanish workers to work for a change of *System* and to refuse to be lulled to political sleep by any mere change of *government*, however many 'concessions' may be promised by the demagogues of Capitalism.[10]

Before 19 July, therefore, the anti-parliamentarians were not supporters of the Republican government, and after the beginning of the Civil War they repeatedly warned the working class not to place any faith in parliamentary institutions. However, such views represented an element of the anti-parliamentarians' response to the events in Spain which was flatly contradicted by the ideas which dominated their propaganda until mid-1937.

SUPPORTING THE REPUBLIC

If a single document encapsulated all the essential features of the anti-parliamentarians' position during the initial period of the Spanish Civil War, it was the resolution adopted at a meeting of the USM on 11 August 1936. This demanded 'that all workers' organisations convene public meetings for the purpose of expressing complete solidarity with the Spanish Government *de facto* and *de jure*', and to criticise the British government for refusing to supply the Republic with arms. Prime Minister Baldwin was censured for not recalling Parliament to session, as was Labour leader Attlee for not demanding that this be done. The USM proceeded to urge 'The recall and dissolution of Parliament and a direct appeal to the electors on this one issue: SUPPORT SPAIN', with 'All Anarchists and Anti-Parliamentarians to vote for and support all candidates standing against Fascism and for practical support of Spain.' If Parliament was not recalled and dissolved there should be a general strike and the establishment of Councils of Action to sit in permanent session until the Spanish crisis was resolved. The resolution ended by repeating its appeal for 'definite action and support of the Spanish Government and the workers of Spain.'[11]

Thus the basic features of the anti-parliamentarians' initial response were: support for the Republican government; respect for capitalist legality; calls for intervention by other nation states; and a readiness to unite with other organisations on the minimum basis of support for the Republic. All of these features arose from the anti-parliamentarians' view that the Civil War was basically a 'fight . . . between military fascism and democracy, even constitutional democracy',[12] and from their support for the latter against the former.

Support for the Republican government was pledged in nearly every issue of *Regeneracion*. More often than not, support for the Spanish working class and support for the Spanish government were represented as inseparable. This could be seen in the frequent use of phrases promising 'complete loyalty through all possible action to the Spanish Government and workers who support it',[13] or supporting 'the properly constituted Government of Spain and its magnificent working class defenders'.[14]

As this last quote indicates, the USM also stressed the legitimacy of the Republican government, describing it, for example, as 'the recognised and legally elected and properly constituted government of Spain'.[15] This was also a feature of the APCF's response. Although the group had argued in the light of the attempted coup that 'Constitutionalism . . . has surely now proved a failure',[16] there was nonetheless a strong element of constitutionalism in much of what the APCF wrote about Spain. For example, the APCF criticised the fascists for their 'breaches of international law' in attempting to overthrow 'an orthodox democratic government'.[17]

It was in such terms that both groups couched their appeals to the governments of other nation states (principally Britain and France) to intervene in the Civil War on the side of the Republican government. Guy Aldred criticised the British government for adopting a position of 'neutrality between a constitutional government and a fascist counter-revolutionary rebellion'.[18] An article from a Spanish source published in the APCF's press called for an end to the British government's arms embargo: 'There is not a single convincing argument to prevent the supply of arms to the legally and democratically constituted government of Spain'.[19] The APCF itself criticised the British government for refusing military aid to the Republic when 'the Spanish Government satisfies the legal requirements according to orthodox international legal standards'.[20]

The anti-parliamentarians' support for democracy against fascism, and their appeals to capitalist states to intervene in Spain, were taken to their logical conclusion in a leaflet published by the USM around the end of 1936. The author, T. L. Anderson, argued that Italy and Germany were frustrated at the deadlock in the Civil War and would soon embark on an outright invasion of Spain. If this happened the British government would then feel compelled to intervene militarily as well. In such circumstances, Anderson argued, 'the immediate purpose of the Spanish Workers and the British forces – the smashing of fascism – would be common to both. Where would be the logic of supporting one and opposing the other . . . If war comes as a struggle between the Democratic and the Fascist states the duty of Socialists is to take a hand in it.'[21] Encouraging the working class to identify its interests with those of 'its own' ruling class has always been an essential precondition for enlisting workers to fight in inter-capitalist wars, and there can be no escaping the fact that this was the role Anderson's argument would have played had the scenario he envisaged come about.

Ironically, only a few months earlier Anderson had written an anti-war article in which he had observed: 'It is a tribute to the power of words that millions of human slaves will march forth to slaughter each other in the most diabolical manner, at the behest of their oppressors. In 1914 it was "Gallant Little Belgium"; today it is "Defenceless Abyssinia"; tomorrow – what?'.[22] The answer that Anderson had given to his own question would be put into words by USM member Ethel MacDonald in October 1937: 'Anti-Fascism is the new slogan by which the working class is being betrayed.'[23]

In their approach to co-operation with other organisations the anti-parliamentarians set aside long-established principles in favour of a single criterion: support for the Republic. If there had been a general election in 1936, as the USM demanded, and all anarchists and anti-parliamentarians had voted for all candidates standing against fascism, this would have entailed supporting, among other parties, the CPGB – the very organisation the APCF had been founded to oppose!

The APCF adopted a similarly unprincipled approach towards the anti-fascist alliance of republican and left wing organisations in Spain. In February 1937 the group published a pamphlet in which Frederica Montseny of the Iberian Anarchist Federation (FAI) defended the

Spanish anarchists' co-operation with other parties on the minimal basis of support for the Republic: 'If on July 19th we had attempted, as we could have done, to proclaim Libertarian Communism in Catalonia, the results would have been disastrous . . . *The fact is that we were the first to modify our aspirations, the first to understand that the struggle against international fascism was in itself great enough.'* The same pamphlet also quoted another of Montseny's speeches in which she had said: 'In these tragic times, we must put aside our point of view, our ideological conditions, in order to realise the unity of all anti-fascists from the Republicans to the Anarchists.'[24] The APCF endorsed these sentiments by publishing them without criticism. Clearly, therefore, the anti-parliamentarians' support for the Republican government entailed the indefinite postponement, or complete abandonment, of any revolutionary aspirations or principles.

Nevertheless, the need for unity among the various organisations claiming to represent the working class was one of the strongest lessons the APCF drew from the initial events of the Civil War. The way in which Republicans, Socialists, Communists and Anarchists had united to resist the fascist coup was held up as something worth emulating in Britain. In September and October 1936 the APCF urged 'All Unattached Anti-Parliamentarians, Socialists, Anarchist-Communists and Revolutionaries' to join in a 'genuine Revolutionary United Front' against 'the common enemy – international capitalism and fascism'.[25] A small step in this direction was taken when the APCF and the London *Freedom* Group suspended publication of their respective journals in order to produce jointly the monthly *Fighting Call*.

The USM, however, paid little attention to the APCF's calls for unity. Indeed, from the beginning of the Civil War until spring 1937, relations between the APCF and the USM were extremely hostile, because of the fierce competition between the two groups to gain official recognition from the anarcho-syndicalist National Confederation of Labour (CNT), and to become the Spanish organisation's accredited representative in Britain. Guy Aldred was adamant that the CNT–FAI's British 'franchise' should be awarded to him, by virtue of his long record of commitment to the anarchist cause and because 'The United Socialist Movement was the first organisation in Great Britain to rally to the cause of the Spanish Workers, and to insist on the Anarchist character of the Spanish struggle'.[26] Aldred poured scorn on the competing 'bid' of the APCF. Referring to the nineteen leaflets in the *Regeneracion* series, he alleged that his rivals had 'never thought of Spain, till I started the leaflets'.[27]

This quarrel was complicated when Emma Goldman, who had dropped out of political activity in the late 1920s to earn a living by lecturing as a literary critic, suddenly reappeared in the anarchist movement after the outbreak of the Civil War and began to organise support for the CNT–FAI around herself, completely ignoring those such as Aldred who had maintained an active commitment to revolutionary activity during less thriving periods in the anarchist movement's fortunes.[28] This stirred the resentment Aldred had felt towards Goldman ever since their bitter quarrel during 1924–5 over whether or not the Bolsheviks were persecuting genuine revolutionaries. In Aldred's view Goldman was simply exploiting the Civil War in order to 'regain the position she lost through her petty-bourgeois careerism'.[29] Furthermore, Aldred felt that Goldman and the *Freedom* Group – and thus, by association, the APCF too – were conspiring to settle old scores and force him out of the anarchist movement.[30]

All things considered, therefore, Aldred was not at all pleased when the role of officially representing the CNT–FAI in Britain was assigned to a Bureau in London closely associated with *Freedom* and the APCF.

Yet the APCF's success in gaining the CNT–FAI's official 'blessing' rebounded to its own disadvantage in the end, as it turned the group into little more than a 'servicing organisation' for the Spanish anarcho-syndicalists. The *Fighting Call*, and *Advance* when it resumed publication, both consisted almost entirely of material lifted directly from the CNT–FAI *Boletin de Informacion*, with no critical comments added and hardly any editorial articles written by the APCF itself. By confining themselves to such activity the APCF made practically no direct contribution towards the development of a more critical attitude to what was happening in Spain, whereas the USM, because it was less restricted in its allegiance to the CNT–FAI, was able to do so.

THE BEGINNINGS OF A REVOLUTIONARY CRITIQUE

In September 1936 *Regeneracion* published an appeal from Guy Aldred's French comrade André Prudhommeaux, who was now in Barcelona working for the CNT–FAI, asking for arms, money and trained soldiers to be sent to Spain, and for the anarcho-syndicalist ideas of the CNT–FAI to be publicised in Britain.[31] Although it was Aldred's ambition to see an Anti-Parliamentary 'Column' sent from Glasgow,[32] Prudhommeaux suggested a much smaller delegation. Accordingly, Ethel MacDonald was chosen to make the journey to Spain, accompanied by Jane Patrick, who had been invited by the CNT in her personal capacity as an experienced printer.[33] Although Patrick had been a member of the APCF since its formation, she did not go to Spain as its official delegate. For some obscure reason the APCF disowned her when she left for Spain, and while she was there she was supported from funds raised by the USM.

MacDonald and Patrick left Glasgow on 19 October 1936, travelling via Nimes where a base relatively close to the Spanish border could be provided by Prudhommeaux's comrades. After arriving in Barcelona, however, they soon encountered problems. A letter from the APCF disowning Patrick had arrived ahead of them, and they immediately fell under suspicion. Back in Glasgow there was an angry confrontation between USM and APCF members, which resulted in the APCF dispatching a second letter to explain that while they no longer considered Patrick to be a member of their group they had not intended to cast doubt on her integrity as a revolutionary.[34] Their credentials thus established, Patrick served for a time on the Committee of Defence in Madrid, while MacDonald worked for the Information in Foreign Languages section at the CNT–FAI headquarters in Barcelona, where she made regular English-language broadcasts on the CNT Radio Barcelona.

The pair also kept in regular contact with their comrades in Glasgow, and their first-hand reports of what was happening in Spain gradually began to put forward a very different view of the issues at stake in the Civil War, compared to the position that the anti-parliamentary groups had thus far adopted.

Although the APCF had argued in May 1936 that only through the mass pressure of its own strikes and demonstrations could the working class hope to gain anything for itself, during the rest of 1936 the anti-parliamentarians had neglected this principle and put most of their energy into urging various governments to act on the working class's behalf. What impressed Ethel MacDonald, however, was the way in which the Spanish workers, rather than relying on the politicians of the Republican government to resist the fascist coup, had immediately set about organising and fighting the Civil War on their own initiative. In this sense the Civil War was 'the living demonstration of the power of the proletariat, the living truth of the force of direct action'.[35] MacDonald reversed the relative emphases that the anti-parliamentarians had placed on parliamentary and governmental action as opposed to the direct action of the workers themselves – she argued that 'We know too well that Capitalism will never assist us'[36] – and urged 'direct action in solidarity with the Spanish struggle by workers in other lands. How? By sending arms, yes; but by the social revolution primarily.'[37] This line of thought was taken up by Guy Aldred. In February 1937 he wrote: 'Parliamentarism will not save the Spanish workers' struggle, which is our struggle. Only Direct Action can do that . . . Liquidate Parliamentarism in Anti-Parliamentarism. Translate words into act. Face Fascism with determination, industrial solidarity, and the Social General Strike.'[38]

The USM also began to reassess the issues at stake in the Civil War. Previously it had been seen as a straight fight between democracy and fascism, with little attention paid to the point that these were simply two competing forms of political rule based on the same underlying capitalist society. In February 1937, however, Ethel MacDonald pointed out that 'Fascism . . . is but another name for Capitalism',[39] while Guy Aldred made these remarks about the democratic face of the capitalist Janus:

> The official government slogan in Spain is 'the democratic republic'. This means capitalism, even if of a liberal, reformist type. It means exploitation, even though in a less oppressive form than under Franco. Hence, this slogan does not express the aspirations in the civil war, of at least a large section of the Spanish masses. They want, not democratic capitalism, but no capitalism; they want to make a workers' revolution, and establish workers' collectivism.[40]

After this criticism of what the Republican forces were fighting for had been made, slogans in support of the Spanish government became as rare in the USM's press in 1937 as they had been common in 1936, and CNT–FAI leaders such as Frederica Montseny were criticised retrospectively for having joined the Republican government formed by Largo Caballero in November 1936.[41]

Meanwhile, although the USM was revising its position on Spain at a much faster rate and becoming more openly critical of the CNT–FAI than the APCF was, after reaching their nadir during the winter of 1936–7 relations between the USM and APCF began to improve. This may have been due in part to Frank Leech's resignation from the APCF around April 1937. There was no love lost between Leech and members of the USM, and his presence in the APCF was frequently cited as a stumbling block in the way of closer co-operation. The reason for Leech's departure from the APCF is obscure. In May 1937, under the name of the 'Anti-Parliamentary Volunteers', he published a pamphlet called *The Truth about Barcelona*, based entirely on a *Boletin de Informacion* received from the CNT–FAI.[42] In August 1937 he formed the Glasgow Anarchist-Communist Federation, which became part of the Glasgow Group of the Anarchist Federation of Britain during the Second World War, and will be discussed in the following chapter.

The friendlier relations which had begun to exist between the APCF and the USM became evident in May 1937, when the two groups co-operated to publish the one-off *Barcelona Bulletin*. This consisted mainly of Jane Patrick and Ethel MacDonald's eye-witness accounts and analysis of the week of street fighting in Barcelona between the Stalinist-dominated Generalitat (regional government of Catalonia) on one side and the CNT–FAI and the 'Trotskyist' POUM on the other. It was one of the first publications to describe what had happened during the 'May Days' from a point of view sympathetic to the CNT–FAI and the POUM. The *Barcelona Bulletin* also contained an article titled 'Win The War! – But Also The Revolution' by Willie McDougall of the APCF, which seems to have been one of the few occasions on which a member of the APCF argued against defence of the Republic and in favour of revolution.[43]

Jane Patrick left Spain immediately after the May Days and arrived back in Glasgow towards the end of the month. In 1938 she joined the USM. Ethel MacDonald stayed on in Spain and at one point was arrested and imprisoned by the Generalitat, charged with having revolutionary literature in her possession and an out-of-date residence permit. In view of the Stalinist repression directed against the CNT–FAI and POUM in the aftermath of the May Days, 'considerable anxiety regarding [Ethel MacDonald's] welfare' was 'felt by her relatives and comrades' in Glasgow.[44] The APCF took the initiative in forming an Ethel MacDonald Defence Committee, in which the USM also participated.[45] Eventually MacDonald was released unharmed, escaped from Spain at the beginning of September 1937, and after visiting comrades in France and Holland en route arrived back in Glasgow in November. The Defence Committee was disbanded after learning that MacDonald was out of danger, but the anti-parliamentarians continued to campaign for action in support of CNT–FAI and POUM prisoners and refugees right up to, and indeed after, the end of the Civil War.

After the *Barcelona Bulletin* the USM published no other journals, apart from single issues of the *Word* (May 1938) and *Hyde Park* (September 1938), until May 1939, when the threat of world war provided the impetus for the *Word* to be revived and another spell of sustained activity began. The APCF's press took over the role of providing a forum for the continued development of the critical attitude towards the Civil War pioneered by members of the USM.

In September 1937, for example, the APCF's *Workers' Free Press* reprinted an article from *International Council Correspondence*. This argued that the CNT–FAI's anti-fascist alliance with the Socialist and Communist Parties had been 'a united front with capitalism, which can only be a united front *for* capitalism'. Anti-fascism amounted to telling the working class to 'co-operate with one enemy in order to crush another, in order later to be crushed by the first':

> The People's Front is not a lesser evil for the workers, it is only another form of capitalist dictatorship in addition to Fascism . . . from the viewpoint of the interests of the Spanish workers, as well as of the workers of the world, there is no difference between Franco-Fascism and Moscow-Fascism, however much difference there may be between Franco and Moscow . . . The revolutionary watchword for Spain is: Down with the Fascists and also down with the Loyalists.[46]

The following month the APCF published an article that Ethel MacDonald had sent from Barcelona in August 1937, which also opposed the anti-fascist alliance with democratic capitalism in favour of social revolution against *all* forms of capitalist domination:

> Fascism is not something new, some new force of evil opposed to society, but is only the old enemy, Capitalism, under a new and fearful sounding name . . . Under the guise of 'Anti-Fascism' elements are admitted to the working class movement whose interests are still diametrically opposed to those of the workers . . .Anti-Fascism is the new slogan by which the working class is being betrayed.[47]

In the second issue of *Solidarity*, successor to the *Workers' Free Press*, the APCF published an unsigned report received from Spain. Surveying the previous two years of the Civil War, it argued: 'All this could have been avoided (2 million dead) if the workers had taken control and eliminated the government, thus killing at one stroke, a great force that has been working with Franco all along the line. The proletariat of Spain was lulled into political unconsciousness by the government which was supposed to be leading it.' The article described the Popular Front as a 'capitalist government'.

However, the very same issue of *Solidarity* also contained several hangovers from the position adopted by the APCF during the initial period of the Civil War. On the front page there was an appeal from the CNT–FAI, calling for 'GENERAL STRIKES TO MAKE THE GOVERNMENTS RECOGNISE THE LEGAL RIGHTS OF THE SPANISH PEOPLE'. Elsewhere there was a resolution from the Earnock branch of the Lanarkshire Miners' Union, calling on the TUC to 'declare a General Strike until the legal right to purchase arms has been restored to the Spanish Government' by the British government. Another article criticised the British government's 'damnable treachery to Loyalist Spain' – 'Loyalists' being supporters of the Republican government described elsewhere in the paper as capitalist and anti-working class![48]

Thus the APCF never shook itself entirely free of its original attitude towards events in Spain. In its various publications nearly all the articles that adopted a revolutionary position originated outside the group; with Ethel MacDonald, the *International Council Correspondence* group, or the dissident CNT–FAI faction, The Friends Of Durruti, whose view of the Civil War, concluding that 'Democracy defeated the Spanish people, not Fascism', was published in *Solidarity* in mid–1939.[49]

SPAIN: A TESTING GROUND

After more than a decade of counter-revolution, the outbreak of the Civil War in Spain aroused the anti-parliamentarians in Britain almost as much as the revolution in Russia had done nearly 20 years before. But the alacrity with which they seized hold of its radical veneer of spontaneity and direct action was matched by the torpor that characterised their analysis of the struggle's real political and social content. As the events of the Civil War unfolded, the issues at stake became clearer. The USM went furthest in rejecting its initial support for Republican capitalism, and in developing a revolutionary attitude to events. The APCF itself showed few signs that it was capable of carrying out a comparably rigorous critique of its own position, but took vicarious credit from publishing the views of groups such as the one around *International Council Correspondence*.

As we will see in the following chapter, by the time of the outbreak of the Second World War the ideas developed in a rudimentary way by some of the anti-parliamentarians since 1937 put them in a much stronger position to respond in a revolutionary manner than they had been at the start of the war in Spain. Although it was not until the war years themselves that the anti-parliamentarians' critique of democracy, fascism and anti-fascism reached a more coherent level, sufficient groundwork had been carried out to ensure that there would be no farcical repetition in 1939 of the tragic position adopted by the anti-parliamentary communists in 1936.

8 The Second World War

'CONVERT THE IMPERIALIST WAR INTO CIVIL WAR'

In May 1939 the APCF published an appeal to the working class titled 'Resist War!', the opening two paragraphs of which expressed in a nutshell the position adopted by the group throughout the Second World War:

> Workers! The Capitalist system – production for Profit instead of for use – is the cause of War! In the struggle for markets, in which to realise their profits, the Capitalists of the world clash, and then expect their 'hands' to become 'cannon fodder'!
>
> ALL the Capitalists are aggressors from the workers' point of view. They rob you until you are industrial 'scrap', and will sacrifice you 'to the last man' to defend their imperial interest![1]

By analysing war as competition amongst rival capitalists pursued by military means, the APCF rejected the ruling class's portrayal of the impending conflict as essentially a democratic crusade against fascism: 'Big Business in this country [Britain] . . . is not concerned about democracy. They would destroy capitalist democracy and every vestige of workers' democracy to ensure the continuity of capitalism (i.e. their profits).'[2] The USM took the same view. In Guy Aldred's opinion, the 'crimes of Fascism' provided 'no excuse for supporting the hypocrisy of pseudo-democracy . . . Why should young men go forward to fight to acquire more territory to be plundered and exploited by American millionaires? Why should they conceive American democracy to be something superior to German Fascism?'.[3] USM member Annesley Aldred (son of Guy Aldred and Rose Witcop) made the same point in March 1940: 'It makes no difference to the effect of a bomb whether it is dropped with the hatred of a Fascist Dictator or the love and kisses of a Democratic Prime Minister . . . In every case it is the workers who are killed. And any form of government which condones that killing must be intolerable to the workers.'[4]

Besides the APCF and USM, the ideas and activities of a third anti-parliamentary group – the Glasgow Anarchist Federation – will also be discussed in this chapter. The Glasgow Anarchist Federation emerged during 1940, when the Glasgow Anarchist–Communist Federation (formed on Frank Leech's initiative in 1937), and another Glasgow organisation called the Marxian Study Group, began joint activity as the Glasgow Group of the Anarchist Federation of Britain. The Glasgow Anarchists produced a few issues of a small journal called the *Anarchist*, but their principal mouthpiece was the newspaper *War Commentary*, produced by the AFB in London. The first issue of *War Commentary*, published in November 1939, put forward views on the war similar to those expressed by the APCF and USM:

> the present struggle is one between rival Imperialisms and for the protection of vested interests. The workers in every country, belonging to the oppressed class, have nothing in common with these interests and the political aspirations of the ruling class. Their immediate struggle is their *emancipation*. *Their* front line is the workshop and factory, not the Maginot Line where they will just rot and die, whilst their masters at home pile up their ill-gotten gains.[5]

This analysis was shared by the Glasgow Anarchists. Glasgow Group member Eddie Shaw, for example, wrote that the only winners in the war would be 'the small minority who own and control the means of production and who are the only ones likely to benefit from the conquest of trade routes and foreign markets, which the sacrifice of millions of innocent people has made possible'.[6]

At the outbreak of the conflict the anti-parliamentary groups all called for the war between the fascist and democratic capitalist states to be turned into a war between the capitalist and working classes. The APCF's slogan in 1939 was: 'DOWN WITH NAZISM AND FASCISM, but also DOWN with ALL IMPERIALISM, BRITISH and FRENCH included!'.[7] This was elaborated three years later:

> We stand for the victory over Hitlerism and Mikadoism – by the German, and the Japanese, workers, and the simultaneous overthrow of all the Allied Imperialists by the workers in Britain and America. We also wish to see the reinstitution of the Workers' Soviets in Russia and the demolition of the Stalinist bureaucracy. In a word, we fight for the destruction of ALL Imperialism by the Proletarian World Revolution.[8]

The demand raised by revolutionaries during the First World War for the 'imperialist war' between nations to be turned into a 'civil war' between classes was repeated by Annesley Aldred in 1939:

> Democracy is, alike with the Fascism which it is to oppose, merely a phase of the same Capitalist system. Is it not obvious, therefore, that if there must be war, it should be a war . . . to overthrow the system that is responsible for all war? It should not be an internecine war between the workers of different nations, but a war in which they stand shoulder to shoulder, and refuse to be any longer the victims of Capitalist exploitation.[9]

The anti-parliamentarians' opposition to *all* sides in the conflict was not altered by Russia's entry into the war in mid-1941. As a capitalist state itself, it was only to be expected that Russia would be drawn into the armed struggle for markets between the imperialist rivals. In 1939 the Glasgow Anarchists had planted themselves firmly within the anti-parliamentary tradition of analysing Russia as a state capitalist regime by publishing a pamphlet, written by the Russian anarcho-syndicalist G. Maximov, called *Bolshevism: Promises and Reality*. This characterised the Russian economy in the following terms:

> Agriculture and industry are organised on the bourgeois principle of the profit-system, i.e. on the exploitation and appropriation by the state of surplus value which is swallowed by the bureaucracy. Industry organised on the capitalist principle makes use of all the capitalist principles of exploitation: Fordisation, Taylorisation, etc.[10]

Maximov denied that the Russian regime could be regarded as progressive in any sense and called on the Russian working class and peasantry to revolt as they had done in 1917, only this time *against* the Bolsheviks.

When the APCF stated in its appeal to 'Resist War!' that 'ALL the Capitalists are aggressors from the workers' point of view', it referred not only to the avowedly capitalist democracies such as Britain and the USA, and the fascist states such as Germany and Italy (the APCF argued that 'Fascism, is but a consequence of Capitalism'),[11] but also to Russia. As Marxian Study Group member James Kennedy pointed out in *Solidarity* in 1939: 'Wage labour is the basis of capitalism. Russian society is no exception . . . Wage labour gives rise to commodity production and capitalist relations, therefore, the control of the means of production and exchange in the hands of the State and not the proletariat.'[12] The USM likewise 'decline[d] to conceive that it is possible, from any point of view, to differentiate the USSR from the general run of capitalist countries'.[13] According to Guy Aldred, since Russia was a capitalist state its intervention in the war was no less motivated by capitalist imperatives than was the involvement of all the other belligerent states: 'the foundation of the USSR social economy is a system of hired labour and commodity production. Consequently, the Soviet Union, like the rest of the capitalist states, needs foreign markets and spheres of political and economic interest. Foreign markets and spheres of influence make for an imperialist policy and militarism.'[14]

Stalinist Russia's alliance with the democratic states bolstered the anti-parliamentarians' argument that the conflict had nothing to do with a crusade for democracy, since they could point out that there were more similarities between the political organisation of capitalism in Nazi Germany and Stalinist Russia than there were between Stalinist Russia and the Allied democracies. Referring to the so-called 'communism' in Russia, USM member John Caldwell argued: 'This "communism" of the strike-breaker, the dungeon-keeper, the executioner and the hired apologist is *not* the Communism our fathers preached and suffered to propagate. It resembles more that other form of bastard socialism, born in similar circumstances in war-exhausted Germany – the creed of the Nazi.'[15] Guy Aldred also drew a parallel between Stalinism and fascism when he observed: 'Democracy, free speech, free press, the inalienable right of private judgement do not exist in the Soviet Union any more than they do in Germany or Italy.'[16]

STATE INTERVENTION IN THE ERA OF CAPITALIST DECADENCE

The anti-parliamentarians based their refusal to take sides in the war in part on an appraisal of the state as a product of the division of society into classes, used by the ruling class to enforce and maintain its own domination over all other classes in society. Under capitalism the state could clothe itself in a variety of guises, but whether fascist, democratic or whatever, it remained nonetheless an instrument of capitalist domination over the working class. By dismissing the differences between democratic and fascist forms of political rule as superficial compared to the capitalist mode of production common to both, the anti-parliamentarians could argue that the democratic and fascist states were basically the same. From the working class's point of view, therefore, there was nothing to choose between them.

During the war some anti-parliamentarians developed another method of approaching this same conclusion. The APCF argued not only that the various nation states were all equally capitalist, but also that they were all equally totalitarian – or tending to become so – and that this was a historical tendency accelerated by the war. This view was summed up by the German revolutionary emigré 'Icarus' (Ernst Schneider), writing in 1944: 'The present imperialist war anticipates and precipitates the economic and political forms to come. Under the smokescreen of freeing Europe from "Totalitarianism", this very form of monopoly capitalism is developing everywhere.'[17]

As Icarus's remark suggests, in the APCF's view changes in the political organisation of capitalism were bound up with capitalist economic developments. In a 1940 appeal 'To Anti-parliamentarians' – based word-for-word on an article which had appeared five years earlier in *International Council Correspondence* – the APCF explained this link by situating totalitarianism in the context of capitalism's movement through ascendant and decadent phases: 'we have definitely left the era of democracy, the era of free competition. This democracy which served the conflicting interests of small capitalists during the developing stage, is now no longer compatible. Monopoly capitalism in a period of permanent crisis and war finds dictatorship and terror the only means to ensure it a tranquil proletariat.'[18] The APCF's 'Principles And Tactics' (1939) observed: 'Even for Capitalist purposes, Parliament is more and more being "consulted" AFTER the event.'[19] Concluding that parliamentary democracy was becoming increasingly obsolete (a conclusion strengthened after the beginning of the war when the Emergency Powers Act gave the government authority to legislate without reference to Parliament), and thus that 'the question of parliamentary activity is of very much decreasing importance', the APCF's appeal argued that 'the name anti-parliamentary therefore is historically outdated and should be discarded'.[20] Consequently, in October 1941 the APCF abandoned its old title and began calling itself the Workers' Revolutionary League.

Another article putting forward the view that totalitarianism was part of capitalism's strategy for self-preservation in its era of decadence and permanent crisis was published in *Solidarity* at the beginning of 1941. The author, M.G., argued that

> Capitalism in crisis cannot afford to indulge in democracy. The insoluble contradictions of the system are so manifest that it is no longer possible for the ruling class to find even a breathing space within the framework of the old parliamentary regime. In order to stave off for a time at least the inevitable collapse, it renounces so-called democratic rule and resorts to the most flagrant and unabashed methods of class domination, otherwise fascism.[21]

In short, as Icarus wrote in 1944: ' "Nationalisation" is on the way, with or without Hitler, because there is no other outlook for capitalist imperialism. The inevitable form of organised capitalism is Nazism (Fascism). What has happened in Italy, Russia, Poland, Germany, Austria, and so on, is developing in Britain and everywhere else.'[22]

For reasons which F.A. Ridley explained in 1942, this developing tendency towards generalised state capitalism had been greatly accelerated by the specific needs of capital during wartime:

> modern war itself is pre-eminently a totalitarian regime . . . consequently, the democratic powers, when faced with the necessity to wage on their own behalf a war that is necessarily conducted in the manner that is natural to their totalitarian opponents, must become, in fact, totalitarian themselves in order to carry it on at all effectively.[23]

In other words (as the APCF put it): 'Democratic capitalism can only fight fascist capitalism by itself becoming fascist.'[24]

STATE INTERVENTION IN WARTIME BRITAIN

During the war the anti-parliamentarians in Britain found plentiful evidence to support their contention that the democratic regimes were abandoning their liberal facade and resorting to totalitarian forms of political rule.

Introducing an extension of the Emergency Powers Act in the Commons in May 1940, Clement Attlee stated: 'It is necessary that the Government should be given complete control over persons and property, not just some persons of some particular class of the community, but of all persons, rich and poor, employer and workman, man or woman, and all property.'[25] The entire productive apparatus became oriented towards war production at the expense of every other sector. Food and clothing were rationed, consumer goods and services were severely restricted in range and quantity, gas and electricity were diverted from domestic supply to the war economy, and so on. There was an official ban on strikes, enforced overtime, state direction of where workers were employed, suspension of agreements regarding working conditions, internal surveillance, internment of 'aliens', and censorship of the media. Workers also had to be mobilised to transform the armed forces from relatively small, professional units into mass conscript armies. Most of the rest of this chapter concentrates in greater detail on some aspects of the imposition of a centralised state capitalist war economy in Britain, and on the resistance offered by the anti-parliamentary communists.

From November 1939 Defence Regulation 18B enabled the Home Secretary to order, at his own discretion, the detention of any person 'of hostile origin or associations', and anyone 'recently concerned in acts prejudicial to the public safety or the defence of the realm or in the propagation or instigation of such acts'.[26] In May 1940 the Regulation's powers were broadened to permit the internment of members of any organisations which might be used 'for purposes prejudicial to the public safety, the defence of the realm, the maintenance of public order, the efficient prosecution of any war in which His Majesty [sic!] may be engaged, or the maintenance of supplies or services essential to the life of the community'.[27] At the end of 1943 Guy Aldred and J. Wynn published a well-documented pamphlet subtitled 'Investigation of Regulation 18B; its origin; its relation to the constitution; with first-hand accounts of what suffering has been involved for those who have been arrested and interned under it.' This argued that the Regulation had in effect established unrestrained executive power – in other words, a form of dictatorship: 'no man who differs from his fellows in his opinion of the Government's policy and dares to voice that opinion is safe from sudden and secret arrest . . . As matters now stand there is no judicial safeguard for the liberty of the subject against arbitrary acts of the executive'.[28]

Regulation 18B was mainly used to intern members of the British Union of Fascists, and people of Italian or German nationality or descent (some of whom had fled their native countries because of their opposition to fascism). In addition it was also used against some Irish Republicans in Britain, and at least once to jail a striking shop steward (John Mason of Sheffield in August 1940). However, since the Regulation was operated entirely at the discretion of the Home Secretary, *no-one* was beyond its reach: 'All that now stands between any citizen and his secret and hurried incarceration in a gaol or prison camp is the incalculable whim of whoever may chance to be in the office of Home Secretary.'[29] Hence the title of Aldred and Wynn's pamphlet: *It Might Have Happened To You!*

In the same month (May 1940) that the Home Secretary was granted potentially dictatorial powers through the extension of Regulation 18B, the Emergency Powers Act was also extended to empower the Minister of Labour to direct labour and set wages, hours and conditions of work in 'key' establishments. Around the same time, the Conditions of Employment and National Arbitration Order ('Order 1305') was introduced. This outlawed strike action unless disputes had first exhausted a set negotiation procedure involving the Ministry of Labour and the National Arbitration Tribunal. In effect, workers could only strike legally if they had the state's permission!

The Essential Works Order, introduced in March 1941, gave the state further control over labour by obliging workers to obtain the National Service Officer's permission if they wanted to change jobs. So rarely was this granted that virtually the only way workers could leave workplaces controlled by the Order was by provoking their own dismissal. Under the EWO workers could also be prosecuted and imprisoned for absenteeism or for failing to carry out any 'reasonable order' issued by the boss. By the end of 1941 nearly six million workers were working in industries controlled by the EWO or the similar Docks Labour and Merchant Navy Orders.

By December 1941 growing labour shortages had necessitated the introduction of industrial conscription for women aged 20–30. 'Mobile' women (meaning those without family responsibilities) could be sent to work in any part of the country, while 'immobile' women were directed to employment nearer home.

At the beginning of 1944 the 'Bevin Boy' scheme was introduced involving the initially-optional but later compulsory conscription of one in ten young men into coalmining rather than into the armed forces. This measure provoked the Tyneside and Clydeside apprentices' strikes of March–April 1944. When four members of the Trotskyist Workers' International League were prosecuted for supporting the Tyneside strike, an Anti-Labour Laws Victims Defence Committee was formed in which members of the Glasgow Anarchist Federation were involved.[30] The state's response to the apprentices' strikes was the introduction of Regulation 1AA, which prescribed five years' imprisonment and/or a £500 fine for 'any person who declared, instigated, made anyone take part in, or otherwise acted in furtherance of a strike amongst workers engaged in essential services'.[31]

In 1944 *Solidarity* summarised the burden of such legislation from the working class's point of view:

> Industrial conscription has been introduced in the form of the EWO. Workers are forced to stay in poorly paid monotonous jobs, which require them to work overtime to have a wage in keeping with the increased cost of living. Labour is directed from 'non-essential' to 'essential' work, young women are transferred from factory to factory to suit the needs of capitalism. And now, the youth of the country is being forced, willy nilly, down the mines.[32]

Add to this the struggle against military conscription (a struggle in which the anti-parliamentarians were actively involved, and which will be discussed later), and it becomes obvious why the APCF should have thought James Connolly's remarks about war so pertinent as to reprint them in *Solidarity* 27 years after they were first uttered: 'In the name of freedom from militarism it establishes military rule; battling for progress it abolishes trial by jury; and waging war for enlightened rule it tramples the freedom of the press under the heel of a military despot.'[33]

WARTIME STRIKES AND ANTI-PARLIAMENTARY PROPAGANDA

Paradoxically, the rapid and extensive growth of state power during the war, aided and abetted by organisations traditionally regarded as defenders of working-class interests, created conditions in which some aspects of anti-parliamentary propaganda could actually gain a hearing among the working class more readily than before. Extensive state intervention in the direction of labour power and production, and the co-operation of official labour organisations in drawing-up and operating labour legislation, meant that radical anti-state and anti-trade union propaganda was bound to strike a sympathetic chord with at least some sections of the working class.

Before looking at this more closely, however, it would be wise to sound a note of caution. It is not disputed here that most British workers believed sincerely in the justice and necessity of waging a war against fascism. What they did object to in many cases was the introduction of 'fascist' measures 'at home' in order to prosecute the war. There was a widespread feeling among working-class people of wanting to fight the war on their own terms, and not at the beck and call of notoriously anti-working class politicians (such as Churchill) who had not hidden their sympathies towards fascism before the war. As the figures for wartime strikes testify, workers were willing to take action in defence of hard-won rights on numerous occasions, even if it involved setting aside 'higher considerations' and coming into conflict with the bosses, the state, the law and their own 'official representatives' (see Table 8.1).

Table 8.1 Disputes involving stoppages (all industries), 1939–45

	Stoppages	*Workers involved*	*Working days 'lost'*
1939	940	337 000	1 356 000
1940	922	299 000	940 000
1941	1 251	360 000	1 079 000
1942	1 303	456 000	1 527 000
1943	1 785	557 000	1 808 000
1944	2 194	821 000	3 714 000
1945	2 293	531 000	2 835 000

Source: Department of Employment and Productivity, 1971.

At such moments certain elements of anti-parliamentary propaganda coincided with what militant workers were beginning to conclude from their own experiences. The crucial point of divergence was that militant working-class action never broke out of its anti-fascist context. 'Industrial conflict arose from a wide range of circumstances relating to the industrial interests of particular groups of workers; it did not arise because of any substantial opposition to the Second World War itself.'[34] In other words, workers were prepared to oppose the capitalist state and the capitalist trade unions, but mainly in order to prosecute more effectively the capitalist war.

Nevertheless, the Glasgow Anarchist Federation (most of whose members were industrial workers attracted to the group because of their experiences during the war) certainly believed that wartime conditions provided a fertile soil for its ideas. A 'Clydeside Worker', writing in *War Commentary* in 1943, observed how state power and an anti-statist opposition could grow hand-in-hand: 'in the atmosphere of Political Dictatorship, such as prevails today, with all its trappings, regional Gauleiters, total negation of representation, total conscription of labour, with their resultant starvation wages, the Clydeside worker is taking to Anarchism, the road to freedom, just like water fills the hollows of a plain'.[35] On the integration of trade unions into the state, Eddie Fenwick of the Glasgow Group argued that the anti-strike position adopted by the unions had undermined their traditional hold over the working class:

> When they openly form a united front with the ruling class for the avowed purpose of strike-breaking then surely their days are numbered . . . The trade union machine as at present constituted is disintegrating before our eyes. It will survive only as long as the workers take to forge in struggle their new and revolutionary forms of organisation.[36]

While the actions of the state and trade unions during the war helped to emphasise the relevance of anti-parliamentary ideas to some militant workers, the single most important factor which created this situation was the Communist Party's sudden swing to fanatical support for the war following Germany's attack on Russia in mid-1941. The practical consequences of this overnight reversal jeopardised the leadership of and control over the actions of militant workers that the Communist Party had been able to exercise until then in several key areas and industries. 'Whenever the workers did come out on strike against their hellish conditions', reported Alex Binnie of the revived Clyde Workers' Committee in 1943, 'they found that this party [the CPGB], instead of giving them support, tried to get them back to work in order that production would go on'.[37] It was this which gave groups which still supported the continuing class struggle, such as the anti-parliamentary communists, the opportunity to step into the breach.

Reports in *War Commentry* written by Glasgow Anarchist Federation members show how the Anarchists intervened on the margins of some industrial disputes during the war and tried to propagandise the lessons of such struggles. In November 1941, for example, the Glasgow Anarchists supported a strike by Glasgow Corporation bus drivers and conductors at the city's Knightswood depot against the introduction of a new running-time schedule. The bus workers' union opposed the strike, 'Yet several hundred workers had so little respect for the good faith of their trade union', reported the local evening paper, 'that they refused their appointed spokesmen's guidance'.[38] The Labour-controlled Corporation Transport Committee also condemned the strike, expressing its astonishment at its employees' failure to take account of 'the serious time in which we were living'.[39] The Committee sent dismissal notice to the strikers and replaced the strike-bound services with 80 Army and Air Force buses. Despite solidarity from other depots the Knightswood strikers were forced back to work. The Transport Committee's actions met with bitterness among the strikers. According to Frank Leech, ' "*Did our boys join up to be used against their fellow workers*" was one of the questions.'[40] Such incidents, involving anti-working class actions by the local state and Labour Party, were grist to the mill of the Anarchists' propaganda.

Towards the end of 1943 Glasgow Anarchist Federation members were also involved on the periphery of strike action in the Lanarkshire coalfield, where the APCF, USM and Anarchist Federation all had active affiliated groups around Blantyre, Burnbank, Hamilton and Motherwell. On 20 September 1943 500 miners went on strike at Wester Auchengeich pit after the colliery contractor had accused 3 miners of malingering. The action spread to Cardowan colliery, where 1000 miners joined the strike with their own demand for the release of 16 colleagues who had been jailed for non-payment of fines imposed for taking part in a strike the previous May. By 28 September the strike had spread throughout Lanarkshire, and to West Stirlingshire and East Dunbartonshire.

The National Union of Scottish Mineworkers President, CPGB member Abe Moffat, blamed the strike on incitement by 'a group of people identified with the Anarchist movement, ILP and so-called militant miners, who are definitely opposed to the war against Fascism'.[41] *War Commentary* responded by admitting that 'our Scottish comrades have been carrying on propaganda in the coalfields since the beginning of the war', but maintained that 'the strike was the spontaneous result of the men's resentment at lying accusations made by a coal contractor against three strippers at Wester Auchengeich colliery, and the imprisonment of 16 Cardowan miners for refusal to pay fines imposed on them for participating in an "unofficial" stoppage last May'.[42]

The leaders of the NUSM 'immediately set to work to discredit the strikes in every way' and tried to 'force the men back to work'. On 29 September the NUSM Executive suspended three Cardowan branch officials for supporting the strike. The following day, however, a mass meeting of strikers overwhelmingly rejected a Communist-proposed resolution calling for work to be resumed in the interests of the war effort and for negotiation of the miners' demands to be left in the hands of the union executive, and voted to continue the strike for the release of the imprisoned miners and the reinstatement of the suspended officials.

On 1 October the imprisoned miners were freed after paying their fines under pressure from Moffat, and the strike ended. Lord Traprain, the Ministry of Fuel and Power's Regional Controller, 'thanked the trade union officials for their tireless efforts to ensure a resumption and noted with deep satisfaction that these efforts met with considerable success'.[43]

A third strike in which the Glasgow Anarchists were involved took place at Barr and Stroud's engineering factory in Glasgow when 2000 women went on strike on 13 December 1943 in support of a pay demand. At the beginning of the strike the men in the factory voted to support the women's strike fund, but did not actually join the strike themselves – in limited numbers – until 6 January 1944. This lack of basic solidarity forced the women to reluctantly abandon the strike on 11 January 1944.[44]

The strike displayed several features which the Glasgow Anarchists could use in their propaganda. The TGWU and AEU had both urged a return to work: 'The role of the trade union bureaucrats was the same despicable one they have adopted throughout the period of the war.' Since three-quarters of the women did not belong to any union, however, the strike bypassed official union forms and procedures (one woman who had argued that 'success could only be achieved through recognised channels of negotiation' was voted off the strike committee by 'an overwhelming majority').[45] The Anarchists emphasised the positive potential of this aspect of the strike:

> You have demonstrated that you can organise without the Trade Unions. The 'leaders' are against you. Their funds are closed to you. And yet you have taken part in one of the most solid strikes of recent years. The form of organisation you have set up i.e. the Strike Committee and the Hardship Committee is the beginning of the form of organisation advocated by Syndicalists, whether you know it or not. You must extend this form of organisation.

The formation of committees to organise food supplies and to spread the strike to other workers were among the suggestions made. Ultimately, wrote Frank Leech: 'We would like to see you forming Committees to prepare for the taking over of the factory and commencing the production of the goods you require.'[46]

TRADE UNIONS AND WORKERS' COUNCILS

The Glasgow Anarchist Federation's most interesting account of wartime industrial action was a pamphlet published in February 1945 called *The Struggle in the Factory*. Written under the pen-name 'Equity' by a worker in the Dalmuir Royal Ordnance Factory, it described how, following Russia's entry into the war, the CPGB shop stewards at Dalmuir had 'proceeded to sabotage all direct action' by the workers and 'linked themselves with the policy of the employing class, their lackeys the Trade Union leaders, and the Labour leaders'.[47]

As such the pamphlet conveyed basically the same points that other Anarchist Federation members had expressed in articles published in *War Commentary*; as Equity pointed out, 'the history of Dalmuir ROF . . . is the history of any other war-time factory'.[48] What was distinctive about Equity's pamphlet was that, unlike the articles written by most other Glasgow Anarchists, it did not propose 'anarcho-syndicalism' or 'revolutionary industrial unionism' as the solution to the problems it had identified. Instead, Equity explained the reactionary nature of trade unionism in a way that called into question the viability of *any* form of unionism created as an alternative to the existing trade unions.

In *The Struggle In The Factory*, and in articles published in *War Commentary*, Equity argued that 'the function of Trade Unionism was to bargain for reforms',[49] and that by performing this role trade unions 'could, and did, win advantages in wages and conditions during the growth and expansion of the Capitalist System'.[50] However, this period of ascendancy had now come to an end – 'The present capitalist system of society has ceased to expand'[51] – and the capitalist class had 'no more reforms to give'.[52] The material basis of trade unionism as a reformist working-class movement had therefore vanished. 'The Unions have moved towards their eclipse as working class organisations, and they now proceed rapidly along the road towards complete integration with the capitalist state machine.'[53] With each national capital only able to survive in an increasingly competitive world market by attacking the wages and conditions of its own working class, the new function of trade unionism had become that of 'accepting on behalf of the workers, all kinds of anti-working class measures', 'announc[ing] further reductions in working conditions'[54] and 'organis[ing] poverty on behalf of capitalism'.[55]

Equity's writings thus related the function of trade unionism, and the limits of what it might be able to achieve on behalf of the working class, to capitalism's movement through different historical periods (ascendance and decadence). As we have already seen, this was the approach adopted by the European left or council communists, and the APCF had also begun to take up some of these ideas since the mid-1930s. It is interesting, therefore, to find a pamphlet published in the name of the Anarchist Federation arguing from within the same current of thought.

During the war the APCF applied the same theory of capitalist decadence to the development of its ideas about the emergence of class consciousness. In its 1940 appeal 'To Anti-parliamentarians', the APCF argued, as Equity would later, that 'During the upswing period of capitalism, when it was developing and expanding, it was possible to grant concessions to the working-class because of the increase in productivity and the resultant increase in profits'. However, this upswing period belonged to the past: 'The present period of capitalist decline is one in which no concessions are possible for the working class.'[56] Through their experience of bankrupt capitalism's inability to grant even the most basic of their needs in its period of permanent crisis, working-class people would become conscious of the necessity for a complete change in the organisation of society: 'Though their primary demands will be for reforms the logic of events will force the pace. Capitalism cannot grant what is required. Grim necessity will compel the workers to social revolution.'[57]

The instruments of this revolution would be workers' councils, arising from the working class's struggle for basic needs – increasingly informed by a consciousness of the need to destroy the existing system – combined with the necessity to wage these struggles outwith and against existing forms of organisation. The basic outline of this process had already become apparent during the war, when the trade unions' opposition to strikes had forced workers to pursue their demands by creating new, 'unofficial' organisational forms.

The APCF's belief that workers' councils were 'the real fighting organisations of the working class'[58] distinguished the group from the 'old' labour movement, which saw revolution in terms of the conquest of power by a *party*. In a call 'For Workers' Councils' published in *Solidarity* in 1942, the basic features of the council form of organisation were outlined by Frank Maitland. The councils would be *universal*, organising all workers 'of whatever race, sex, religion, age or opinion'; *industrial*, 'organised in units of factory, workshop, store, yard, mine or other enterprise'; *proletarian* in composition, 'representing only the working class'; *democratic*, 'organised in the simplest possible way, with the participation of *all* workers'; and *revolutionary*, fighting for 'the overthrow of capitalist authority'. Maitland also stressed that workers' councils would be *independent* bodies, 'in the sense that they must be class organisations, that is, not councils initiated or controlled by any particular party or subscribing to a particular programme or financed by a particular union – they must represent the workers *as workers*'.[59] This emphasis on the councils' independence dovetailed precisely with the APCF's attachment to the principle of working-class self-emancipation.

THE PARTY AND THE WORKING CLASS

The role political parties could play in the emergence of revolutionary consciousness was the subject of an important debate in *Solidarity* during the war.

The first contribution to the discussion was an article titled 'The Party and the Working Class', which had originally appeared in *International Council Correspondence* in September 1936. The APCF attributed the article to Paul Mattick, but its author was actually Anton Pannekoek. Pannekoek argued against the traditional conception of the party as 'an organisation that aims to lead and control the working class'. He did not oppose revolutionaries joining together to form organisations distinct from the rest of the working class, but these would be 'parties in an entirely different sense from those of today', since their aim would not be 'to seize power for themselves'. Instead, they would act as propaganda groups – 'organs of self-enlightenment of the working class by means of which the workers find their way to freedom'. The actual revolutionary struggle itself, however, would be 'the task of the working masses themselves . . . The struggle is so great, the enemy so powerful that only the masses as a whole can achieve a victory'.[60]

Replying to Pannekoek in the following issue of *Solidarity*, Frank Maitland took up an opposite point of view. While Pannekoek had stated that 'The belief in parties is the main reason for the impotence of the working class', Maitland argued that the party had an indispensable role to play in the class struggle as the bearer of consciousness to the workers:

> the great mass of proletarians live and engage in the class struggle, without being conscious of the struggle, without understanding it . . . The class struggle by itself will not educate and organise the masses . . . It still remains for the conscious minority to enlighten the masses . . . A party is necessary as the brain of the class, the sensory, thinking and directing apparatus of the class, of tens and hundreds of millions of people.

While rejecting 'The social-democratic conception of a parliamentary party and the communist idea of a party dictatorship', Maitland maintained that the solution to the party question was not to 'get rid of the party' (as Pannekoek had argued), but to 'struggle for the control of the party by the working class, in opposition to the control of the working class by the party'.[61]

Paul Mattick was next to enter the debate, ostensibly to defend Pannekoek's position against Maitland. In doing so, however, Mattick went much further than Pannekoek in denying the party's role altogether. Taking as his starting-point 'parties as they have actually existed,' rather than 'Maitland's conception of what a party ought to be', Mattick pointed out that parties 'have not served the working class, nor have they been a tool for ending class rule'. The 'decisive and determining' source of revolutionary consciousness would not be political parties but 'the actual class struggle': 'The "consciousness" to rebel against and to change society is not developed by the "propaganda" of conscious minorities, but by the real and direct propaganda of events. The increasing social chaos endangers the habitual life of greater and ever greater masses of people and changes their ideologies.'[62]

After they had appeared in *Solidarity*, Pannekoek, Maitland and Mattick's articles were also published in *Modern Socialism*, a journal edited in New York by Abraham Ziegler. Ziegler's comments on the debate were duly printed in *Solidarity*. This seems to have been the final contribution. Ziegler rejected Maitland's support for a 'Leninist "leadership" party' which would 'guide [the workers] to victory', and he also disagreed with Pannekoek and Mattick's view that revolutionary consciousness was a more or less spontaneous product of the class struggle. On the other hand, Ziegler agreed with Pannekoek on the desirability of parties acting as 'non-power, non-leadership' groups 'in the interests of working class enlightenment'. Alongside this he also cited Kautsky and Lenin's view that revolutionary consciousness had to be injected into the class struggle from outside by radicalised members of the bourgeois intelligentsia. This synthesis of positions was to be found in Daniel De Leon's conception of the party 'as a teacher, not as a leader over the working class'. As an 'educational–propaganda organisation' the party had an essential role to play in the struggles of the working class.[63]

The APCF's views on the subject shied away from either extreme. Some of the group's statements, such as the following, suggested that like Mattick they believed revolutionary organisations had little to contribute to the emergence of class consciousness: 'Relative poverty must of necessity become absolute in a declining capitalism. This will cause an increasing unwillingness to tolerate capitalism; a willingness to RESIST its encroachments and finally a revolution against it. Socialism will follow.'[64] As with Mattick's belief that increasing social chaos would change people's ideas, this implied that revolutionary consciousness was economically determined and inevitable, and left no useful role for intervention by organised groups.

At other times, however, *Solidarity* also expressed the opposite point of view. At the end of 1942, for example, it observed that 'political clarity and understanding do not develop simultaneously with awakening class-consciousness . . . spontaneity of action and revolutionary fervour do not always embody the necessary knowledge of proletarian strategy and tactics'. Moving in Maitland's direction, the APCF argued that 'those already conscious and politically advanced workers' had a duty to 'come together in common unity' in order to 'give a clear cut and directive lead to the social aspirations of their less politically advanced fellow workers'.[65]

Even so, this view did not seek to deny completely the importance of workers' own experiences, since intervention by organised groups would only be effective if the revolutionary ideas they put forward could be tested against reality and recognised as correct: 'propaganda is not the only factor in making the workers realise the opposition of their interests to those of the ruling class. Class antagonism arises not because of propaganda but because a divergence of economic interest actually exists . . . Regarding propaganda, the workers compare what is said with what is done.'[66] In other words, it was not a question of workers learning *either* from experience *or* from propaganda; in practice, *both* sources had positive contributions to make.

Of all the contributors to the debate the APCF was closest to Pannekoek's position. Like Pannekoek, the APCF rejected 'the orthodox party conception', meaning the idea of parties as power-seeking minorities. Nevertheless, the APCF still believed that as an organised revolutionary group it had an important role to play in the class struggle: 'It is our mission to educate, agitate and enthuse; perhaps even to inspire. We will gladly give service as propagandists, as advisers or as delegates. But we do NOT seek to boss or control. We would impel, not compel, seeking the maximum self-initiative and direct action of the workers themselves.'[67] Ultimately, the only guarantee against a party seizing power and exercising a dictatorship over the working class would be for groups such as the APCF to 'sow as much socialist propaganda as possible', so that working-class people would be 'as immune as possible from the danger of various types of Fuhrers, who, on the promise of solving the problems they must ultimately solve themselves, will but change the form of slavery'.[68]

INDIVIDUAL WAR-RESISTANCE

Although the anti-parliamentary groups all started off by calling for industrial action against the war, such appeals received no large-scale response. For this reason the anti-parliamentarians' own opposition to the war was mainly forced to take the form of 'direct individual action'.[69] As Frank Leech observed: 'We Glasgow Anarchists issued a leaflet calling workers to resist conscription by a General Strike . . . there was no response. Ever since, in common with other groups and individual workers, we have fallen back on individual resistance.'[70]

Such action was an important feature of the anti-parliamentary groups' activities. A measure of the earnestness with which the principle of refusing involvement with any part of capitalism's military apparatus was treated can be ascertained from the minutes of a USM group meeting held in May 1942:

> Comrade Lennox informed the Group that she had been strongly advised to obtain a gas-mask, and that she intended acting on this advice. In view of this decision she felt she could not continue membership of the USM. After the discussion the Chairman expressed the feeling of the Group in informing Comrade Lennox that this was a private matter and did not affect membership of the Group; though several members considered it a matter of principle not to possess or carry a gas-mask.[71]

Participation in Air Raid Precautions work and compulsory fire-watching schemes was also shunned. As Anarchist Federation member Eddie Fenwick explained when prosecuted for refusing to firewatch at his workplace, since the 'owners of private property had denied him the elementary rights of man, he was entitled to refuse to protect private property'.[72] When Frank Leech was fined for refusing to comply with the firewatching regulations, and then imprisoned after declining to pay, he went on hunger strike in Barlinnie Prison, Glasgow, explaining afterwards that he would not 'be used by any ruling class in their wars . . . I am determined that our dictators will only conscript my dead body. Not whilst there is breath in it will I submit to them'. After going without food for 17 days Leech was released when friends paid his fine.[73]

The main focal point of the anti-parliamentarians' individual resistance was opposition to military conscription. During the First World War Lenin had argued that workers should not refuse to enter the armed forces: 'You will be given a gun. Take it and learn the military art. The proletarians need this knowledge not to shoot your brothers, the workers of other countries . . . but to fight the bourgeoisie of your own country.'[74] The anti-parliamentarians rejected this tactic:

> militarisation is intended to accustom the masses to submissiveness and ready obedience. This, in turn, leads to a psychology which

> would be, to say the very least, unfavourable for a flowering of real workers' democracy. Rather it would encourage the growth of the stifling fungi of bureaucracy and despotism all over again. On this triple count, therefore, militarism should be resisted in every possible way.

The same article also argued against the idea that communists should enlist in order to subvert the armed forces:

> military authorities will not regard with detached benevolence the consistent spreading of revolutionary thoughts and literature . . . work under such conditions must entail the watering down of these ideas to such an extent as will present no danger to the authorities. That leads one to ask whether entry into imperialist armies for this purpose is worth while at all.[75]

This article's observation that workers in uniform were rarely 'hemmed off entirely' from contact with the rest of their class was later taken up by another article on the same topic: 'The majority of the members of the forces are members of the working class, and their outlook is just as progressive as the outlook of the best of the workers . . . the members of the forces, having strong working-class connections, will – in a period of crisis – develop a revolutionary outlook.'[76] In general, therefore, anti-parliamentarians eligible for conscription opted to try their luck before the Conscientious Objectors' Tribunals.

The APCF, USM and Glasgow Anarchist Federation were all active to varying degrees in the Glasgow and West of Scotland No-Conscription League. Willie McDougall of the APCF and Guy Aldred both served spells as Chair of the organisation. In 1940 Aldred wrote a pamphlet for the NCL's Advisory Bureau titled *The C.O., the Tribunal, and After*, which explained the rights of C.O.s, described the Tribunal and Appeal procedures, and offered legal advice. Having often been on the receiving end at courts of law, Aldred was well qualified for the task of advising C.O.s, and the *Word*'s reports of C.O. Tribunals and Appellate Courts frequently mentioned his appearances on behalf of the defendants.

In August 1940 four members of the Glasgow Anarchist Federation – James Kennedy, Frank Dorans, Eddie Shaw and Frank Leech – were prosecuted for allegedly inciting people to evade the duties and liabilities relating to conscription laid down in the National

Service (Armed Forces) Act. The basis of the charge was that they had advertised the offer of information and advice for prospective C.O.s and had held mock tribunals to help C.O.s prepare their cases. The four defendants were found not guilty, however, since in the judge's opinion their actions had not technically amounted to 'incitement'.[77]

The anti-parliamentary groups' members experienced varying degrees of success in their own appearances before the Tribunals. Since as a rule the anti-parliamentarians did not conceal their willingness to fight in the *class* war, in many cases they naturally failed to satisfy the Tribunals' requirement that defendants had to have a conscientious objection to *all* use of force. Once the process of Tribunals and Appeals had been exhausted, unsuccessful C.O.s were required to undergo medical examination before being enlisted. Refusal to submit to examination was a criminal offence. In April 1944 Frank Leech reported that 'Dozens of our members have served twelve months' sentences for refusing M.E. [Medical Examination]'.[78]

Court appearances were frequently used as an opportunity to denounce conscription and the capitalist war. At his trial in September 1941 for refusing medical examination, Glasgow Anarchist James Dick stated his refusal to fight in a war 'for the defence of those in this country like Churchill, who helped build up Fascism and praised Hitler and Mussolini for the grand work they were doing for civilisation!'. This speech earned Dick a further 14 days' imprisonment for contempt of court on top of the customary 12 months for refusing medical examination.[79]

Aided by experts such as Aldred, other C.O.s made full use of all legal technicalities, loopholes and procedural irregularities. One of the craftiest defences was offered by Glasgow Anarchist Eddie Shaw. After two years of court appearances and prison sentences Shaw was required to attend for examination at the Medical Board centre in Dumbarton Road, Glasgow, at 2.30 pm on 21 June 1944. He was taken from custody at Marine Police Office and arrived at Dumbarton Road at 2.20. After refusing examination he was taken back to the Police Office, arriving there just after 2.25. Six days later he was sentenced to 12 months' imprisonment. Shaw then lodged an appeal, pleading that he had been physically prevented from submitting himself for examination because he had been in police custody at the appointed time! Suitably confounded by the ingenuity of the appeal, the judge quashed the conviction and awarded Shaw ten guineas expenses.[80]

USM members Annesley Aldred, Johanna Haining and John Caldwell all succeeded in gaining unconditional exemption at the first or second attempt.[81] Leigh Fisher of Burnbank, Lanarkshire, was less fortunate. Like Eddie Shaw, he too spent nearly two years being dragged through court appearances and prison sentences until the Appellate Tribunal finally decided in November 1942 that he could register as a C.O. if he resumed his previous employment or found work in the building trade.[82]

William Dick, an APCF C.O., appeared before the Tribunal in June 1942. Unusually, he put forward a pacifist defence – 'My oppposition to war, although it is connected with my opposition to the State and to the State organisation of Society, proceeds definitely from clear moral opposition to violence' – and was granted unconditional exemption.[83]

During the war the USM's *Word* recounted the details of Guy Aldred's repeated imprisonments during 1916–19 for resisting conscription, and also published accounts of the general history of Conscientious Objection to the First World War. One of the purposes this served was to attack supporters of the Second World War who had been C.O.s during the 1914–18 conflict. The most frequent targets of such criticism were the Clydeside politicians Patrick Dollan and Thomas Johnston. Both had a reputation for being C.O.s during the First World War, but they supported the second and were now 'enjoying places of honour in the State' as Lord Provost of Glasgow (Dollan) and Regional Defence Commissioner for Scotland (Johnston). Guy Aldred considered that this was 'hypocritical' and suggested: 'If you despise the 1940 conchies, sack the 1916 ones also' (many private employers and more than a hundred local government bodies sacked or suspended C.O.s in their employ).[84]

The about-turn of former opponents of war such as Johnston and Dollan was of course regarded as further proof of the corrupting effect of parliamentarism. The 'practising conscientious objectors of 1914–1918' had been transformed into 'stern practising militarists' by a 'growing adaptability to ideas of reformism, and a growing parliamentary sense of responsibility to capitalist institutions'.[85]

The theme of contradiction and inconsistency also featured in the USM's attacks on the CPGB. Before the outbreak of the war the USM criticised the CPGB for proposing to abandon the position of 'turning imperialist war into civil war', and for campaigning in support of a war for democracy.[86] When Russia signed a Non-Aggression Pact with Germany in 1939 and the CPGB reversed its position, the USM criticised the hypocrisy of today's friendly alliance with yesterday's bitterest enemy. Russia's entry into the war in 1941, which caused yet another somersault, simply added to the abundance of inconsistencies which characterised the CPGB's record. The lone CPGB MP Willie Gallacher frequently bore the brunt of the USM's attacks; in 1942 Aldred commented: 'Every Socialist will recall how [Gallacher] was for a "People's Peace" and for the sabotage of war when Stalin made his famous pact with Hitler; and how, when Hitler broke the pact, he became the jingo of jingoes, in defence of the Soviet Union! The man's contradictions and worthlessness defy full recording.'[87]

STRANGE BEDFELLOWS

In June 1943, after another fruitless attempt by the CPGB to affiliate to the Labour Party, the ferocity of Aldred's opposition to the Communist Party provoked him to urge workers to 'rally round the Labour Party Executive in its firm struggle against the Communist Party conspiracy for power and dictatorship'.[88] This call was quickly condemned by *Word* reader V. Wilson, who argued that compared with the 'Labour guardians of Capitalist-Imperialism' the CPGB was merely 'a handful of irresponsible clowns'.[89] Wilson suggested that Aldred's appeal had been made 'in a moment of aberration'. Yet there were several other occasions during the war when the *Word*'s readers found good cause to criticise alliances proposed or actually entered into by Aldred.

Although the USM's opposition to the war was initially founded on revolutionary principles, the group soon exhibited a willingness to ally itself with other organisations and individuals who were against the war for all sorts of different reasons. This led to the formation of some absurdly unholy alliances – or perhaps 'broad church' might be a more appropriate term, since a striking feature of the *Word* was the number of articles it contained written by Unitarian, Baptist and Humanist Reverend Ministers who opposed the war on Christian–Pacifist grounds.

As editor of the *Word*, Aldred also gave considerable space and coverage to the articles and speeches of anti-war labour movement politicians such as Creech Jones, John McGovern, Rhys Davies and Fred Jowett. Davies and Jowett had both been members of the 1924 Labour government so vehemently criticised in the past by Aldred, but these previous antagonisms were temporarily forgiven for the sake of preserving anti-militarist unity.

Another of Aldred's opportunist liaisons was with Alexander Ratcliffe, secretary of the Scottish Protestant League and editor of its newspaper, *Vanguard*. This association illustrated very well how two people could oppose the same thing for totally different reasons. Like the *Word*, Ratcliffe's paper criticised Patrick Dollan for the hypocrisy of supporting war in 1939 after opposing it in 1914 – but it also attacked him on the sectarian and racist grounds that he was a 'Papist' and an 'Irish-Paddy'. Aldred rejected such 'prejudice and abuse',[90] but even so he regularly published articles by Ratcliffe in the *Word* throughout the war. In contrast the Glasgow Anarchists refused to allow the Protestant League's bookshop in Glasgow to distribute *War Commentary*, because the League was anti-Semitic (apparently *Vanguard* tended to 'devote half its space to statements to the effect that "the Jew So-and-So" has been appointed to this or that').[91]

Aldred's most unlikely alliance by far, however, was the one he concocted with the Marquis of Tavistock, Hastings Russell, who later became the Duke of Bedford. Alec Kaye, a USM member in London, warned Aldred about Bedford in May 1940:

> I attended Lord Tavistock's peace meeting at the Kingsway Hall . . . The meeting reeked with propaganda for the British People's Party, an obviously camouflaged Fascist movement. I recognised several known Fascist supporters as stewards . . . Tavistock is not all that he appears to represent. If I ever heard a whitewashing of Hitler, it was by him. Even when he regretted the brutalities, he still had some justification for such acts.[92]

As well as being an apologist for Nazism, Bedford was a believer in Social Credit monetary theories, and articles written by him about this subject, plus others advocating a negotiated peace with Germany, filled numerous pages of the *Word* every month.

In 1984 Aldred's relationship with Bedford was defended by John Caldwell, who related that the pair first met as speakers at an anti-war meeting in Glasgow:

> Tavistock mentioned he was having difficulty having his pamphlet printed because of the war and the fear it gave publishers . . . [Aldred] sympathised with the Marquis in the frustra-

> tion of not being able to spread his anti-war message. The Strickland Press had just opened . . . There was printing capacity to spare. In this way, when no one else dared to do so, Aldred became printer to the Duke of Bedford.

According to Caldwell, ‘Neither influenced the other, nor subsidised, nor subverted the other’.[93]

In fact, the association between Aldred and Bedford went much further than the disinterested commercial relationship described by Caldwell. Aldred held Bedford in rare esteem – ‘He is a man of fearless integrity’[94] – and in August 1941 went so far as to suggest the formation of a Socialist–Pacifist coalition with Bedford at its head: ‘We would have him the leader of the opposition to the present Government, and so the next Prime Minister.’[95] As we will see later, Aldred also accepted some of Bedford’s Social Credit ideas.

The flood of readers’ letters to the *Word* agreeing with Aldred’s proposal for a Bedford-led Socialist–Pacifist alliance illustrated the sort of audience the paper was reaching – and addressing – during the war. Nevertheless, there was a minority of readers who were severely critical of Aldred’s opportunism, and whose views deserve to be restated. Alec Kaye, whose criticism of the Duke of Bedford has already been quoted, argued in June 1940 that ‘Genuine Socialists’ could not enter into any ‘Popular Front for peace’ with ‘pseudo-Socialists and peace-lover-cum-fascist advocates’.[96] In November 1944 Daryl Hepple of Gateshead described the *Word*’s contents as ‘a hotch-potch of Socialism, Social Credit, Freethought and Pacifism, not forgetting pandering to Labour MPs, who happen to be Pacifists, several reverent gentlemen and much boosting of the Non-Socialist Duke of Bedford. Strange bedfellows indeed for one who claims to be an Anarchist.’ The *Word*’s ‘sentimental bourgeois pacifism . . . Asking rival Capitalist gangsters to negotiate a just peace’ made as much sense as it would to ‘ask a lion to turn vegetarian’.[97] In 1945 John Fairhead of Woking attacked Aldred’s ‘uncritical and completely comradely alliance with men of the type of Rhys Davies and the Duke of Bedford . . . In so far as you oppose the cancer of Stalinism, more power to your elbow; in so far as you continue to dally with the day-dreams of an anachronistic anarchism, may you be damned.’[98]

Aldred replied to such criticism by stressing the value of free speech and the need to discard ‘sectarian considerations’. Defending the heterogeneity of the *Word*'s contributors in May 1942 he wrote: 'I do not worry whether I share their views or otherwise. I simply say to myself: Is this a truthful man? Does he write sincerely? Has he a message? Will his views bear discussion and help mankind? If the reply is "Yes", I publish the article. I am not a censor but a defender and advocate of freedom of speech, thought and writing.'[99] Two months later Aldred justified the *Word*'s editorial policy in similar terms: 'The *Word* is a forum of democracy and its columns are closed to none. It is open to all heretical opinion, and since we believe violence and exploitation to be wrong, to all Pacifist and all Socialist opinion.'[100]

THE APCF AGAINST SECTARIANISM

Like the *Word* under Guy Aldred's editorship, the APCF's paper *Solidarity* was also a forum for the expression of a wide range of views – though not of the sort that the *Word*'s revolutionary critics condemned. Class struggle anarchists such as Albert Meltzer and Mat Kavanagh, council communists Anton Pannekoek and Paul Mattick, the Trotskyist Frank Maitland, Spartacist Ernst Schneider ('Icarus'), F. A. Ridley of the ILP and James Kennedy of the Marxian Study Group – all contributed to a fruitful interplay of ideas on many topics.

Solidarity's editorial policy typified the APCF's view of its own relationship to other revolutionary groups. Believing that no single party would 'ever have in its ranks ALL the BEST elements in the working class', the APCF rejected the spectacle of 'numerous competing bodies all play-acting at being THE vanguard'.[101] No party could claim to have held the correct position on every issue in the past, nor could any group be certain that it would take the right line on every question which might arise in the future. Many of the issues separating revolutionaries would be settled only by the future course of the class struggle itself 'rendering obsolete or clarifying many of the errors previously held'.[102] In the meantime, revolutionaries had enough in common to adopt a more co-operative attitude and practice: 'Pending the final show-down with capitalism there will arise many issues upon which all revolutionaries, irrespective of section, SHOULD agree. For such objects we ought to put our party loyalty second to class loyalty which all profess, in order to attain the *maximum possible striking power*.'[103] In practical terms this meant the formation of revolutionary alliances 'either for an agreed limited programme or for any single issue arising in the class struggle'.[104]

The APCF's belief that 'All educational or agitational propaganda that awakens or deepens class consciousness should be welcomed'[105] was another anti-sectarian attitude taken seriously by the group. In 1941, for example, the *Word* acknowledged 'the splendid propaganda zeal of our comrade, W. C. McDougall, of the APCF, editor of *Solidarity*. His circulation of pamphlets and papers is a feature of Glasgow activity in war time. Last month he circulated nearly 300 *Word*s.'[106] Besides selling the USM's paper the APCF also distributed *War Commentary*, the main paper of the Glasgow Anarchist Federation.[107]

Another of the APCF's anti-sectarian initiatives was the establishment of the weekly Workers' Open Forum in Glasgow in October 1942, based upon the slogans: 'A Workers' Council for eliminating error. All parties invited. Let the Truth prevail!'. By mid-1943, according to a report in *Solidarity*, the Open Forum had been addressed by speakers from the Anarchist Federation, SPGB, SLP, Workers' International League, ILP, Common Wealth, Peace Pledge Union, No-Conscription League, the Secularists, a Single Tax group and 'unattached but prominent Industrial Unionists, etc'.[108] As the war dragged on, the activities carried out by the APCF in its own name were 'largely submerged . . . in the interests of the Workers' Open Forum'.[109]

The following passage, from the APCF's 'Principles and Tactics', encapsulates the group's modest estimation of its own self-importance and its unshakeable belief in the working class's capacity to emancipate itself through its own efforts:

> Instead of struggling for supremacy, revolutionary parties should aim as far as possible at complete liquidation into the workers' soviets, where they can advance their policies by courage, initiative and example. Practical, instead of abstract problems, will be on the order of the day, and the best solutions, irrespective of who advocates them, should be adopted without prejudice. We will find, in practice, that the Vanguard interpenetrates and overlaps all existing parties; and that workers, previously of no party at all, are able to contribute in a surprising degree and to over-shadow many who were previously considered as indispensable and of the elite![110]

THE END OF THE WAR

The anti-parliamentary groups had all expected that as in 1917–18 the war would end in revolution. In 1941 Guy Aldred predicted: 'Demobilisation and other difficulties would bring about a crisis: for the war represented a breakdown of Capitalist Democracy and faced it with Revolution.'[111] In 1943 Glasgow Anarchist Eddie Shaw envisaged widespread revolution as the various nation states disintegrated under the stress of the conflict,[112] while Frank Maitland anticipated that 'the invasion of Europe will produce revolts and revolutionary attempts'.[113]

Events in Italy in 1943 encouraged such thinking. In March a strike at the Turin FIAT–Mirafiori plant spread throughout the city, and then to large factories in Milan. Around 300 000 workers were involved. The strikes provoked a crisis within the Italian ruling class, and Mussolini was dismissed as head of government. These events were regarded as the first steps in the direction of far greater changes. The Glasgow Anarchists' 'Manifesto on Italy' proclaimed that the Italian workers had

> struck the first real blow against Fascism since this war started – a blow for Social Revolution, AND ANARCHY . . . Forward to the call of the Italian workers, beckoning you to a new world, free for ever from war, poverty and enslavement. Prepare for action, HANDS OFF THE ITALIAN WORKERS. No Arms, Men or ammunition to crush the revolutionary Italian workers.[114]

A similar appeal was made in 1944 after the start of the Civil War in Greece. When British troops were dispatched to aid the Greek government against the 'Communist' guerillas, a Glasgow Anarchist leaflet 'distributed widely on the Clyde' warned: 'Workers, your brothers in uniform are being used as the advance guard of reaction . . . It is in our interests not to allow ourselves to be used as blacklegs against fellow-workers in other lands.'[115] At a 'Withdraw From Greece' protest meeting chaired by Willie McDougall in Glasgow in January 1945, the Anarchist Federation speaker Jimmy Raeside 'was very warmly received for his forthright call to industrial action'.[116]

As it turned out, of course, 1945 saw no repetition of the revolutionary upheavals that ended the First World War. The enduring popularity of anti-fascism was insurance against revolution in the victorious Allied countries, since revolution would have required a massive *break* with this ideology which had helped to sustain the war effort for six years. At the end of the First World War the defeated powers had been those most prone to insurrection, but the military occupation of the defeated powers' territory at the end of the Second World War effectively ruled out any prospect of working-class uprisings there. The victorious ruling classes were as mindful as the anti-parliamentarians of the spectre of 1917–18, and used every means at their disposal against the workers of the countries they had supposedly come to liberate to ensure that this spectre did not become incarnate.

For Guy Aldred the war ended with a parliamentary campaign in Glasgow Central in the 1945 general election – a far cry from the revolutionary crisis he had predicted in 1941. Opposition to the oppressive measures introduced during the war was a prominent theme of Aldred's election address:

> I am opposed to conscription. I am opposed to the control of labour. Control Finance. Control Foreign Policy. Control the social use of all wealth that is socially produced. But control the individual free man or free woman by controlling and directing his or her own labour power! I say no. My programme is: end all control, all direction of labour; end conscription and regimentation.[117]

There were also faint echoes of the 1922 'Sinn Fein' candidature in Shettleston. Aldred declared that he would not indulge in any electioneering or canvassing, and emphasised that he was '*not* seeking a career';[118] the candidature was simply a means to 'register opinion and the growth of an idea'.[119] Another echo of 1922 was a mention of the soviet system advocated prominently in the Shettleston address: 'Parliamentarism, talking-shop politics, ought to be liquidated in an economic and culturally organised society, with an industrial franchise, and direct control of representation at every point by the common people: the wealth producers.'[120]

Alongside these ideas were reformist demands such as a call for an end to 'secret diplomacy'. The blatant contradiction here between advocating *world* socialism one moment and popular control of 'foreign' policy the next was typical of the whole address. The influence of the currency crank Duke of Bedford was also evident:

> The doctrine of social credit cannot be substituted for Socialism, but the idea that money is merely a medium or measure of exchange, and *not* a commodity in itself, is a sound one. Money, so long as money is tolerated – and I believe in the complete abolition of the money system – should be reduced to true use-function . . . Labour ought to be free and wealth, which is social, ought to be socialised.[121]

Such ideas were totally at odds with the ABC of communism usually propagated by the anti-parliamentarians. If wealth was socialised – as Aldred demanded – access to it would be open to everyone without restriction on a free and equal basis; there would be no need for money or any other system of exchange. The existence of money, precisely as a medium or measure of exchange, implies commodity production and the exclusion of a section of society from the control or use of wealth. In other words, 'merely' capitalism. Money can never function as anything but a commodity in itself; indeed, it epitomises commodities, since its *only* use is to store or exchange wealth and it has no true use-function whatsoever.

On polling day Aldred made no advance on his previous forays into the electoral field. The seat was won by a Conservative with 9365 votes, while Aldred came bottom of the poll with 300.

Remaining true to the anti-parliamentary tradition, on the day of the election members of the Anarchist Federation 'toured the Glasgow streets with the loudspeaker, exposing politics and politicians, and advising workers to stop using their votes and start using their brains'.[122]

9 A Balance Sheet

After the Second World War the anti-parliamentary communist groups entered a period of decline from which they would not recover – although the ideas they had propagated survived to be taken up by a later generation of revolutionaries.[1] Towards the end of the war a split developed amongst the Glasgow Anarchists over their relations with the *War Commentary* group in London. One faction began publishing a paper called *Direct Action*, focusing mainly on workplace struggles to compensate for *War Commentary*'s alleged lack of industrial coverage. Here the anarcho-syndicalist strand which had always been present within the Glasgow Anarchist Federation came to the fore. A second, less active group formed around Frank Leech, Jimmy Raeside and Eddie Shaw. These were the 'anarchist working men', mentioned in George Woodcock's history of anarchism, that Woodcock describes as regarding the individualist anarchist Max Stirner's *The Ego And His Own* (1845) as 'still a belated gospel'.[2] This group was apparently held together by Shaw and consequently fell apart when he emigrated. Frank Leech died in January 1953.[3]

The old guard of the United Socialist Movement – Jane Patrick, Ethel MacDonald, Guy Aldred and John Caldwell – continued to publish the *Word*. Between 1946 and 1962 Aldred stood for Parliament in four Glasgow constituencies – Bridgeton, Camlachie, Central (twice) and Woodside – never collecting more than the meagre handfuls of votes that he had picked up in his earlier electoral efforts. John Caldwell says of Aldred during this period: 'the ranks were thinning around him. The old Anarchists and "antis" were fading from the scene.'[4] After Aldred's death in October 1963, Caldwell took over as editor of the *Word* until it finally ceased to appear in 1965. The Workers' Open Forum – into whose activities the *Solidarity* group dissolved itself at the end of the war – continued to provide a common meeting ground on a regular basis in Glasgow well into the late 1950s. Willie McDougall, a leavening influence in many initiatives such as the Open Forum, remained an active communist until his death at the age of 87 in 1981.[5]

John Caldwell's comment on the disappearance of the Workers' Open Forum – 'the end of the period of proletarian meetings in austere halls of wooden benches and bare floors'[6] – captures the feeling of the vanishing era in which the anti-parliamentary communists had been active. The art of open-air speaking – the street-corner oratory upheld as an alternative to sending men and women to Parliament – died in the increasing roar of motorised traffic. Traditional speaking pitches were bulldozed away by the redevelopment of inner city areas. Audiences disappeared through the dispersal of working-class communities to new, suburban housing schemes and through the trend toward atomised forms of entertainment such as television. These changes were all manifestations of the post-war economic boom, when steadily rising standards of living, low unemployment, wider provision of social welfare and confident promises of a permanently crisis-free capitalism all seemed to make a nonsense of the anti-parliamentarians' earlier references to the irreversible decay and impending bankruptcy of the capitalist system.

Surveying the activities and achievements of the anti-parliamentary communist groups during 1917–45, it is obvious that their worth cannot be assessed according to their numerical support or influence within the working class. In these terms the anti-parliamentary communists had precious little to show for all their tireless efforts. Rather, it was in terms of helping to sustain a genuinely revolutionary tradition in Britain that the anti-parliamentarians made an enormous and invaluable contribution.

During the inter-war years only the anti-parliamentary communist groups and a tiny handful of others kept alive a vision of an authentic alternative to capitalism. In the anti-parliamentarians' conception of socialism/communism, the wealth of society would no longer be owned and controlled by a self-interested minority of the population, but would become the common possession of all the world's inhabitants. The slavery of wage labour, and its relentless toll on the physical and mental well-being of those forced to depend on it, would be replaced by the voluntary co-operation of free and equal individuals engaged in enjoyable productive activity, in which the boundaries between work and play would disappear. The subordination of human needs to the dictates of production for profit via the market, and the domination of every area of human activity by money and exchange relationships, would give way to production for the satisfaction of every individual's freely-chosen needs and desires, and unrestricted access for all to the use and enjoyment of abundant quantities of wealth. Class-divided society and the system of competitive national blocs, with their necessary attendant apparatus of armed forces, frontiers, police, courts, prisons and so on, would give way to a harmonious, classless world community of liberated men and women.

Who else besides the anti-parliamentary communists was putting forward such a vision of emancipation? Certainly not the organisations popularly associated with socialism/communism: the Labour Party striving to demonstrate that it could manage capitalism more effectively and more responsibly than its Conservative opponents, and the Communist Party tying itself in knots in its role as apologist for every political twist and turn made by the despicably anti-working class Russian regime!

The anti-parliamentary communists not only promoted a goal worth fighting for; by constantly stressing that the overthrow of capitalism could only come about through the actions of a majority of class-conscious working-class people organising and leading themselves, they also defended the only method by which this goal could be achieved. The labour movement was dominated by the idea that the instrument of social change would be the conquest of power by a minority of the working class organised in a political party. In this matter the social democratic and Leninist parties differed only in the sense that the former saw this as a peaceful parliamentary process, while the latter laid more emphasis on the violent minority coup. Meanwhile, on every occasion where these parties did win and hold power they did so as oppressors of the working class and as upholders of the very system that they had purported to oppose.

The conclusion drawn by the anti-parliamentarians was that social revolution could no longer be defined in terms of a party taking power. Revolutions could only succeed if the conscious mass of working-class people themselves determined the course of events throughout every phase of the struggle. Working-class people had to begin to organise their struggles by themselves, keeping all initiative in their own hands and organising independently of all organisations or institutions that would defuse, divide or divert the workers' own collective power and consciousness. This could be done through forms of organisation such as mass assemblies open to everyone actively involved in the struggle, and where necessary through the election of mandated and recallable delegates. Eventually such forms of organisation – the soviets or workers' councils – could be used by working-class people to establish their own power over society, and to reorganise production and distribution on a communist basis.

During a period spanning nearly 30 years, in which occurred such momentous events as two world wars, the Russian revolution, the great economic crisis of the late 1920s and early 1930s and the Spanish Civil War, it is only to be expected that the anti-parliamentary communists occasionally faltered in their response to some events. The *Dreadnought* group's proposals for post-revolutionary transitional measures, which they described as communist but which were in fact capitalist; Guy Aldred's reluctance until 1925, for reasons of personal animosity, to believe accounts of Bolshevik persecution of revolutionaries; the way in which the anti-parliamentarians refrained from extending their analysis of Russia as a state capitalist regime back to the period before 1921; the *Dreadnought* group's confusions over nationalisation; Aldred's flirtation in the 1930s with the Trotskyist idea that Russia was in some way a 'workers' state'; the anti-parliamentary communist groups' support for the capitalist democracy of the Spanish Republic against its fascist opponents at the beginning of the Civil War in 1936; the USM's anti-war alliances during 1939–45 with pacifists, Labour politicians, fascist apologists and religious and racial bigots . . . these are just some of the positions taken up by the anti-parliamentarians which anyone assessing their history would be completely justified in criticising and rejecting. It is a catalogue of errors which should dispel any notion that the anti-parliamentarians were flawless heroes who never put a foot wrong. Nevertheless, the anti-parliamentarians were able to correct many of these mistakes themselves, and even where they did not their errors can still be fruitful if revolutionaries learn from them and do not condemn themselves to repeating them.

It is also to be expected that during the decades since the end of the Second World War some of the anti-parliamentarians' perspectives were called into question by subsequent events. For example, it might appear at first sight that the APCF, which argued that capitalism had entered a period of permanent crisis and decay in which it was unable to grant even the simplest demands of the working class, and that whatever the outcome of the Second World War Western capitalism would evolve towards fascist-type totalitarian forms of political rule, was spectacularly wrong in its predictions.

But what of the expectations of the great majority, who believed that they were fighting a war to end all wars and for a new era of peace, freedom and prosperity? During the 1950s and 1960s it seemed as if these hopes had been fulfilled . . . as long as one closed one's eyes to the sight of the rival superpowers armed to the teeth and engaged in endless proxy wars in South East Asia, the Middle East and elsewhere, to the growing poverty and destitution in the Third

World, to what was happening in Stalinist Russia and Eastern Europe, to the Western European fascist states in Spain and Portugal, and so on. More than 20 million people were killed in the first 40 years of so-called peace after 1945. The war for which the superpowers are currently preparing could quite easily destroy the whole planet, and all its inhabitants, if it is ever allowed to begin. The so-called freedom enjoyed by striking coalminers in Britain during 1984–5 – consisting of roadblocks, curfews, pass laws, centrally-controlled national riot police, arbitrary arrest and imprisonment, political courts and so on – show that when called upon to do so the ruling class has no compunction about letting slip its democratic facade and resorting to naked coercion and violence to defend its rotting system. Increasing state repression, and ultimately war, are the ruling class's only remaining answers to the inexorable economic crisis into which the world has plunged, and to the working class's resistance to the austerity which is being forced upon it. So much for peace, freedom and prosperity.

Every capitalist solution to the world's problems has been tried and has failed. The communism advocated by groups such as the anti-parliamentary communists in Britain during 1917–45 remains the only genuine and as yet untried alternative to the existing system. Faced with the choice of war or revolution, barbarism or communism, it is up to the working-class people of the world to take up the ideas put forward by the anti-parliamentary communists, and destroy capitalism before it destroys us.

Notes and References

1 'Anti-Parliamentarism' and 'Communism'

1. *Workers' Dreadnought*, 15 September 1917.
2. Minutes of WSF General Meeting 19 March 1917, Pankhurst Papers.
3. *Spur*, May 1917.
4. *Woman's Dreadnought*, 27 January 1917.
5. *Workers' Dreadnought*, 26 January 1918.
6. Minutes of WSF Executive Committee meeting 26 July 1918, Pankhurst Papers.
7. *Workers' Dreadnought*, 16 February 1918.
8. Ibid., 1 June 1918.
9. Ibid., 7 December 1918.
10. Minutes of WSF General Meeting 15 November 1918, Pankhurst Papers.
11. *Workers' Dreadnought*, 2 November 1918.
12. Ibid., 30 November and 7 December 1918.
13. Marx, 1977, p. 66.
14. *Spur*, June 1918.
15. Caldwell, 1983, p. 17.
16. *Red Commune*, February 1921.
17. *Workers' Dreadnought*, 22 March 1919.
18. Minutes of WSF Executive Committee meeting 28 March 1919, Pankhurst Papers; *Workers' Dreadnought*, 14 June 1919.
19. Minutes of WSF Executive Committee meeting 12 June 1919, Pankhurst Papers.
20. *Spur*, May 1919.
21. Letter dated 16 July 1919 in *Communist International*, September 1919.
22. Letter dated 28 August 1919 in Lenin, 1969, pp. 243–5.
23. *Commune*, June 1924.
24. *Worker*, 13 December 1919.
25. *Spur*, January–February 1920
26. Jones, 1982, pp. 205–7.
27. *Spur*, October 1919.
28. Ibid., January 1921.
29. Ibid., May 1920.
30. Ibid., July 1920.
31. Ibid., October 1920.
32. Ibid., August 1920.
33. *Workers' Dreadnought*, 10 April 1920.
34. Minutes of WSF Executive Committee meetings 20 February and 3 March 1920, Pankhurst Papers.
35. Minutes of WSF Executive Committee meeting 10 June 1920, Pankhurst Papers; *Workers' Dreadnought*, 12 June 1920.

36. *Workers' Dreadnought*, 26 June and 3 July 1920.
37. *Forward*, 26 June – 2 October 1920.
38. *Spur*, March 1919; *Communist*, May 1919; Communist League leaflet, file 48, Pankhurst Papers.
39. *Spur*, May 1920.
40. Ibid., August 1920.
41. Ibid., August 1920 and April 1921.
42. Lenin, 1975, pp. 85 and 87 (emphases in original).
43. Letter dated 8 July 1920 in Lenin, 1969, p. 261.
44. *Workers' Dreadnought*, 2 October 1920.
45. Ibid., 16 October 1920.
46. Pankhurst, 1921, pp. 45–6.
47. *Workers' Dreadnought*, 11 December 1920.
48. Ibid., 18 and 25 December 1920, 1 and 8 January 1921.
49. Ibid., 1 January 1921.
50. Ibid., 15 January 1921.
51. *Red Commune*, February 1921.
52. *Workers' Dreadnought*, 30 July and 17 September 1921.
53. McGovern, 1960, pp. 95–6.
54. *Workers' Dreadnought*, 8 October 1921.
55. Ibid., 11 February 1922.
56. Ibid., 23 September 1922.
57. Ibid., 28 October 1922.
58. Caldwell, 1978, p. 231.
59. Aldred, 1922.
60. *Workers' Dreadnought*, 19 February 1921.
61. Ibid., 25 November 1922.
62. *Commune*, November 1923.
63. Milton, 1973, pp. 298–300.
64. *Workers' Dreadnought*, 10 November 1923.
65. Leaflet reprinted in *Commune*, November 1923 (emphases in original).
66. *Workers' Dreadnought*, 17 November 1923.
67. *Commune*, December 1923–January 1924.
68 Ibid., October 1924.
69. 'Platform of the Communist International adopted by the First Comintern Congress' in Degras, 1956, p. 18 (emphasis in original).
70. 'Theses on Bourgeois Democracy and Proletarian Dictatorship adopted by the First Comintern Congress' in ibid., p. 13.
71. *Spur*, July 1917.
72. *Workers' Dreadnought*, 3 December 1921.
73. ECCI circular letter on Parliament and Soviets in Degras, 1956, p. 67.
74. 'Theses on Communist Parties and Parliament adopted by the Second Comintern Congress' in ibid., pp. 153–4.
75. Ibid.
76. Lenin, 1975, p. 104.
77. Ibid., p. 52 (emphases in original).
78. *Workers' Dreadnought*, 27 September 1919.
79. Letter dated 16 July 1919 in *Communist International*, September 1919.

80. *Workers' Dreadnought*, 24 March 1923.
81. Aldred, 1923, p. 6
82. Aldred, 1922.
83. *Spur*, May 1918.
84. Ibid., May 1920.
85 *Red Commune*, February 1921.
86 *Workers' Dreadnought*, 30 July 1921.
87. Ibid., 24 September 1921.
88. *Red Commune*, February 1921.
89. *Workers' Dreadnought*, 6 October 1923.
90. Gallacher, 1966, pp. 152–4.
91. *Workers' Dreadnought*, 2 December 1922.
92. *Spur*, June 1918.
93. Ibid., May 1918 (emphases in original).
94. *Worker*, 22 July 1922 (emphasis in original).
95. *Workers' Dreadnought*, 24 March 1923.
96. Ibid., 24 September 1921.
97. Ibid.
98. Ibid., 27 August 1921.
99. Ibid.
100. Ibid., 1 December 1923.
101. *Spur*, March–April 1918.
102. *Workers' Dreadnought*, 31 July 1920.
103. Ibid., 24 March 1923.
104. Pannekoek, 'World Revolution and Communist Tactics' in Smart, 1978, pp. 110–11 (emphasis in original).
105. *Workers' Dreadnought*, 21 April 1923.
106. Ibid., 15 April 1922.
107. Ibid., 24 March 1923.
108. *Commune*, December 1924.
109. *Spur*, March 1919.
110. *Workers' Dreadnought*, 3 July 1920.
111. Ibid., 1 June 1918.
112. *Red Commune*, February 1921.
113. Aldred, 1922.
114. *Workers' Dreadnought*, 4 February 1922.
115. Ibid., 2 November 1918.
116. Ibid., 16 February 1918.
117. Ibid., 27 April 1918.
118. *Spur*, June 1918.
119. *Workers' Dreadnought*, 26 November 1921.
120. Ibid., 13 August 1921.
121. Ibid., 10 December 1921.
122. Ibid., 23 September 1922.
123. Ibid., 21 February 1920.
124. Ibid., 20 May 1922.
125. Ibid.
126. Ibid., 26 November 1921.
127. *Spur*, August 1917.
128. *Workers' Dreadnought*, 15 April 1922.

129. *Spur*, September 1917.
130. Aldred, 1919a, pp. 4–5.
131. *Woman's Dreadnought*, 3 March 1917.
132. *Spur*, August 1917.
133. Ibid., May 1918.
134. *Workers' Dreadnought*, 10 December 1921.
135. Ibid., 1 April 1922.
136. Ibid., 18 March 1922.
137. *Spur*, August 1917.
138. *Workers' Dreadnought*, 26 November 1921.
139. *Spur*, May 1918.
140. *Solidarity*, June–July 1939.
141. *Woman's Dreadnought*, 3 March 1917.

2 The Russian Revolution

1. *Spur*, May 1917.
2. Ibid., July 1917 (emphasis in original).
3. Ibid., October 1917.
4. *Woman's Dreadnought*, 9 June 1917
5. Ibid., 24 March 1917.
6. Ibid., 30 June 1917.
7. *Workers' Dreadnought*, 11 August 1917.
8. Ibid., 29 September 1917.
9. Ibid., 17 November 1917.
10. *Spur*, January–February 1918.
11. Carr, 1966, p. 10.
12. Minutes of WSF General Meeting 13 August 1917, Pankhurst Papers.
13. *Workers' Dreadnought*, 29 December 1917.
14. Ibid., 5 January 1918.
15. Ibid., 12 January 1918.
16. Pollitt, 1940, pp. 109–10.
17. *Workers' Dreadnought*, 2 March 1918.
18. Ibid., 1 June 1918.
19. Ibid., 19 January 1918.
20. Ibid., 13 December 1919.
21. Ibid., 31 August 1918.
22. Ibid., 12 July 1919.
23. Ibid., 12 April 1919.
24. Ibid., 1 May 1920.
25. Ibid., 6 August 1921.
26. Ibid., 3 December 1921.
27. See ibid., 14 June and 29 November 1919, 21 February and 3 July 1920.
28. Aldred, 1920, p. 18.
29. *Spur*, June 1920.
30. Ibid., September 1919.
31. *Workers' Dreadnought*, 10 December 1921.
32. Ibid., 24 December 1921.

33. *Red Commune*, February 1921.
34. *Workers' Dreadnought*, 21 February and 3 July 1920.
35. Ibid., 3 July 1920.
36. Ibid.
37. Ibid., 26 May 1923.
38. Ibid., 29 November 1919.
39. Ibid., 21 February and 3 July 1920.
40. Ibid., 3 July 1920.
41. Serge, 1972, p. 357.
42. Nove, 1969, p. 114.
43. Ibid., p. 55.
44. *Workers' Dreadnought*, 25 March 1922.
45. Ibid., 17 September 1921.
46. Ibid., 3 August 1918.
47. Ibid., 21 January 1922.
48. Ibid., 20 May 1922.
49. Ibid., 7 July 1923.
50. Ibid., 31 May 1924.
51. Ibid., 17 September 1921.
52. Ibid., 24 December 1921.
53. Ibid., 4 March 1922.
54. Ibid., 18 March 1922 (emphasis in original).
55. Carr, 1966, p. 357.
56. *Workers' Dreadnought*, 6 May 1922.
57. Ibid., 13 October 1923.
58. Ibid., 9 December 1922.
59. Ibid., 8 October 1921.
60. Ibid., 24 December 1921.
61. Ibid., 2 February 1924 (emphases in original).
62. Ibid., 15 July 1922.
63. Ibid., 28 January 1922.
64. Ibid., 24 December 1921.
65. Ibid., 28 January 1922.
66. Ibid., 17 September 1921.
67. Ibid., 30 July 1921.
68. Ibid., 17 September 1921.
69. Ibid., 4 November 1922.
70. Degras, 1956, p. 225.
71. *Spur*, May 1920.
72. Ibid., August 1920.
73. Ibid., May 1920.
74. Ibid., August 1920.
75. The Manifesto of the Fourth (Communist Workers') International (KAI) was published in the *Workers' Dreadnought* between 8 October and 10 December 1921 (emphases in original).
76. *Commune*, November 1923 (emphasis in original).
77. Ibid., September 1923.
78. Ibid., June 1924.
79. Ibid., August 1924.

80. Ibid., (emphasis in original).
81. Ibid., December 1924.
82. Ibid., April 1925.
83. *Workers' Dreadnought*, 29 July 1922.
84. Ibid.
85. Ibid., 17 June 1922.
86. See Daniels, 1960, p. 159 and Schapiro, 1955, pp. 327–8.
87. *Commune*, November 1925.
88. *Workers' Dreadnought*, 28 January 1922.
89. Ibid., 8 October 1921.
90. Ibid., 31 May 1924.

3 The Labour Party

1. Aldred, 1940d, p. 39.
2. Aldred, 1955–63, vol. I no. 5, p. 113.
3. Aldred, 1955–63, vol. I no. 11, p. 260.
4. Aldred, 1923, p. 3.
5. Aldred, 1948, p. 33.
6. Quoted in Aldred, 1942a, p. 15.
7. *Commune*, September 1923.
8. Ibid., August 1924.
9. Klugmann, 1968, p. 20.
10. Minutes of WSF Executive Committee meeting 22 March 1917, Pankhurst Papers.
11. Minutes of WSF General Meeting 15 April 1918, Pankhurst Papers.
12. Minutes of WSF Finance Committee meeting 12 September 1918, Pankhurst Papers; *Workers' Dreadnought*, 2 November 1918.
13. *Workers' Dreadnought*, 28 July 1917.
14. Quoted in Aldred, 1942b, p. 47.
15. *Workers' Dreadnought*, 13 April 1918.
16. Ibid., 30 November 1918.
17. Ibid., 15 December 1917.
18. Ibid., 9 March 1918.
19. Ibid., 27 October 1917 and 2 March 1918.
20. Ibid., 6 July 1918.
21. Ibid., 13 April 1918.
22. Ibid., 27 October 1917.
23. Ibid.
24. Ibid., 17 November 1917.
25. Ibid., 28 July 1917.
26. Aldred, 1923, p. 11.
27. *Workers' Dreadnought*, 21 February 1920.
28. Ibid., 18 January 1919.
29. See Degras, 1956, p. 3.

30. Ibid., pp. 25–6.
31. Minutes of WSF Bow branch meeting 19 May 1919, Pankhurst Papers.
32. Minutes of WSF Executive Committee meeting 22 May 1919, Pankhurst Papers.
33. *Workers' Dreadnought*, 14 June 1919.
34. Minutes of WSF Executive Committee meeting 12 June 1919, Pankhurst Papers.
35. *Workers' Dreadnought*, 21 February 1920.
36. Minutes of WSF Executive Committee meeting 7 August 1919, Pankhurst Papers.
37. Bush, 1984, p. 231.
38. *Workers' Dreadnought*, 14 February 1920.
39. See ibid., 20 March 1920 for the full text of both resolutions and an account of the proceedings.
40. Kendall, 1969, p. 208.
41. Minutes of WSF Executive Committee meeting 3 March 1920, Pankhurst Papers.
42. *Workers' Dreadnought*, 8 May 1920.
43. Lenin, 1975, p. 85.
44. Ibid., pp. 90–1.
45. Minutes of WSF Executive Committee meeting 30 March 1920, Pankhurst Papers.
46. *Workers' Dreadnought*, 3 July 1920.
47. *Spur*, July 1920.
48. *Workers' Dreadnought*, 14 and 21 February 1920.
49. Ibid., 21 February 1920.
50. Ibid., 24 July 1920.
51. Lenin, 1975, p. 91.
52. Hulse, 1964, p. 177.
53. Degras, 1956, p. 125.
54. Communist International, Publishing House, 1921, p. 74.
55. Lenin, 1969, pp. 267–71.
56. See Rosmer, 1971, pp. 76–7.
57. Pankhurst, 1921, pp. 45–6.
58. *Workers' Dreadnought*, 31 July 1920.
59. Letter dated 8 July 1920 in Lenin, 1969, p. 261.
60. MacFarlane, 1966, p. 94.
61. See Klugmann, 1968, pp. 230–4.
62. *Workers' Dreadnought*, 5 February 1921.
63. Ibid., 30 July 1921.
64. Ibid., 13 August 1921.
65. See 'Communist Party Affiliation to the Labour Party', 1974, pp. 16–34.
66. See MacFarlane, 1966, p. 109.
67. *Commune*, September 1923.
68. *Workers' Dreadnought*, 13 August 1921.
69. Ibid., 16 June 1923.
70. Ibid., 22 December 1923.
71. Ibid., 15 December 1923.

72. Ibid., 17 May 1924.
73. Pollitt, 1940, pp. 197 and 199.
74. See figures in Kendall, 1974, pp. 118–31.
75. Lazitch and Drachkovitch, 1972, p. 263.
76. Ibid., p. 364.
77. *Workers' Dreadnought*, 11 February 1922.
78. Ibid., 23 September 1922.
79. Ibid., 7 July 1923.
80. See *Worker*, 15 and 29 July, 19 and 26 August, and 9 and 16 September 1922.
81. *Commune*, November 1923.
82. *Workers' Dreadnought*, 30 June 1921.
83. Quoted in Branson, 1979, p. 128.
84. *Workers' Dreadnought*, 6 October 1923.
85. *Commune*, February 1924.
86. Ibid., March 1924.
87. *Workers' Dreadnought*, 26 January 1924.
88. Ibid., 23 February 1924.
89. Quoted in Aldred, 1942b, p. 31.
90. *Workers' Dreadnought*, 8 March and 12 April 1924.
91. Aldred, 1928, p. 6.

4 Trade Unions and Industrial Organisation

1. *Workers' Dreadnought*, 30 October 1920.
2. Ibid., 13 September 1919.
3. Ibid., 15 February 1919.
4. Circular concerning 'Activity on the Industrial Field' from E. T. Whitehead, CP(BSTI) Secretary, to Party branches, 12 July 1920, file 124, Pankhurst Papers.
5. *Workers' Dreadnought*, 21 April 1923.
6. Ibid.
7. Aldred, 1919b, p. 7.
8. *Workers' Dreadnought*, 28 July 1923.
9. Aldred, 1919b. See Author's Note to 1919 edn. and Section II (emphasis in original).
10. *Workers' Dreadnought*, 4 February 1922.
11. Ibid., 19 February 1921.
12. Circular from E. T. Whitehead, CP(BSTI) Secretary, to Party branches, 10 June 1920, file 125, Pankhurst Papers.
13. *Workers' Dreadnought*, 12 July 1919.
14. Ibid., 28 July 1923.
15. Resolution XI, Rank and File Convention Draft Agenda, file 32e, Pankhurst Papers.
16. Quoted in Hinton, 1973, p. 119.
17. Murphy, 1972.
18. See the 'Communist Party Notes' published in the *Workers' Dreadnought* from July 1920 onwards.

19. South Wales Miners' Federation Unofficial Reform Committee, 1973.
20. Peterson, 1976, p. 26 (emphasis added).
21. *Workers' Dreadnought*, 3 July 1920.
22. CP(BSTI) Suggested Circular to Branches, Number Four, no date, file 125, Pankhurst Papers.
23. CP(BSTI) Report of Industrial Sub-committee, Draft for Final Revision, no date, file 5a, Pankhurst Papers.
24. Klugmann, 1968, pp. 20–1.
25. Aldred, 1929, p. 83 (emphases in original).
26. *Word*, August 1939.
27. Campbell, 1979, p. 87.
28. McShane and Smith, 1978, pp. 77–8.
29. See Kirkwood, 1935, Chapters 8–10.
30. See Aldred, 1940e, pp. 52–64.
31. *Worker*, 2 August 1919.
32. *Spur*, March 1919.
33. Statistics in this section are from the Board of Trade Statistical Department, 1926.
34. McShane and Smith, 1978, p. 136.
35. Regional and occupational figures from Astor *et al.*, 1922.
36. Quoted in Francis and Smith, 1980, p. 32.
37. Hinton and Hyman, 1975, p. 14.
38. *Workers' Dreadnought*, 10 June 1922.
39. Quail, 1978, p. 303.
40. Leaflet issued by John McGovern, Treasurer, APCF Defence and Maintenance Fund, Shettleston, 1921, bundle 2, Aldred Collection.
41. See Holton, 1976.
42. *Workers' Dreadnought*, 27 August 1921.
43. Ibid., 28 January 1922.
44. Ibid., 21 April 1923.
45. Ibid., 27 August 1921 (emphasis added).
46. Ibid., 11 February 1922.
47. Ibid., 23 September 1922.
48. Ibid., 5 November 1921.
49. Gorter, 'The Organisation of the Proletariat's Class Struggle' in Smart, 1978, p. 157.
50. KAPD, no date, p. 72.
51. *Workers' Dreadnought*, 5 November 1921.
52. Gorter, 'The Organisation of the Proletariat's Class Struggle' in Smart, 1978, p. 162.
53. Ibid., p. 159.
54. *Workers' Dreadnought*, 10 May 1924.
55. Ibid., 4 February 1922.
56. Ibid., 8 September 1923.
57. Ibid., 14 July 1923.
58. Ibid., 8 September 1923.
59. Ibid., 1 September 1923.
60. Ibid., 4 August 1923.
61. Ibid., 7 July 1923.

62. Ibid., 4 and 18 August, 1 September and 20 October 1923.
63. Ibid., 19 January 1924.
64. Ibid., 7 July 1923.
65. *Spur*, March 1920.
66. Ibid., October 1920.
67. Richards, 1983, p. 198 (emphases in original).
68. *Workers' Dreadnought*, 5 January 1924.
69. Aldred, 1955–63, vol. II no. 3, p. 359.
70. Aldred, 1955–63, vol. II no. 5, p. 113.
71. *Spur*, August 1919.
72. Ibid.
73. *Commune*, September 1923.
74. Aldred, 1940d, pp. 58–9.
75. *Spur*, March 1917.
76. Ibid., July 1917.
77. *Workers' Dreadnought*, 23 June and 7 July 1923.
78. *Commune*, November 1925.
70. Ibid., March 1924.
80. *Spur*, October 1918.
81. Ibid., October 1920.

5 The Late Twenties and Early Thirties

1. *Workers' Dreadnought*, 30 July 1921.
2. *Red Commune*, February 1921.
3. *Workers' Dreadnought*, 5 February 1921.
4. Ibid., 17 June 1922.
5. Ibid., 29 July 1922.
6. Aldred, 1948, p. 18.
7. McGovern, 1960, p. 55.
8. Authier and Barrot, 1976, p. 197 (author's translation).
9. Challinor, 1977, p. 223.
10. Pankhurst, 1926.
11. Pankhurst, 1927a and 1927b.
12. Pankhurst and Stefanovici, 1930.
13. Pankhurst, 1930.
14. Statistics in this section are from the Department of Employment and Productivity, 1971.
15. *Commune*, May 1925.
16. Ibid., November 1925.
17. Aldred, 1945c, p. 10.
18. See Berkman, 1925.
19. See *Commune*, November 1925, February and December 1926, September–October, November and December 1927, and March 1928.
20. Ibid., November 1925.
21. Ibid., January 1926.
22. Ibid., February 1926.
23. Ibid., November 1925 and May 1926.
24. Aldred, 1934a, p. 37.

25. Aldred, 1940a, pp. 46–7.
26. *Commune*, July 1928 (emphases in original).
27. Ibid., May 1927 (emphasis in original).
28. Ibid., September–October 1927.
29. *Council*, February 1933.
30. *Commune*, September–October 1927 (emphasis in original).
31. See ibid., March 1928 and *Commune Anti-Parliamentary Communist Gazette*, March 1929.
32. *Council*, February 1933.
33. See letter from Basil Taylor to Guy Aldred, 8 April 1934, bundle 195, Aldred Collection.
34. *Council*, November 1932.
35. Trotsky, 1967, pp. 234–56.
36. *Commune*, September 1925.
37. Aldred, 1926b, p. 32.
38. *Commune*, January 1925.
39. Aldred, 1926b, p. 11.
40. *Commune*, February 1926.
41. Ibid., June 1925.
42. Ibid., July 1928.
43. Aldred, 1926b, p. 29.
44. Aldred, 1929, pp. 14 and 16.
45. *Commune*, July 1928 (emphasis in original).
46. Aldred, 1926b, p. 29.
47. *Commune*, July 1928.
48. Aldred, 1928, p. 10.
49. *Commune*, October 1926.
50. Aldred, 1928, p. 10 (emphases in original).
51. *Commune*, October 1926.
52. *Workers' Dreadnought*, 27 October 1917.
53. *Woman's Dreadnought*, 3 March 1917.
54. Ibid.
55. Ibid., 5 May 1917
56. Ibid., 2 June 1917.
57. *Workers' Dreadnought*, 13 November 1920.
58. *Spur*, November 1920.
59. *Workers' Dreadnought*, 1 March 1919.
60. Ibid., 30 August 1919.
61. Ibid., 8 March 1919.
62. Ibid., 11 August 1923.
63. Ibid., 13 January 1923.
64. *Commune*, September 1925.
65. *Commune Special Anti-Parliamentary Communist Gazette* 12 June 1926.
66. *Commune*, September–October 1927.
67. *Commune Anti-Parliamentary Communist Gazette*, January 1929.
68. *Council*, October 1931.
69. *Commune*, January 1926.
70. Ibid., October 1925.

71. Ibid., June 1925.
72. Ibid., May 1926.
73. *Commune Special Anti-Parliamentary Communist Gazette*, 16 May 1926.
74. Ibid., and *Commune*, July 1926.
75. *Commune*, March 1928.
76. Ibid., October 1923.

6 The Split in the APCF and Formation of the USM

1. *Council*, January 1932 (emphasis in original).
2. *Commune Anti-Parliamentary Communist Gazette*, May 1929.
3. *Council*, December 1931.
4. Ibid., June 1932.
5. *Commune Anti-Parliamentary Communist Gazette*, May 1929.
6. *Council*, October 1931.
7. *Word*, March 1944.
8. *Council*, February 1933.
9. See Caldwell, 1981.
10. See Glasgow Free Speech Council of Action leaflet, 'A Call for United Action', 1931, in bundle 56, Aldred Collection.
11. *Council*, October 1931.
12. Ibid., May 1933.
13. Ibid., June 1932.
14. Ibid., October 1931.
15. Ibid., December 1931.
16. Ibid., May 1932 (emphasis in original).
17. Ibid., June 1932.
18. Aldred, 1935, p. 97.
19. Aldred, 1942a, pp. 75–6.
20. *Word*, March 1944.
21. Guy Aldred to Sandy Whyte, 12 April 1934, bundle 195, Aldred Collection.
22. The Minute Book of the Workers' Open Forum is in bundle 127, Aldred Collection.
23. *New Spur*, March 1934.
24. Ibid., February and March 1934.
25. Aldred, 1934f, pp. 3 and 5–6.
26. Ibid., p. 3.
27. *Socialist May Special*, May 1934 (emphasis in original).
28. Aldred, 1934d, p. 6.
29. *Socialist May Special*, May 1934 (emphasis in original).
30. Ibid.
31. Aldred, 1934f, p. 5.
32. Aldred, 1934d, p. 16.
33. Aldred, 1934e, p. 8.
34. *Socialist May Special*, May 1934.
35. See correspondence between Guy Aldred, Tom Taylor (Organising

Secretary, ILP Glasgow Federation) and Fenner Brockway (ILP National Administrative Council), May–June 1934, bundle 7, Aldred Collection.

36. See minutes of Workers' Open Forum/United Socialist Movement meetings 28 June and 5 and 12 July 1934, bundle 127, Aldred Collection.
37. See *United Socialist*, October 1934.
38. Letter to the *Evening Times* (Glasgow), 23 July 1931 in Aldred, 1940f, p. 29.
39. See Caldwell, 1978, p. 235.
40. Minutes of USM meeting 16 October 1934, bundle 128, Aldred Collection.
41. Aldred, 1934b.
42. Aldred, 1934c.
43. Text of proposed amendment in bundle 26, Aldred Collection.
44. See correspondence between Frank Leech and Guy Aldred, March 1934, in bundle 230, Aldred Collection.
45. Aldred's foreword to Trotsky, 1934, pp. 2–3.
46. *United Socialist*, October 1934.
47. Aldred, 1935, p. 40.
48. Ibid., p. 55.
49. Ibid., pp. 55 and 39.
50. Anti-Parliamentary Communist Federation, 1935, p. 6.
51. Ibid., pp. 18–19.
52. Ibid., p. 10.
53. Ibid., pp. 19 and 28.
54. Ibid., p. 21.
55. *Attack*, May 1936.
56. Aldred, 1935, p. 24.
57. Luxemburg, 1935, pp. 13–14.
58. Ibid., p. 20.
59. Ibid., p. 23.
60. Ibid., pp. 23–4.
61. Ibid., p. 26.
62. APCF foreword to ibid., p. 3.
63. Aldred, 1935, p. 102.
64. *International Council Correspondence*, June 1935.
65. Aldred, 1935, p. 61.
66. Minutes of USM meeting 7 May 1935, bundle 128, Aldred Collection.
67. See letter from Guy Aldred to Vera Buch Weisbord, 17 June 1935, bundle 13, Aldred Collection; Weisbord, 1977, p.312.
68. Minutes of USM meeting 7 May 1935, bundle 128, Aldred Collection.
69. Letter reprinted in *News From Spain*, 1 May 1937.
70. Guy Aldred to the *Evening Citizen* (Glasgow), 8 September 1936 in Aldred, 1940f, p. 44.
71. *Word*, May 1938.
72. Socialist Anti-Terror Committee, 1938, pp. 1–5.
73. See minutes of USM meeting 21 March 1938, bundle 129, Aldred Collection.

74. Letter from B. Meehan to USM Chairman, 25 June 1935, bundle 101, Aldred Collection.
75. Minutes of USM meeting 2 July 1935, bundle 128, Aldred Collection.
76. See minutes of USM meetings 16 October 1935 and 28 January and 4 February 1936, bundle 128, Aldred Collection.
77. Bricianer, 1978, p. 243.
78. Aldred, 1935, Chapter 11.
79. *Attack*, May 1936.
80. Ibid.
81. Aldred to the *Evening Times* (Glasgow), 24 August 1935 in Aldred, 1940f, p. 37.
82. Mattick, 1970, p. viii.
83. Marx and Engels, 1968, pp. 181–2.
84. *Living Marxism*, Spring 1940.
85. Ibid.
86. Ibid.
87. International Communist Current, no date, p. 12.
88. Appel, 1985, p. 28.
89. 'APCF Aims' published in Anti-Parliamentary Communist Federation, 1935, p. 30 and Luxemburg, 1935, pp. 27–8.
90. *Advance*, May 1936.
91. Ibid.
92. Ibid.
93. Aldred, 1940c, p. 7.

7 The Civil War in Spain

1. Sylvia Pankhurst, 'The Red Twilight' (unpublished typescript), file 26c 73–2, Pankhurst Papers.
2. *Advance*, May 1936.
3. *Regeneracion*, 2 August 1936.
4. Caldwell, 1976, p. 213.
5. Quoted in Jones, 1982, p. 206.
6. *Advance*, September 1936.
7. *Workers' Free Press*, September 1937.
8. *Solidarity*, June–July 1939.
9. Ibid., November 1940–January 1941.
10. *Advance*, May 1936 (emphases in original).
11. Resolution published in *Regeneracion*, 16 August 1936.
12. *Regeneracion*, 5 August 1936.
13. Ibid., 8 August 1936.
14. Ibid., 18 August 1936.
15. Ibid., 26 August 1936.
16. *Advance*, September 1936.
17. Ibid., August–September 1936.
18. *Regeneracion*, 8 August 1936.
19. *Fighting Call*, November 1936.
20. Ibid., 1 February 1937.

21. 'If War Comes . . . What Then?', (no date), bundle 56, Aldred Collection.
22. *Advance*, May 1936.
23. *Workers' Free Press*, October 1937.
24. Montseny, 1937, pp. 5 and 13 (emphasis in original).
25. See *Advance*, September 1936 and *Fighting Call*, October and November 1936.
26. *Regeneracion*, 21 February 1937.
27. Guy Aldred to Jane Patrick, 30 November 1936, bundle 141, Aldred Collection.
28. See unpublished manuscript by Guy Aldred attacking Emma Goldman in bundle 105, Aldred Collection.
29. Guy Aldred to André Prudhommeaux, 15 October 1936, bundle 110, Aldred Collection.
30. See Guy Aldred to Jane Patrick, 30 November 1936, bundle 141, Aldred Collection.
31. *Regeneracion*, 9 September 1936.
32. Ibid., 23 September 1936.
33. See minutes of USM meeting 20 October 1936, bundle 129, Aldred Collection.
34. See minutes of USM meeting 12 November 1936, bundle 129, Aldred Collection.
35. Text of radio broadcast (no date) published in *News From Spain*, 1 May 1937.
36. *Regeneracion*, 21 February 1937.
37. Text of radio broadcast (7 March 1937) published in *News From Spain*, 1 May 1937.
38. *Regeneracion*, 21 February 1937.
39. Ibid., 28 February 1937.
40. *News From Spain*, 1 May 1937.
41. Ibid.
42. Anti-Parliamentary Volunteers, 1937.
43. *Barcelona Bulletin*, 15 May 1937.
44. *Advance*, 19 July 1937; 2nd edn, 7 August 1937.
45. See minutes of USM meetings 10 and 31 August 1937, bundle 129, Aldred Collection, and *Workers' Free Press*, September 1937.
46. See *International Council Correspondence*, August 1937 and *Workers' Free Press*, September 1937 (emphasis in original).
47. *Workers' Free Press*, October 1937.
48. *Solidarity*, August 1938.
49. Ibid., June–July 1939.

8 The Second World War

1. *Solidarity*, May 1939.
2. Ibid., March–April 1939.
3. *Word*, May 1939.
4. Ibid., March 1940.

5. *War Commentary*, November 1939 (emphases in original).
6. Ibid., mid-April 1943.
7. *Solidarity*, mid-October 1939.
8. Ibid., October–November 1942.
9. *Word*, August 1939.
10. Maximov, 1939, p. 21.
11. *Solidarity*, June–July 1939.
12. Ibid., March–April 1939.
13. Aldred, 1945c, p. 5.
14. Ibid., p. 4.
15. *Word*, January 1944.
16. Ibid., May 1939.
17. *Solidarity*, September 1944.
18. Ibid., September–October 1940. See also 'Anti-Parliamentarism and Council Communism' in *International Council Correspondence*, October 1935.
19. *Solidarity*, June–July 1939.
20. Ibid., September–October 1940.
21. Ibid., November 1940–January 1941.
22. Ibid., May 1944.
23. Ibid., August–September 1942.
24. Ibid., May 1944.
25. Quoted in Calder, 1971, p. 124.
26. Aldred and Wynn, 1943, p. 2.
27. Ibid., p. 10.
28. Ibid., p. 4.
29. Ibid., p. 2.
30. See *War Commentary*, August 1944.
31. Croucher, 1982, p. 241.
32. *Solidarity*, May 1944.
33. Ibid., June–July 1942.
34. Croucher, 1982, p. 373.
35. *War Commentary*, April 1943.
36. Ibid., mid-May 1944.
37. *Solidarity*, June–July 1943.
38. *Evening Times* (Glasgow), 12 November 1941.
39. Ibid., 11 November 1941.
40. *War Commentary*, December 1941 (emphasis in original).
41. *Word*, November 1943.
42. *War Commentary*, October 1943 Supplement.
43. *Evening Times* (Glasgow), 1 October 1943. Account of strike compiled from *Evening Times* (Glasgow), 23 September–5 October 1943; *War Commentary*, October 1943 Supplement; and *Word*, November 1943.
44. Account of strike compiled from *Evening Times* (Glasgow), 13 December 1943–11 January 1944; *Solidarity*, December 1943–January 1944; and *War Commentary*, January, mid-January and February 1944.
45. *Evening Times* (Glasgow), 28 December 1943.
46. *War Commentary*, January 1944.
47. Equity, 1945, pp. 5 and 16.

48. Ibid., p. 3.
49. *War Commentary*, 14 July 1945.
50. Equity, 1945, p. 21.
51. Ibid.
52. *War Commentary*, 24 February 1945.
53. Ibid., 14 July 1945.
54. Equity, 1945, pp. 20–1.
55. *War Commentary*, 7 April 1945.
56. *Solidarity*, September–October 1940.
57. Ibid.
58. Ibid.
59. Ibid., October–November 1942 (emphases in original).
60. Ibid., November 1940–January 1941.
61. Ibid., February–April 1941.
62. Ibid., August–September 1941.
63. Ibid., February–April 1942.
64. Ibid., November 1940–January 1941.
65. Ibid., October–November 1942.
66. Ibid., September–October 1940.
67. Ibid., November 1940–January 1941.
68. Ibid., February–April 1941.
69. Aldred, 1945c, p. 16.
70. *War Commentary*, mid-April 1944.
71. Minutes of USM meeting 11 May 1943, bundle 97, Aldred Collection.
72. *War Commentary*, mid-April 1943.
73. Ibid., November and December 1943, mid-February and mid-April 1944.
74. Lenin, 1970, pp. 64–6.
75. *Solidarity*, August–September 1942.
76. Ibid., February–May 1943.
77. *Anarchist*, no. 2, no date [August 1940] and no. 3, no date [September 1940]; *Solidarity*, September–October 1940; *War Commentary*, August and October 1940; *Word*, September 1940.
78. *War Commentary*, mid-April 1944.
79. *War Commentary*, December 1941; *Word*, December 1941.
80. *War Commentary*, mid-October 1942, mid-January, mid-April, July and mid-October 1944; *Word*, October 1942 and November 1944.
81. *Word*, February 1941, December 1942 and April 1945.
82. Ibid., August and December 1941, December 1942 and January 1943.
83. *Word*, July 1942; *Solidarity*, August–September 1942.
84. *Word*, July 1940.
85. Aldred, 1942b, p. 3.
86. *Word*, August 1939.
87. Aldred, 1942a, p. 65.
88. *Word*, June 1943.
89. Ibid., August 1943.
90. Ibid., June 1940 and January 1941.
91. *War Commentary*, 13 January 1945.
92. *Word*, May 1940.

93. Caldwell, 1984, pp. 9–10.
94. Aldred, 1942a, p. 77.
95. *Word*, August 1941.
96. Ibid., June 1940.
97. Ibid., November 1944.
98. Ibid., March 1945.
99. Ibid., May 1942.
100. Ibid., July 1942.
101. *Solidarity*, June–July 1939.
102. Ibid., February–April 1941.
103. Ibid., September–October 1940 (emphasis in original).
104. Ibid., June–July 1939.
105. Ibid., June–July 1943.
106. *Word*, March 1941.
107. See *War Commentary*, February and April 1940.
108. *Solidarity*, June–July 1943.
109. Ibid.
110. Ibid., June–July 1939.
111. Minutes of USM Study Circle meeting 8 May 1941, bundle 130, Aldred Collection.
112. *War Commentary*, mid-April 1943.
113 *Solidarity*, June–July 1943.
114. *War Commentary*, mid-September 1943.
115. Ibid., 30 December 1944.
116. Ibid., 27 January 1945.
117. Aldred, 1945a and 1945b.
118. Ibid., (emphasis in original).
119. *Word*, December 1945.
120. Aldred, 1945a.
121. Ibid., (emphasis in original).
122. *War Commentary*, 14 July 1945.

9 A Balance Sheet

1. See Wildcat, 1986.
2. Woodcock, 1970, p. 91.
3. See Freedom Press Group, 1953.
4. Caldwell, 1976, p. 265.
5. See Jones, 1982, pp. 205–7.
6. Caldwell, 1976, p. 215.

References/Select Bibliography

Advance (Glasgow) May 1936–August 1937.

Aldred Collection, Mitchell Library, Glasgow.

G. Aldred (1919a), *The Case For Communism* (London: Bakunin Press, 1919).

——— (1919b), *Trade Unionism and the Class War* (London: Bakunin Press, 1919).

——— (1920), *Michel Bakunin Communist* (Glasgow/London: Bakunin Press, 1920).

——— (1922), *General Election, 1922: To the Working-Class Electors of the Parliamentary Division of Shettleston* (Glasgow: Alexander Wood, October 1922).

——— (1923), *Socialism And Parliament* (Glasgow/London: Bakunin Press, 1923).

——— (1926a), *'Labour' In Office: A Record* (Glasgow: Bakunin Press, 1926).

——— (1926b), *Socialism Or Parliament: The Burning Question of Today* (Glasgow: Bakunin Press, 1926.)

——— (1928), *Government By Labour: A Record of Facts* (Glasgow: Bakunin Press, 1928).

——— (1929), *At Grips With War* (Glasgow: Bakunin Press, 1929).

——— (1934a), *Bakunin: I 1814–64 Bakunin & Herzen* (Glasgow: Guy Aldred, no date).

——— (1934b), *Glasgow Municipal Election, 1934* (Glasgow: W. Dick, 1934).

——— (1934c), *Municipal By-Election 1934* (Glasgow: W. Dick, December 1934).

——— (1934d), *Socialism And Parliament Part I Socialism Or Parliament: The Burning Question of Today* (Glasgow: Guy Aldred, 1934).

——— (1934e), *Socialism and the Pope* (Glasgow: Guy Aldred, 1934).

——— (1934f), *Towards The Social Revolution? Whither The ILP?* (Glasgow: Guy Aldred, 1934).

——— (1935), *For Communism* (Glasgow: Guy Aldred, 1935).

——— (1940a), *Bakunin* (Glasgow: Bakunin Press/Strickland Press, 1940).

——— (1940b), *The C.O., The Tribunal And After* (Glasgow: Strickland Press, 1940).

——— (1940c), *Dogmas Discarded: An Autobiography of Thought*, Part I (Glasgow: Strickland Press, 1940).

——— (1940d), *Dogmas Discarded: An Autobiography of Thought*, Part II (Glasgow: Strickland Press, 1940).

——— (1940e), *John Maclean* (Glasgow: Bakunin Press/Strickland Press, 1940).

——— (1940f), *Letters to the Editor* (Glasgow: Bakunin Press/Strickland Press, 1940).

——— (1940g), *Pioneers of Anti-Parliamentarism* (Glasgow: Bakunin Press/Strickland Press, 1940).

——— (1940h), *Studies in Communism* (Glasgow: Bakunin Press/Strickland Press, 1940).

——— (1942a), *Socialism And Parliament Part I Socialism Or Parliament: The Burning Question of Today* (Glasgow: Strickland Press, 1942).

——— (1942b), *Socialism And Parliament Part II Government By Labour: A Record of Facts* (Glasgow: Strickland Press, 1942).

——— (1944), *A Call To Manhood* (Glasgow: Strickland Press, 1944).

——— (1945a), *General Election, 1945* (Glasgow: Alexander Smith, 1945).

——— (1945b), *General Election, 1945: Address to the Services* (Glasgow: Alexander Smith, 1945).

——— (1945c), *Peace Now – And For Ever* (Glasgow: Strickland Press, 1945).

——— (1948), *Rex V. Aldred: London Trial, 1909, Indian Sedition, Glasgow Sedition Trial, 1921* (Glasgow: Strickland Press, 1948).

——— (1955–63), *No Traitor's Gait!*, vol. I no. 1–vol. III no. 1 (Glasgow: Strickland Press, 1955–63).

——— and J. Wynn (1943), *It Might Have Happened to You!* (Glasgow: Strickland Press, 1943).

Anarchist (Glasgow) August–September 1940.

Anti-Parliamentary Communist Federation (1935), *The Bourgeois Role of Bolshevism: Its Relation to World Communism* (Glasgow: Anti-Parliamentary Communist Federation, no date).

Anti-Parliamentary Volunteers (1937), *The Truth About Barcelona* (Glasgow: Anti-Parliamentary Volunteers, May 1937).

J. Appel (1985), 'Discussion on the Report by Radek on the Tactics of the International' in *Communist Bulletin*, no. 9 (Autumn 1985).

J. Astor *et al.* (1922), *The Third Winter of Unemployment* (London: P. S. King, 1922).

Attack (Glasgow) May 1936.

D. Authier and J. Barrot (1976), *La Gauche Communiste en Allemagne 1918–21* (Paris: Payot, 1976).

Barcelona Bulletin (Glasgow) May 1937.

A. Berkman (ed.) (1925), *Letters From Russian Prisons* (New York: Albert & Charles Boni, 1925).

Board of Trade Statistical Department (1926), *Statistical Abstract for the United Kingdom 1910–24* (London: HMSO, 1926).

N. Branson (1979), *Poplarism 1919–25* (London: Lawrence & Wishart, 1979).

S. Bricianer (1978), *Pannekoek and the Workers' Councils* (St Louis: Telos Press, 1978).

J. Bush (1984), *Behind The Lines: East London Labour 1914–19* (London: Merlin Press, 1984).

A. Calder (1971), *The People's War: Britain 1939–45* (London: Granada, 1971).

J. Caldwell (1976), 'The Red Evangel: A Biography of Guy Aldred' (unpublished typescript).

———— (1978), 'Guy Alfred Aldred, Antiparliamentarian, 1886–1963: A Memoir' in I. MacDougall (ed.), *Essays In Scottish Labour History* (Edinburgh: John Donald, 1978).

———— (1981), 'The Battle for Glasgow Green' in Scottish Labour History Society *Journal*, no. 16 (1981).

———— (1983), 'Guy Alfred Aldred' in *Black Star*, no. 1 (October 1983).

———— (1984), Letter concerning Guy Aldred and the Duke of Bedford in *Black Star*, vol. 2 no. 2 (February 1984).

A. Campbell (1979), review of I. MacDougall (ed.), *Essays in Scottish Labour History* in Society for the Study of Labour History *Bulletin*, no. 39 (Autumn 1979).

E. Carr (1966), *The Bolshevik Revolution 1917–23*, vol. III (London: Macmillan, 1966).

R. Challinor (1977), *The Origins of British Bolshevism* (London: Croom Helm, 1977).

Commune (Glasgow) May 1923–April/May 1929.

Commune Special Anti-Parliamentary Communist Gazette (Glasgow) May 1926–May 1929.

Communist (London) May–August 1919.

Communist International (Petrograd) May 1919–February 1921.

Communist International, Publishing House (1921), *The Second Congress of the Communist International* (USA: Publishing House of the Communist International, 1921).

'Communist Party Affiliation to the Labour Party: Transcript of the Meeting of 29 December 1921' (1974) in Society for the Study of Labour History *Bulletin*, no. 29 (Autumn 1974).

Council (Glasgow) October 1931–May 1933.

R. Croucher (1982), *Engineers At War* (London: Merlin Press, 1982).

R. Daniels (1960), *The Conscience of the Revolution* (Cambridge, Mass.: Harvard University Press, 1960).

J. Degras (ed.) (1956), *The Communist International 1919–43: Documents*, vol. I (London: Oxford University Press, 1956).

Department of Employment and Productivity (1971), *British Labour Statistics: Historical Abstract 1886–1968* (London: HMSO, 1971).

Equity (1945), *The Struggle in the Factory* (Glasgow: Anarchist Federation, February 1945).

Evening Times (Glasgow).

Fighting Call (Glasgow/London) October 1936–February 1937.

Forward (Glasgow) June–October 1920.

H. Francis and D. Smith (1980), *The Fed: A History of the South Wales Miners* (London: Lawrence & Wishart, 1980).

Freedom Press Group (1953), 'Frank Leech' in *Freedom* 17 January 1953.

W. Gallacher (1966), *Last Memoirs* (London: Lawrence & Wishart, 1966).

J. Hinton (1973), *The First Shop Stewards' Movement* (London: Allen & Unwin, 1973).

——— and R. Hyman (1975), *Trade Unions and Revolution* (London: Pluto Press, 1975).

B. Holton (1976), *British Syndicalism 1900–14* (London: Pluto Press, 1976).

J. Hulse (1964), *The Forming of the Communist International* (California: Stanford University Press, 1964).

Hyde Park (Glasgow) September 1938.

International Communist Current (no date), *The Decadence of Capitalism*, 2nd edn (London: International Communist Current, no date).

International Council Correspondence (Chicago) October 1934–December 1937

B. Jones (1982), 'William C. McDougall' in *History Workshop Journal*, no. 13 (Spring 1982).

L. Jones (1972), 'Sylvia Pankhurst and the Workers' Socialist Federation: The Red Twilight, 1918–24' (University of Warwick: unpublished M.A. thesis, 1972).

KAPD (no date), 'Theses on the Role of the Party in the Proletarian Revolution' in *Revolutionary Perspectives*, no. 2 (no date).

W. Kendall (1969), *The Revolutionary Movement in Britain 1900–21* (London: Weidenfeld & Nicolson, 1969).

——— (1974), 'The Communist Party of Great Britain' in *Survey* vol. 20 no. 1(90) (Winter 1974).

D. Kirkwood (1935), *My Life of Revolt* (London: George Harrap, 1935).

J. Klugmann (1968), *History of the Communist Party of Great Britain*, vol. I (London: Lawrence & Wishart, 1968).

B. Lazitch and M. Drachkovitch (1972), *Lenin and the Comintern*, vol. I (California: Stanford University Press, 1972).

V. Lenin (1969), *British Labour and British Imperialism* (London: Lawrence & Wishart, 1969).

——— (1970), *Lenin on War and Peace: Three Articles* (Peking: Foreign Languages Press, 1970).

——— (1975), *'Left-Wing' Communism, An Infantile Disorder* (Peking: Foreign Languages Press, 1975).

Living Marxism (Chicago) February 1938–Fall 1941.

R. Luxemburg (1935), *Leninism or Marxism* (Glasgow: Anti-Parliamentary Communist Federation, no date).

L. MacFarlane (1966), *The British Communist Party* (London: MacGibbon and Kee, 1966).

J. McGovern (1960), *Neither Fear Nor Favour* (London: Blandford Press, 1960).

H. McShane and J. Smith (1978), *Harry McShane: No Mean Fighter* (London: Pluto Press, 1978).

K. Marx (1977), *The Civil War in France* (Peking: Foreign Languages Press, 1977).

——— and F. Engels (1968), *Selected Works* (London: Lawrence & Wishart, 1968).

P. Mattick (1970), 'Introduction' in *New Essays* (Westport, Connecticut: Greenwood Reprint Corporation, 1970).

G. Maximov (1939), *Bolshevism: Promises and Reality* (Glasgow: Anarchist Federation, no date).

A. Meltzer (1976), *The Anarchists in London 1935–55* (Sanday: Cienfuegos Press, 1976).
N. Milton (1973), *John Maclean* (London: Pluto Press, 1973).
F. Montseny (1937), *Militant Anarchism and the Reality in Spain* (Glasgow: Anti-Parliamentary Communist Federation, February 1937).
J. Murphy (1972), *The Workers' Committee* (London: Pluto Press, 1972).
New Essays (Chicago) Fall 1942–Winter 1943.
New Spur (Glasgow) December 1933–April 1934
News From Spain (Glasgow) May 1937.
A. Nove (1969), *An Economic History of the USSR* (London: Allen Lane, 1969).
Pankhurst Papers, International Institute of Social History, Amsterdam.
S. Pankhurst (1921), *Soviet Russia As I Saw It* (London: Dreadnought Publishers, 1921).
——— (1926), *India and the Earthly Paradise* (Bombay: 1926).
——— (1927a), *Delphos: The Future of International Language* (London: Kegan Paul, Trench, Trubner, 1927).
——— (1927b), *Is An International Language Possible?* (London: Morland Press, no date).
——— (1930), *Save The Mothers* (London: Alfred Knopf, 1930).
——— (1932), *The Home Front* (London: Hutchinson, 1932).
——— (1977), *The Suffragette Movement* (London: Virago, 1977).
——— and I. Stefanovici (1930), *Poems of Mihail Eminescu* (London: Kegan Paul, Trench, Trubner, 1930).
R. Peterson (1976), 'The General Strike: Fifty Years On' in *World Revolution*, no. 6 (March 1976).
H. Pollitt (1940), *Serving My Time* (London: Lawrence & Wishart, 1940).
J. Quail (1978), *The Slow Burning Fuse* (London: Paladin, 1978).
Red Commune (Glasgow) February 1921.
Regeneracion (Glasgow) July 1936–March 1937.
V. Richards (1983), *Lessons of the Spanish Revolution*, 3rd edn (London: Freedom Press, 1983).
A. Rosmer (1971), *Lenin's Moscow* (London: Pluto Press, 1971).
L. Schapiro (1955), *The Origin of the Communist Autocracy* (London: G. Bell, 1955).
V. Serge (1972), *Year One of the Russian Revolution* (London: Allen Lane, 1972).
M. Shipway (1985), 'Anti-Parliamentary Communism in Britain 1917–45' (University of Manchester: unpublished Ph.D. thesis, 1985).
D. Smart (ed.) (1978), *Pannekoek and Gorter's Marxism* (London: Pluto Press, 1978).
Socialist Anti-Terror Committee (1938), *Against Terrorism in the Workers' Struggle* (Glasgow: Socialist Anti-Terror Committee, March 1938).
Socialist May Special (Glasgow) May 1934.
Solidarity (Glasgow) August 1938–September 1944.
South Wales Miners' Federation Unofficial Reform Committee (1973), *The Miners' Next Step* (London: Pluto Press, 1973).
Spur (London) January 1917–April 1921.

L. Trotsky (1934), *The Soviet Union and the Fourth International* (Glasgow: Guy Aldred, 1934).

L. Trotsky (1967) *The Revolution Betrayed* (London: New Park Publications, 1967).

United Socialist (Glasgow) October 1934.

War Commentary (London) November 1939–August 1945.

V. Weisbord (1977), *A Radical Life* (Bloomington: Indiana University Press, 1977).

K. Weller (1985), *'Don't Be A Soldier!': The Radical Anti-War Movement in North London 1914–18* (London: Journeyman Press, 1985).

Wildcat (1986), *Class War on the Home Front* (Manchester: Wildcat, 1986).

Woman's Dreadnought (London) January 1917–July 1917.

G. Woodcock (1970), *Anarchism* (Harmondsworth: Penguin Books, 1970).

Word (Glasgow) May 1938–December 1945.

Worker (Glasgow) July–September 1922.

Workers' Dreadnought (London) July 1917–June 1924.

Workers' Free Press (Glasgow) September 1937–May/June 1938.

Index